PRAISE FOR
THE SCANDAL OF
THE KINGDOM

For many of us, the parables of Jesus are delightful but mysterious, and at times even scandalous. Dallas Willard opens up for us the beauty of these parables with such uncanny skill and grace that, in the end, we become captivated by the greatness and goodness of God.

RICHARD J. FOSTER, AUTHOR, *CELEBRATION OF DISCIPLINE* AND MANY OTHER BOOKS

Over the years of reading and listening to Dallas Willard, I was always longing for a more refined and robust understanding of what he thought Jesus meant by "kingdom of God." I am thrilled to see that longing satisfied in his probing of the kingdom of God by examining the deposits of the kingdom as taught in Jesus' parables. In his incomparable manner of attuning all that Jesus taught to a life transformed, *The Scandal of the Kingdom* develops into fruition Willard's fresh and valuable understanding of the kingdom.

SCOT MCKNIGHT, PROFESSOR OF NEW TESTAMENT

I stand in a long line of readers whose prophetic imagination has been profoundly shaped by Dallas Willard. *The Scandal of the Kingdom* worked on me in the way his writing always seems to—pointing to meaning hidden in plain sight in familiar biblical passages, using grounded (and occasionally provocative) language to offer a pathway for converting intellectual insight into embodied practice. Another great work from a great mind and even greater life.

TYLER STATON, NATIONAL DIRECTOR, 24-7 PRAYER USA, AND LEAD PASTOR, BRIDGETOWN CHURCH

THE SCANDAL
OF THE
KINGDOM

THE SCANDAL
OF THE
KINGDOM

HOW THE **PARABLES OF**
JESUS REVOLUTIONIZE LIFE WITH GOD

DALLAS WILLARD

ZONDERVAN
BOOKS

ZONDERVAN BOOKS

The Scandal of the Kingdom

Copyright © 2024 by Willard Family Trust

Published in Grand Rapids, Michigan, by Zondervan. Zondervan is a registered trademark of The Zondervan Corporation, L.L.C., a wholly owned subsidiary of HarperCollins Christian Publishing, Inc.

Requests for information should be addressed to customercare@harpercollins.com.

Zondervan titles may be purchased in bulk for educational, business, fundraising, or sales promotional use. For information, please email SpecialMarkets@Zondervan.com.

Library of Congress Cataloging-in-Publication Data

Names: Willard, Dallas, 1935-2013, author.
Title: The scandal of the kingdom : how the parables of Jesus revolutionize life with God / Dallas Willard.
Description: Grand Rapids, Michigan : Zondervan Books, [2024]
Identifiers: LCCN 2024021726 (print) | LCCN 2024021727 (ebook) | ISBN 9780310367949 (hardcover) | ISBN 9780310369301 (international trade paper edition) | ISBN 9780310367956 (ebook) | ISBN 9780310367963 (audio)
Subjects: LCSH: Jesus Christ—Parables. | Christian life—Biblical teaching. | BISAC: RELIGION / Biblical Studies / New Testament / Jesus, the Gospels & Acts | RELIGION / Christian Living / Personal Growth
Classification: LCC BT375.3 .W53 2024 (print) | LCC BT375.3 (ebook) | DDC 226.8—dc23/eng/20240604
LC record available at https://lccn.loc.gov/2024021726
LC ebook record available at https://lccn.loc.gov/2024021727

Cover design: Studio Gearbox
Cover photo: Heritage Image Partnership Ltd / Alamy Stock Photo
Interior design: Denise Froehlich

Printed in the United States of America

24 25 26 27 28 LBC 5 4 3 2 1

To Jane Lakes Willard:

Apart from my salvation,
my wife, Jane, is my single greatest blessing.
It's just amazing how God has dwelt in her.
I simply wouldn't have been able to be
much of anything without her.

CONTENTS

FOREWORD

The Swiss psychologist Elisabeth Kübler-Ross once wrote, "Beautiful people do not just happen."[1] Do you know any of these beautiful people? People who shine with an inner luminescence, who radiate a kind of moral beauty? These kinds of people don't "just happen" by accident; they are *formed*, or forged, often in the fire of suffering and pain, over a long period of time, into people of love.

Dallas Willard was (and if we think about life the way he did, still *is*) one of those beautiful people. He was a man who was no stranger to suffering, and yet he grew into a person of defiant joy—a man whose friends and family still speak of his deep capacity for love, the rare kind of saint "of whom the world was not worthy."[2]

Dallas defined beauty as "goodness made manifest to the senses."[3] By his own definition then, I would say he was a beautiful soul. And while his body is gone from this earth, his writings still stand as a living artifact of his mind. But be warned, they have the potential to alter the trajectory of your life, as they have mine.

In the academic world, it's common for a writer or thinker to adopt an intellectual father or mother; a teacher whose body of work forms the shoulders we stand upon, a kind of mind mentor.

Dallas Willard has been that for me. It's hard to express just how deeply he has shaped my view of who Jesus is and what it means to follow him (or, as Dallas would say, "apprentice under him").

Yet it's not just the brilliance of his mind that has been imprinted so deeply on my psyche—his highly original thought, wide-ranging knowledge base, and integration of philosophy, psychology, and spirituality back into unified whole. It's the beauty of his soul, his whole person—his joyfulness, gentle manner, spiritual humility (and authority), and the unhurried pace of his body. Those who knew him best tell stories of hearing him sing hymns throughout the day. This does not surprise me.

And yet he remains an enigma—a happy God-lover captivated by the beauty of the Trinity and deeply aware of God's inner nature of love, as well as one of the clearest, most uncompromising voices in centuries to call us to a life of obedience and disciplined discipleship, or, as Dietrich Bonhoeffer put it, to "come and die."[4] I have rarely met someone who combined such peaceful presence with such passion for the disciplined pursuit of the with-God life. Dallas was unafraid to speak of the cross not only as something Jesus *did for us*, but also as something *we do with him*.

If we take the sayings of Jesus at face value, this way of thinking should sound unremarkable, but in the current climate of Christian spirituality, it is a radical idea—ancient, yet out of key with the melody of our time. Dallas wisely understood that the tragic divorce in the Western church of the gospel *of* Jesus from discipleship *to* Jesus (what God has done; what we do) is due, at least in part, to a gross misunderstanding of what Jesus actually said and did—the gospel he actually preached and the path or "way" he called his apprentices to follow.

In reflecting on the dissonance between what we hear in much of Christian preaching and what we read from the lips of Jesus in the Gospels, Dallas writes one of the most important sentences of the book: "In many of our Christian circles, we sub-stituted the message *of* Christ with a message *about* Christ. And when we taught about saving faith, we had replaced the faith *of* Christ with a faith *in* Christ."

Many of us in the modern Western church seem to assume the exact opposite to Kübler-Ross's insight—that if we just go to church regularly and believe the right things, something approx-imating the beauty of Christlike character will just happen. Yet our churches, like our lives, are full of evidence to the contrary.

Dallas would gently but firmly remind us that this is because we must believe (or trust) in the *person* of Jesus Christ himself—not just in his death, but his *life*; not just in his substitutionary atonement, but also in his parables and teachings on how to live with him in God's kingdom. We must place our confidence in *him* to show us the way. As we do this, step by step, we will make steady progress into kingdom living.

But this kind of talk is rare. Survey the topography of the modern church, and you will see just what an iconoclast Dallas was, a singularly unique "voice of one calling in the wilderness."[5]

I believe it will be years before we realize the full weight of Dallas Willard's legacy. I pray my great-grandchildren will look back on his life the way we do on the lives of John Wesley, Ignatius of Loyola, or Mother Teresa—as a key character in the unfolding story of Jesus' people.

We still have so much to learn from him. And thankfully we can. Through the gift of *The Scandal of the Kingdom*, we don't have to guess at what his follow-up to *The Divine Conspiracy* would be; we can read it, slowly (as he would) and thoughtfully. We can absorb it into our lives.

My soul came alive on every page of this book. I found myself falling in love with Jesus even more deeply, grasping his parables and teachings more clearly, and experiencing his love in a whole new way.

The more I read Dallas's words, the more I long to *live* like he did. Even more, to *know God* like he did. Because I see something approximating the beauty of Jesus in Dallas's soul, and there is nothing I want more in all of life.

JOHN MARK COMER

INTRODUCTION

"GIVE 'EM HEAVEN"

"Give 'em heaven."

These three simple words spoken by Dallas Willard to his granddaughter shortly before his passing embody his heart and the heart of this book. They can also be used to describe the incarnation, life, and parables of Jesus. But what does it mean to "give 'em heaven"?

We find an answer when we explore the parables of Jesus because they reveal the kingdom of God in ways that theology and doctrine never could. They appear simple on the surface, yet within them we discover the heart of God and the nature of heaven. One minute we are listening to a story about a disobedient son, and the next minute the unconditional love of the father shocks and unsettles us. The tale of a farmer paying his workers the same amount regardless of how long they worked that day upends our preconceived expectations about fairness and justice. And the mysterious workings of seeds become elaborate metaphors of God's Word growing in our hearts.

Parables turn out to be doorways leading into a beautiful and loving reality, yet they also disrupt our comfortable notions about God and heaven. Once we hear them and begin to think about them, they revolutionize and reorganize the inner fabric of our life.

The parables are a gentle guide into heaven with a revealing power that Jesus used to help his listeners gain a stronger foothold for their faith. Dallas wanted us to appreciate the compassionate heart, wisdom, and faith of Jesus Christ, and how these virtues guided his use of storytelling and his manner of teaching. As you will see in chapter 2, he believed that understanding how Jesus taught is crucial if we want to fully embrace the content of his teaching.

WHY "SCANDAL"?

The title *The Scandal of the Kingdom* comes from Dallas's teaching that Jesus' parables were often considered scandalous, his descriptions of the kingdom being nothing like what the people listening to him expected. Describing the parables this way connects to the fulfillment of the prophecy in Isaiah 8:13–15, which is quoted by Peter (1 Peter 2:4–8 NRSVue), identifying Jesus Christ as the "living stone . . . precious in God's sight . . . a cornerstone chosen and precious" for those who believe. But for those who do not believe, he is the "stone that makes them stumble [*skandalon*] . . . because they disobey the word." We will see in chapter 8 that Jesus referred to himself as the cornerstone the builders (the leaders of Israel) chose to throw away because they did not believe in him.

For some, the parables are life-changing wisdom revealing what's possible when we start living out of the abundance of God's love and the power of his kingdom. But for those who are trying to manage, regulate, and control God, they are indeed scandalous—a stumbling block—ludicrous in their gracefulness, shocking in their unfettered acceptance, and naive because the world just doesn't work that way. The "scandal of the kingdom" is God's seemingly irrational outpouring of love and mercy on sinful humanity (Ephesians 2:4–7). The world will often criticize kingdom ways as being shocking, ludicrous, scandalous, threatening, and even wasteful (the scribes and Pharisees certainly did), but there is great joy in exploring and learning the surprising ways of life in the kingdom of God.

KINGDOM PARABLES

Dallas did not set out to comprehensively review all of the parables, but he focused instead on the ones that illustrate the special kind of life that can be found in the kingdom of the heavens that is now available ("at hand") through Jesus. These stories of everyday people often doing unexpected things reveal the attractive and inviting qualities of the kingdom and its king in such a way that the invitation to enter is irresistible. Jesus was a master storyteller indeed.

The vision of God and his kingdom found in these parables will deepen our faith and guide our lives. They will help us see the radiant beauty of God and his kingdom in ways that help "set the LORD always before me" (Psalm 16:8). They are an indispensable contribution to our ability to love God with all our heart, soul, mind, and strength. They move us to love God passionately, think of him constantly, and persistently seek to do his will.

THE WILLARD FAMILY, FRIENDS, AND EDITORS

CHAPTER 1

THE FAITH
OF CHRIST

*And the Word became flesh and dwelt among us, and we
beheld His glory, the glory as of the only begotten of the
Father, full of grace and truth.*

*John bore witness of Him and cried out, saying,
"This was He of whom I said, 'He who comes after me is
preferred before me, for He was before me.'"*

*And of His fullness we have all received, and grace for
grace. For the law was given through Moses, but grace and
truth came through Jesus Christ.*

JOHN 1:14–17

When I was a young minister studying my Bible, I came to the
realization that something very different went on in the life and
ministry of Jesus when compared with the life and ministry of
the churches I knew. The difference was simple: *We* were spending thousands of dollars and exhausting ourselves trying to get
people to come to church, whereas *Jesus* was hiding from people.
We begged, cajoled, and pleaded with people, whereas *Jesus* said,

"Don't follow me. Don't talk about me. Don't let anyone know I did this."

At times, Jesus even discouraged people from following him. When they said, "Lord, I will follow you wherever you go," he responded with statements such as, "Foxes have holes and the birds of the air have nests, but the Son of Man has nowhere to lay his head. Do you wanna live like that?" (Matthew 8:20, paraphrased). His words often shocked and offended people enough to drive them away. There was nothing more revolting than to suggest that people eat human flesh and drink human blood, but Jesus said just that (John 6:54–56).

As I explored the reasons for these differences, I gradually found that in many of our Christian circles, we substituted the message *of* Christ with a message *about* Christ. And when we taught about saving faith, we had replaced the faith *of* Christ with a faith *in* Christ. Now, I know I'm putting a lot of weight on these small words (*of*, *about*, and *in*), so let me illustrate the difference.

THE FAITH *OF* CHRIST

The gospels of Matthew and Mark tell of the night when Jesus and his disciples were in a boat on the Sea of Galilee and a tremendous storm came up. As the storm raged, Jesus slept right through it (Mark 4:38). How beautifully this glimpse of Jesus at peace illustrates his faith in the kingdom of God. Here we see the faith *of* Christ. He could lie down in the middle of a storm and go to sleep.

What were his disciples doing at the same time? They were *screaming*: "Lord! Save us!" They expected to die any minute. Finally, they woke him up shouting, "Do something, Master!" (see Mark 4:35–41; Matthew 8:23–27; Luke 8:22–25). The disciples had faith *in* Christ. That's why they shouted at him. They didn't fully understand who he was yet, but they had great faith *in* him.

When he got up and calmed the storm, Jesus said, "Why are

you afraid, you of little faith?" (Matthew 8:26 NRSVue). Their faith *in* Christ was good, but it was not the faith *of* Christ, which is strong enough to fend off all fear. They were not integrated into the will and nature of God and God's rule over his world in the way Jesus was. They did not yet understand they were to enter into the kind of life Jesus had in order to attain that degree of faith.

After Jesus calmed the sea, the disciples were in awe. They continued to wonder what kind of person he was that the wind and the sea would respond in obedience to his words (Mark 4:41). This illustrates why the difference between believing *in* Christ and having the faith *of* Christ is significant.

The apostle Paul gives another example of this important difference in his letter to the Galatians. The King James Version is the best reflection of this Greek structure:[*]

> Knowing that a man is not justified by the works of the law, but by the faith *of* Jesus Christ, even we have believed *in* Jesus Christ, that we might be justified by the faith *of* Christ, and not by the works of the law. . . .
>
> For I through the law am dead to the law, that I might live unto God.
>
> I am crucified with Christ: nevertheless I live; yet not I, but Christ liveth in me: and the life which I now live in the flesh I live by the faith *of* the Son of God. (Galatians 2:16, 19–20 KJV, emphasis added)

---

[*] Other translations that reflect this Greek structure include the 21st Century KJV, as well as Blue Red and Gold Letter Edition; Douay-Rheims 1899 American Edition; Geneva Bible 1599 edition; JUB Jubilee Bible 2000; New Matthew Bible; New Revised Standard Version: Updated Edition; Revised Geneva Translation; Wycliffe Bible; and Young's Literal Translation. This is a controversial issue among translators. Some recent versions have "the faithfulness of Christ" (e.g., N. T. Wright's *The Bible for Everyone*, the Common English Bible [CEB], and the New English Translation [NET]).

Paul was pointing out that faith *in* Christ is a part of, and the *entryway* into, having the faith *of* Christ. You and I are to take the faith Christ had into ourselves, becoming the person he has called us to be. This inward faith then radiates through every dimension of who we are and constitutes the basic faith in which we live as disciples of Christ.

IMPARTING NEW LIFE

It is this faith of Christ that was expressed in the message of Christ. And if we want to have the results that Jesus had, we need to *teach what Christ taught, in the manner in which he taught it.*

Jesus Christ preached the kingdom of God, which is the unitary and unifying gospel of the New Testament. At the center of the kingdom of God is the meritorious, vicarious suffering life and death of Jesus Christ, including the cross, the resurrection, and Christ's appearances afterward to the church. All of these together brought the church to the place where it could function as his body on earth as he returned to heaven as its living head. In all of this, we see the full gospel of Jesus Christ.

The *aim* of this gospel is to create new persons. The *mode* is the impartation of life. The *instrument* is the Word of the kingdom that imparts new life. The Word of the kingdom is the instrument Jesus used, and it is the instrument we are to use to impart this new life.

When we preach the kingdom of God, when we teach it through his parables and his life and wisdom, when we show forth its power by the actions we take and the words we use—of blessing, of mastery over evil—we are expressing the kingdom of God in such a way as to impart life and create new persons.

As disciples of Christ, we announce a gospel *about* what Jesus accomplished for us (his birth and death, burial and resurrection, atonement and saving work) because our faith *in* Christ and what he did remains forever foundational. From there we grow in our faith to embrace the *full* New Testament faith—that is, the faith *of* Christ—and we proclaim the message *of* Christ.

The message Jesus taught, and the sole message of the New Testament, is the availability and nature of the kingdom of God. The kingdom of the heavens is now accessible to all people alike.

GOD IS RIGHT HERE

I say, "kingdom of the heavens" because when we read the word *heaven* in our New Testaments, it is plural in its Greek form— *ouranois*, "the heavens." The meaning of the plural "heavens" allows us to see God as being present both in the air around our heads and as far away as we can imagine. Omitting the plural form, as when we say, "Our Father who art in heaven," has frequently come to be thought of as "our Father who is in a faraway heaven." But Jesus wants us to understand that God is "our Father who is always near us." It is precisely from the space immediately around us that God watches and God acts.

Jesus' preaching, parables, and healings depended on God and his kingdom being present around us. Jesus' reassurance of the basic elements of our existence being available—food, drink, clothing, and other needs of life—can only be supported with a clear-eyed vision that a totally good and competent God is right here with us and looking after us. God's presence is precisely what "the heavens" conveys in the biblical record, as well as through much of Christian history. And nothing—no human being or institution, no time, no space, no spiritual being, no event—stands between God and those who trust him.[6] For this reason, the term "the kingdom of the heavens" will be used throughout this book.

KINGDOM NOW

When John the Baptist came, his message was, "Repent, for the kingdom of the heavens is at hand" (Matthew 3:2, paraphrased). When Jesus came, he preached the same message: "Repent. Turn.

For the kingdom of the heavens is here. It is at hand" (Matthew 4:17, paraphrased). Many people think this means, "Feel sorry for your sins, because the kingdom of God is *about* to get here." This idea is often associated with someone walking around with a signboard that reads, "Repent! For the end is near!" If we purge our minds of that image, it will help immensely.

Jesus preached that the kingdom of God is now available. It was not *about* to happen; it was something that *had* happened. Whatever the dimensions of the future realization of God's kingdom may be when he returns in power and glory, the kingdom of God *has come* in Jesus Christ. It came with the king himself at the perfect moment in history.

It is crucial to understand that when Jesus preached that the kingdom was "at hand," he meant it in the way someone might speak while extending a hand toward the dining room and saying, "Here's the dining room," to a guest who has come to their home for dinner.

To so easily turn and walk into the kingdom, as Jesus invites us to do, is a seismic shift and a tremendous transition. John the Baptist's message had been to repent, for the kingdom is *coming*. But Jesus, in his person, brought the kingdom of the heavens into the lives of those around him so they could experience it through his presence in their lives.

Jesus put a face on the kingdom of God.

ARE YOU THE MESSIAH?

I wouldn't be surprised if Jesus and John had many conversations about the coming of the kingdom of God over the course of their lives. I imagine they spent time together during various family gatherings or annual feasts talking about the kingdom's arrival and what it would be like.

A touching exchange between these dear friends and kinsmen further explains this idea about the availability and nature of the kingdom. When John was languishing in prison, he sent a message to Jesus, wistfully asking, "Are you *really* the one?" Jesus responded with signs that he, the king, was indeed present:

> "Go and tell John what you hear and see: the blind receive their sight and the lame walk, lepers are cleansed and the deaf hear, and the dead are raised up, and the poor have good news preached to them." (Matthew 11:4–5 ESV)

That last sign was an especially good one; it's as if Jesus said, "The poor hear some good news *for once*."

Jesus was reminding John where real kingdom power lay. In effect, he was saying, "John, the kingdom is present. Do you see what is happening in these people's lives? These things are happening because I am working with the power of God, which is the kingdom rule of God in human life."

The power of the kingdom marked the message of Jesus, and everyone felt it: "The crowds were astounded" (Matthew 7:28 NRSVue). As he spoke, they couldn't believe what he was saying, and they couldn't *not* believe it, because he spoke with such authority. They began to believe things about themselves they had never thought before—things about the possibilities of their life in God's world. *The poor heard some good news for once.*

GREATER THAN JOHN

At this point, Jesus said something interesting about his cousin, who was a great prophet revered by the people and feared by the leaders:

> "Truly I tell you, among those born of women, no one has arisen greater than John the Baptist; yet the least in the kingdom of the heavens is greater than he." (Matthew 11:11, paraphrased)

Have you ever thought of yourself as greater than John the Baptist? You are indeed greater. This is not because of who you are individually, but because of your place in the kingdom of the heavens.

When we walk in the power of the kingdom of God—as it was present in Jesus Christ himself—we have a greater resource, a greater contact with power, than what was available to even John the Baptist, because we are increasingly integrated into the eternal kind of life God intended us to have. Along with this, we become a vital part of the body of Christ where we complement, strengthen, nourish, and encourage one another in such a way that even the one who is least in the kingdom of the heavens is greater than John the Baptist.

So I want you to put a sign on your bathroom mirror that reads, "I am greater than John the Baptist." And then live up to it.

AN OPEN INVITATION TO EVERYONE

Jesus went on to say:

> "From the days of John the Baptist until now the kingdom of the heavens has suffered violence, and the violent take it by force." (Matthew 11:12, paraphrased)

How does violence align with the good news of the kingdom Jesus talked about? Jesus meant that with his arrival, ordinary men and women could simply walk right into the kingdom of God with no requirements of propriety or the correct procedures or protocols. Only the sincere will of the heart to follow Christ is required to usher us into the kingdom of God by the grace of God.

We see this clearly in the story of a leper who came to Jesus and asked to be healed. Lepers, however, were not supposed to be *coming*; they were supposed to be *going*. Their presence violated the protocols for leprosy, which would have kept this man away from other people. But he had heard what Jesus said in his Sermon on the Mount, and he came right up to Jesus and asked, in effect, "Master, if you would . . ." That is a violence. You can almost hear him pleading, not *that* you would, but *if* you would. He was prepared to be rejected because he had, no doubt, experienced a lot of rejection. So he said, "If you are willing," and Jesus said, "Oh, I'm willing!" (Matthew 8:1–3, paraphrased). That is an example of the kingdom being taken by force.

Many other instances are found throughout the Gospels. A Roman centurion asked Jesus to heal his servant, and Jesus replied, "I will come and heal him," even though entering the home of a Gentile went against Jewish custom (Matthew 8:5–13). A woman with an issue of blood who—knowing she was unclean and would cause anyone who touched her to be considered unclean—still slipped through the crowd, thinking to herself, *If I can just touch the hem of his garment, I will be healed* (Mark 5:25–34, paraphrased). That disregard of common custom was "violent."

With the coming of the Messiah, you didn't need to be a Jew or a person with any other "proper" designation. You didn't need to be healthy, wise, smart, or even clean. The story of the prodigal son beautifully illustrates this. The son "came to his senses" (Luke 15:17 NIV) and prepared his heartfelt apology, but didn't get a chance to say anything. The father ran to him, took him into his arms—pig stink and all—and made every provision for him. That's the violence being spoken of, and that's the message of Christ—the present availability of the kingdom of God.

THE POWER OF LIFE

Given the importance of *kingdom* in the message of Jesus, let's briefly review this concept. A kingdom is a society of people with a structure in which there is one person, a king or queen, to whom all of the citizens offer loyalty, service, and respect. The sovereign's part of this relationship is to provide care, protection, and service for the good of the people. It has always been understood that the welfare of a leader rests upon the welfare of the people.

The kingdom of God is exactly like that. It is a society of persons where there is love, service, and respect for the king; and there is care, protection, and service for those who live in the kingdom. When we speak of the kingdom of God, we are speaking of a kingdom which works more like a family or a well-functioning neighborhood, where people really do *love* one another and care for each other. This kingdom is the range of God's effective will—or simply God acting in this world—where what he wants done is done. Jesus' teaching showed us that the kingdom of God is not a thing of times and places; it is a thing of the heart. It is a life that is lived in vital connection with God himself.

Unlike the kingdom of God, human government functions on principles of force, deception, brutality, and the power of death. All human governments have the power of death, but what they lack is the power of *life*. This is what the kingdom of God has: *the power of life*. Human governments can *kill*. God's government gives *life*. This life is based upon the new birth that is an entry into the kingdom of God.

We are invited to bring our lives into the eternal life of God in his everlasting kingdom, being mindful that eternity is already in progress; it is not something that will start later. The only biblical definition of eternal life is this: "This is eternal life, that they may know You, the only true God, and Jesus Christ whom You have sent" (John 17:3). To "know You" is an interactive relationship in which everything we bring into that relationship becomes eternal.

When we live in the kingdom of God by the Spirit of God, our lives are constantly overflowing with goodness and mercy. We do not make this happen. It is a gift, and we receive it. It is not "eating and drinking, but righteousness and peace and joy in the Holy Spirit" (Romans 14:17), which is not humanly possible. The best advice about how to go to heaven is *to go now* by living your life with God. That is what Jesus was saying when he preached, "Repent, for the kingdom of the heavens is at hand" (Matthew 4:17, paraphrased).

The kingdom of God constantly renews us; it comes to us where we are. It is always "at hand," present with us. When the Bible speaks of heaven, it means God acting in this world—right here, right now. This is real life. That is why Jesus said, "Seek first the kingdom of God and his kind of righteousness, and everything else will be added" (Matthew 6:33, paraphrased).

RSVP

Even though God's actions throughout Israel's history were well-known to them, the Israelites struggled with embracing God as their king. Just as the people of God had refused to speak directly with God at Mount Sinai, insisting that Moses do it for them (Deuteronomy 5:24–27), so they refused to let God govern them directly through his law and through key individuals (usually judges) as needed in specific circumstances.

Eventually, *against God's will*, God gave them a human king (1 Samuel 8:19–21). After Israel's rejection of God as king, the biblical language of God's "heavenly" rule and the "God of heaven"[†] emerged within the Old Testament. This new language was preparing the way for the dramatic announcements of John the Baptist and Jesus: "The kingdom of the heavens is now available; turn in to it!" (Matthew 3:2; 4:17, paraphrased).

People think they must live on their own, using only the resources of their natural abilities. They are out there trying to survive, trying to get their way, trying to secure themselves

---

†   As noted in Ezra 6:10; 7:12, 23; Nehemiah 1:5; 2:4; Daniel 2:28, 44.

and advance themselves. Tremendous unhappiness comes from people struggling to run their own "kingdom" (the things over which they have control) when they are not under God.

It is a tough job. Everyone else is trying to run their kingdom too, and they have little to work with except to covet, fight, and be angry. Life is filled with contempt and all the human disagreements that fuel contempt: "You are different from me. You look funny! I must be better than you, so away with you!" Jesus' brother James said, "You fight and war. Yet you do not have because you do not ask" (James 4:2). Asking comes after we have submitted our kingdom to God's kingdom.

Then along comes the message of Jesus: "Good news! Everyone can come. You do not have to live that way anymore. You can come and live in the kingdom of God now." We can give our kingdom to God. As citizens of God's kingdom, we seek to honor him and pray for his will to be done, starting with our own life, and then we pray for God's will to be done everywhere. Someday it will be. Jesus simply calls us to put our confidence in him and know that he will act on our behalf. That is what eternal life is about—God with us.

We accept the invitation to receive Jesus and his kingdom, and he receives us into his kingdom. As we learn how to live fully in the kingdom of God, we become his disciples and friends (John 15:15). That is a precious distinction because we then work as his friends and live out of kingdom resources. That is our life in Christ and in his kingdom.

THE ALLURE OF GENTLENESS

The gentle invitations and overtures of Jesus we find in his behavior and his parables are his way of moving us toward the kingdom of God. As we close this chapter, consider meditating on the gentle ways of the Messiah as foretold by the prophet Isaiah. Matthew quoted this passage as a description of Jesus:

> "Behold! My Servant whom I have chosen,
> My Beloved in whom My soul is well pleased!
> I will put My Spirit upon Him,
> And He will declare justice to the Gentiles.
> He will not quarrel nor cry out,
> Nor will anyone hear His voice in the streets."

Jesus was not a pushy person.

> "A bruised reed He will not break."

This refers to how a reed, when used as a walking stick, often fractures. If so, you might snap the weakened reed and throw it down. But Jesus is so gentle, he wouldn't even do that:

> "And smoking flax He will not quench,
> Till He sends forth justice to victory."

Candlewicks often smoke after you blow them out, and that smoke can irritate your nose. You might decide to wet your fingers and snuff out the wick to make the smoke stop. But not Jesus: "A smoldering wick he will not snuff out, till he has brought justice through to victory" (NIV).

> "And in His name Gentiles will trust."
> (Matthew 12:18–21; quoting Isaiah 42:1–4)

The gentle God whose only Son "shall not strive, nor cry; neither shall any man hear his voice above the street noise" (Matthew 12:19, paraphrased) invites us to "learn from Me, for I am gentle and lowly in heart" (11:29).

The parables of Jesus reveal what the kingdom of God is like and how things work in that kingdom. In the manner in which they are taught, we learn of a king who loves, cares for, protects, and serves his listeners by presenting his teaching in the gentle ways that mirror his own character. As you study them and meditate on them, they will change your life.

CHAPTER 2

HOW JESUS TAUGHT

And so it was, when Jesus had ended these sayings, that the people were astonished at His teaching, for He taught them as one having authority, and not as the scribes.

MATTHEW 7:28-29

Jesus was the brightest man and the most capable and creative teacher who has ever lived. Please don't let anyone make a simpleton of him. That's what happens when someone believes Jesus just tossed out laws for us to keep. Jesus' teachings went far deeper than laws; they were aimed at the heart. His teachings didn't stop with behavior but rather moved to the center of a person's being and their whole-life condition.

You cannot understand *what* Jesus taught unless you understand *how* he taught. This is extremely important, so we will be looking at it carefully in this chapter. When Jesus taught, he shared what it's like to live under the rule of God. That is a difficult thing to convey.

We expect our teachers to tell us *exactly* the way things are so we can know when we've gotten it right. We want Jesus to teach this way as well because it would help us define our righteousness. We would conclude, *If Jesus said, "Do this," I'm gonna do it. He said that if you ask me to carry your burden one mile, I should take it two. So I have to take it two.* But that isn't how Jesus taught.

Jesus' teaching about life in the kingdom is the indispensable means for our coming to be able to live in the kingdom day by day, moment by moment, comfortably in the care of God and in obedience and service to him. We shut this down when we turn his teaching into legalism. If we don't understand how he taught, legalism will run rampant because we will interpret what he was saying as laws. This is a very common mistake, especially with the Sermon on the Mount and the Sermon on the Plain.

TEACHING TO INFORM

Schools in Western cultures commonly dispense information without inviting any contribution on the students' part. They come to class and take notes to review for a test later, and they often never have to think about the subject again. That kind of knowledge has little value and leaves the students much the same on the inside as when they arrived for their class. I once heard a linguist explain that the only places in the world where teachers are expected to lecture on a subject in this manner are in Western Europe and the United States.

An example of this kind of teaching would be students in engineering school who are learning to build a bridge. They want to be taught the general rules about how it is done. They expect the teacher to lay out the facts and data from start to finish so they know how to make the two ends of the bridge meet in the middle. They want the teacher to start at the beginning and go to the end.

The important thing for a teacher, however, is not to try to cram all the answers into people's heads, but to give them the ideas and turn them loose. We may think that laws and generalizations are more likely to help us steer a safe course through life, but a primary problem is the nature of truth and how it is communicated. So Jesus constantly used careful and creative employment of the power of logical insight throughout his teaching to enable people to come to the truth about themselves and about God from the inside of their own hearts and minds. As students of Jesus, we experience him coming to us in such a way that we are allowed to grow into the truth of the kingdom of God. When we understand it and accept it, we can build our bridge.

TEACHING TO TRANSFORM

Great teachers know that the goal of teaching is to change people's ways of life by presenting the listeners with words and experiences that *impact the active flow of their lives.* Jesus accomplished this by teaching in the context of ordinary life, using illustrations drawn from common occupations and daily activities. Instead of using religious ideas and sacred objects, Jesus used everyday things like money, fruit, vines, feasts, seeds, coins, trees, and sheep. Everybody could understand and identify with what he was saying: "Yes, I've lost a sheep!" Jesus' illustrations and examples made the kingdom of God more accessible.

When Jesus said, "The kingdom of the heavens is like leaven, which a woman took and hid in three measures of meal till it was all leavened" (Matthew 13:33, paraphrased), everyone knew about leaven. He was speaking to them right where they lived. They knew it was the kind of thing that makes bread rise. They recognized it as something that started out small but then expanded, working quietly to penetrate all of the dough. Like leaven, good teaching gets tucked away in your mind and becomes more meaningful as it expands with the passing of time. After the story, bread would be a reminder of the nature of the kingdom of the heavens.

Good teachers say things in ways that ensure their teaching is easily remembered. Without computers, records, handouts, or even pens, Jesus' hearers had to be able to "get it" just from listening. So he found ways to poke holes in what people already believed and shake them up a bit. They didn't have to try to remember what he said because it puzzled them enough to stay with them.

Culture is what people believe without thinking and act on without explanation or justification. Jesus got right to the heart of the assumptions and practices common to the culture of the day. He planted thoughts in people's minds in such a way that those thoughts didn't stop growing. Imagine how people felt when they heard, "It is easier for a camel to go through the eye of a needle than for someone who is rich to enter the kingdom of God" (Matthew 19:24 NRSVue). People's reactions to Jesus' teaching show how effective this method was (Matthew 7:28; Luke 4:32).

In general, the way Jesus taught was to take whatever cultural balloon was floating by and let the air out of it. He went to dinner with a man who had filled his house with wealthy neighbors and relatives and said, "When you have a dinner, don't invite your relatives and your wealthy neighbors" (Luke 14:12, paraphrased). Now, do you think his host said, "Let me write this down so I can remember it when he's gone"? No, he was struck by this contradiction to what he believed. That's how Jesus taught and why people remembered it. Because they remembered it, it changed their lives.

UPSIDE DOWN

Jesus designed his teachings to point out common misunderstandings and errant cultural assumptions in order to realign them with the nature of the kingdom of God. When Jesus said that the poor, the meek, and those who mourn were blessed (Matthew 5:3–12), he was announcing the availability of the kingdom to everyone. *Anyone* who lives in the kingdom of God is blessed. There is no one, no matter how far down on the human scale they may be, that cannot be blessed if they will receive the kingdom through faith in Jesus Christ. No one.

Proclaiming a warning of "woe" to those who are rich, who are full, who laugh, and who are spoken well of by others (Luke 6:24–26) was a further application of this scriptural principle of inversion. If you are poor and you are in the kingdom of God, you are blessed. If you are rich, you can be blessed too, but you can't trust in your riches. Blessing is relativized through the kingdom. This, then, is the Great Inversion between the order of man's kingdom and God's kingdom.

Jesus sometimes highlighted specific behaviors in order to reverse a presumption. When he said, "You have heard that it was said. . . . But I say to you," he was stating a generally accepted idea and then contrasting it with the ways of the kingdom of God (Matthew 5:21–22, 27–28, 31–32, 33–34, 38–39, 43–44).* These creative inversions caused people to pause and think. Jesus wasn't trying to alienate them, but was inviting them to evaluate their beliefs in light of the kingdom.

SHOW AND TELL

Sometimes the behaviors Jesus used in his teaching are misinterpreted as commands when they were only intended as examples to reverse a prevailing presumption. For example, when he said, "Give to everyone who asks of you, and do not refuse anyone who wants to borrow from you" (Matthew 5:42, paraphrased), he was not stating a general command for every situation. But some people have interpreted it that way.

This leads them to think Jesus commanded us to give things away even when there's a good reason not to. They may back

---

* See my *The Divine Conspiracy: Rediscovering Our Hidden Life in God* (San Francisco: HarperSanFrancisco, 1998), 146, for a chart outlining these six contrasting situations.

away from his teachings, thinking, *This is not realistic. I can't do this. It will ruin me!* or they dismiss it, thinking, *This must be for another age.* The result is that Jesus' teachings are set aside because they are read as if he were giving a law. Instead, he is challenging our thinking by giving us an illustration of what a kingdom heart might do in that situation.

Giving to one's neighbor becomes illogical when it is misunderstood as a command. Forcing someone to share is inconsistent with the law of love. It can even *overturn* the law of love because it's possible (perhaps probable?) you will come to resent—even hate—the recipient of the gift you were forced to give.

Jesus' illustrations are projections of the few general commands repeated in the Bible: Love the Lord your God with all your heart, soul, mind, and strength; love your neighbor as yourself (Matthew 22:37–39; Mark 12:29–31). Jesus always comes back to the general command to seek God and God's ways in all things (Matthew 6:33).

So it is wise to examine Jesus' teachings and ask if he is giving a general command or offering an illustration of a kingdom principle and what it might look like. If it's an illustration, ask yourself, *What prevailing cultural presumption is he trying to correct?*

In the illustration of giving to everyone who asks of you, the cultural assumption was that a wise person holds on to as much as possible and rarely, if ever, gives to anyone who asks. Jesus inverted this tendency with the startling recommendation to give to everyone who asks. The general command behind this illustration is to cultivate a generous heart, to have the kind of life out of which a generous and cheerful heart grows (2 Corinthians 9:6–8).

KINGDOM REALITY CHECK

As you read the Bible and observe the world today, you see the many ways God is misunderstood. At times people have even thought they could please God by offering their children as a sacrifice (Leviticus 20:2–5). Imagine a god like that!

We may have a few misunderstandings ourselves. The people to whom Jesus came—the people of Israel—were full of them. Above all, they misunderstood the Messiah. They could only think of a messiah as a political leader and earthly king who would lead Israel to be exalted over all the world. To put this in today's context, they thought a God-sent Messiah would offer the best welfare program and the mightiest arms program.

They misunderstood the Old Testament passages that said the Jewish nation and people were to be a light to the world (Isaiah 49:6; Acts 13:46–48). They thought it meant they were to rule the world. They assumed the kingdom of God had to be like the brutal earthly kingdoms that could administer death but never give life. The people of Israel could not comprehend the kingdom of God and the power of its truth, love, mercy, forgiveness, and gentleness. They could not grasp that such a life was what it meant to live well.

REDEFINING JUSTICE

The teachings of Jesus were sometimes directly opposed to people's beliefs and opinions. His parables often sounded *scandalous*. His descriptions of the kingdom were nothing like what the people listening to him expected. In the kingdom, rebellious sons were welcomed home and rich men had trouble getting into heaven (Luke 15:20–24; Matthew 19:23). The Parable of the Workers in the Vineyard—those who toiled only one hour and were paid the same as those who worked all day (Matthew 20:1–16)—is enough to make you mad. It's unjust! But Jesus was redefining justice. This great inversion is well-expressed by his words, "Many who are first will be last, and many who are last will be first" (Matthew 19:30 NIV).

What Jesus was saying about God and human life was so

revolutionary that he had to tell people, "Do not think that I came to destroy the Law or the Prophets" (Matthew 5:17). When you say that kind of thing to a group of people, it's because you know that's what they're thinking. They thought he had come to destroy the Law and the Prophets because he was proclaiming that all human distinctions no longer mattered in the kingdom of God. He was insisting, as the lovely words of the old hymn say, "Whosoever will may come."[7]

Of course, Jesus practiced what he preached. He was constantly in trouble with the religious leaders for associating with the wrong people: "Now all the tax collectors and sinners were coming near to listen to him" (Luke 15:1 NRSVue). Those were the *wrong* folks.

To many people in Jesus' day, one of the most revolting things about him was his habit of welcoming "sinners"—prostitutes and tax collectors—and eating with them, *whether they washed their hands or not.* Can you imagine it? In that culture, who you chose to eat with said everything about your character, and some of these people were quite notorious. Not only that, but Jesus said these people would go into the kingdom of God before those who thought themselves to be righteous (Matthew 21:31). The religious leaders just couldn't get over his audacity.

Jesus' welcoming nature showcased the remarkable generosity of God and the kingdom of God. He was comfortable with the "wrong people," because he was situated solidly in the kingdom of God. He could be with *anyone*; he could be *anywhere*. This isn't necessarily true of us, but as we grow as his disciples and enter deeper into his kind of life, we can increasingly be like him, perfectly safe and perfectly strong in the kingdom of God.

COMPARE AND CONTRAST

When Jesus was attacked for this culturally unacceptable behavior, he didn't defend himself directly. Instead, he slipped around his opponents' defenses by telling simple stories that showed his listeners the attractive openness of the kingdom. A shepherd sought a lost sheep; a woman sought a lost coin; a father sought a lost son (Luke 15:3–32). In his gentle way, Jesus showed there was hope and restoration for everyone.

Parables became one of the primary ways Jesus disrupted the default way of thinking in his culture. The word *parable* (*parabole*) comes from two Greek words that mean "to place or throw beside." *Para* means "beside," as in parallel lines; *bole* means "to throw or to place." Teaching by parables means placing two things next to each other in order to learn more about them through contrast and comparison.

When the human mind tries to understand something, it works best when it can compare and contrast. If you are painting, you never judge a color simply by looking at that color. You place it against another.

Jesus used this technique because it is so well suited to the human mind. Jesus would present a story about an everyday occurrence, such as a family dispute or common farming situation, and place it beside the kingdom of God to provide clarity about what the kingdom is like. This comparison resulted in a deeper understanding about the nature of the kingdom and how it works.

The first time Jesus told a parable, his disciples asked, "Why do you speak to them in parables?" (Matthew 13:10 NRSVue). We will never understand the Bible, the workings of the kingdom of God, and the message and ministry of Jesus unless we understand the answer to their question.

He answered and said to them, "Because it has been given to you to know the mysteries of the kingdom of heaven, but to them it has not been given. For whoever has, to him more will be given, and he will have abundance; but whoever does not have, even what he has will be taken away from him.

Therefore I speak to them in parables, because seeing they do not see, and hearing they do not hear, nor do they understand. And in them the prophecy of Isaiah is fulfilled, which says:

"'Hearing you will hear and shall not understand,
And seeing you will see and not perceive;
For the hearts of this people have grown dull.
Their ears are hard of hearing,
And their eyes they have closed,
Lest they should see with their eyes and hear with
    their ears,
Lest they should understand with their hearts
    and turn,
So that I should heal them.'" (Matthew 13:11–15)

Notice the two aspects of receiving the secrets of the kingdom of the heavens: the ability to hold on to what we have received (capacity) and our willingness to hear the message (receptivity).

TINY BUCKETS

Jesus didn't say, "I'm not going to give it," but, "It has not been given" (Matthew 13:11). *For to those who have, more will be given* (capacity) is a marvelous law of the kingdom of God that holds true in every realm of life. Jesus is giving them only as much as they have the capacity to receive.

Picture it this way: If I come to you to get some water, you can only give me the amount that fits in my bucket. The folks Jesus was speaking to didn't have very big buckets, so he couldn't give them very much. If I don't even have a bucket (*but from those who have nothing*), I may try to hold the water with my cupped hands, but I'll lose it (*even what they have will be taken away*).

Jesus was unwilling to give his listeners more than they could handle because it wouldn't help them. Through his parables, Jesus gently reached out in love and humility without coercion, giving people truth in ways they could receive and retain.

PRECIOUSNESS OF PERSONS

Some people rejected the message of Jesus, closing their ears and shutting their eyes. This might make us wonder, *Didn't Jesus want to heal them? Didn't God want their hearts to turn to him? Why didn't God just pick them up by the seat of their pants, and throw them into the kingdom?*

Yes, Jesus ached for them to enter the kingdom and be healed, but he would not force them. Jesus' explanation of this first parable underscores the function of all parables. They allow the listener to choose to hear or *not* hear, and to see or *not* see.

Instead of saying, "Hey, you rotten people wallowing in the pigpen, I'm going to drop a spiritual bomb on you and blow you right into heaven!" he told a little story: "Well, there was this fellow who had two sons. And one of them said, 'I'm sick and tired of hanging around here, and I'd like to have my money so I can leave, thank you very much.' And his father just up and gave it to him" (Luke 15:11–12, paraphrased).

You see, the parables are an act of mercy to us because sometimes our hearts are hard. You and I both know that if we directly challenge someone with a hard heart, their heart will get even harder. So in his love, mercy, and compassion, Jesus told a story.

Jesus didn't assault people's minds or give them too much to handle, so they listened. He didn't throw religion at them. He didn't condemn them (John 3:17), because he knew people were already condemning themselves and everyone else. And in the midst of all that condemnation, yelling, rejection, and hustle and bustle came an intriguing story. He told parables to help people begin their exploration of his kingdom.

This manner of teaching reflects the mild and gentle character of Jesus, who will send forth victory over all the earth. He didn't take up swords or use loudspeakers and he will not stoop to human means in order to do it; yet the kingdom of God will come and rule the earth.

In his response to the question of "why parables?" Jesus gave us a revelation of the preciousness of human beings. God has placed in the hands of every person the key to their own heart. It unlocks only from the inside. God has so ordained this truth that he himself will not force a heart open, but he will offer us something that can help us unlock it. That's why Jesus taught the way he did.

OPEN AND SHUT

The prophecy from Isaiah that Jesus used to answer the "why parables?" question was originally given at a time of great national distress (Isaiah 42:18–20; 44:18). Isaiah had a literally earthshaking experience in the temple as he interacted with the Lord (Isaiah 6:4). In effect, God told him to tell the people, "Hear, but don't hear! See, but don't see!" in order to alert them to their problem with their spiritual hearing and their spiritual vision. Many times, we don't hear and don't know we're not hearing; we don't see and don't know we're not seeing.

Jesus said over and over, "He who has ears to hear, let him hear!" (e.g., Matthew 11:15). During my youth, I thought this was a nice little embellishment, like saying, "Well, that's the end of the story." But then I began to realize this was, in many ways, the heart of the matter. Not everyone has ears to hear or eyes to see. Many people use them primarily as filtering and sorting devices.

Teachers see this in classrooms. If a student thinks they already know the subject or have "heard it all before," they simply stop listening. The teacher is faced with the dilemma of how to get through to them when their minds are turned off. Any time the teacher tries to address the material again, it signals the student to switch their mind off again.

In the same way, some people who have heard about God or his kingdom turn their minds off whenever the topic comes up. Not everyone in church (including the teachers) has "ears to hear" because they think they have heard it all before. They aren't listening. Their hearts are closed. So how do we get around this?

Whether it's ears that don't hear, eyes that don't see, or hearts that don't understand, the insensitivity of the heart is the issue. God told Isaiah, "Make the heart of this people fat" (Isaiah 6:10 KJV). A fat heart is insensitive because fat insulates the heart.

God saw the insensitivity of the Israelites' hearts and commanded them to "circumcise" their hearts (Deuteronomy 10:16). Paul experienced the same condition when he wrote, "Real circumcision is a matter of the heart" (Romans 2:29 NRSVue). Circumcision of the heart cuts away the layers of callousness so the person can hear, see, and understand. In Jewish culture, circumcision in its very nature was a symbol of vulnerability and tenderness, but it primarily referred to a tender heart. A circumcised heart is one that is receptive to God.

SOFTENING THE HEART

When Jesus said, "Therefore I speak to them in parables, because seeing they do not see, and hearing they do not hear, nor do they understand" (Matthew 13:13), he was probably thinking something like this: *At this moment they don't seem ready to hear or see. If I tell them a story about a woman who searched her entire house for one lost coin, they will be able to see and hear that kind of thing. It will be something they will remember for a while and the deeper meaning will reveal itself in time.*

Jesus was aware that the hardness of their hearts was connected to their will. They didn't *want* to hear. They didn't *want* to understand. So the question became, "Should we just give up on them?" And Jesus' answer is, "No, we will give them what they can receive."

The parables of Jesus came to people in such a way that they could grow into the truth of the kingdom. His teaching style provided people the opportunity to take responsibility for opening the door to their heart, seeking the truth and hunting for even more truth. By the time listeners were able to discern the truth (rather than being lectured at), they may have even been able to stand it.

The genius of Jesus as a teacher is clearly seen in his respectful and merciful approach. He wasn't just delivering information; he was presenting people with a *different kind of life* than the one they were accustomed to. Teaching in parables helped him give people a vision of how life in the kingdom of God fit into their everyday, ordinary life.

PONDERING THE PROSE

Jesus used these masterful teaching methods to change people's lives, but many people do not want to change. Human beings, in general, are afraid of change and thus resist it. Apart from Christ, humans are dominated by fear and pride. In some cases, fear overrides pride; in other cases, pride wins over fear. In both cases, they cause a hardness of heart.

The parables and paradoxes Jesus presented required processing time. They helped people warm up to ideas they might have initially resisted. He gave them something they could keep working on without getting into a confrontational struggle.

If you confront people and tell them "how it is," they will stiffen up inside and respond with an argument about who's right and who's wrong. But suppose you tell them a story about a man who had two sons, and he said to them both, "Go work in the vineyard." And one son said, "Sure, Dad," but took off for the pool hall instead. And the other said, "No way!" as he also took off for the pool hall. But halfway down the road, the second son turned around and said, "Nah, you know, I'd better go do this for my dad." When Jesus asked, "Which one did the will of the father?" how would they quarrel with that? (Matthew 21:28–31, paraphrased).

Now suppose Jesus had said, "Listen, you children of Israel. You know what you've done. *You're* the ones who said to God, 'I'm going,' but you went to the pool hall instead." In truth, that's the way they were. They talked a lot about God but their hearts had gone to the pool hall. Using stories allowed the listeners' hearts, which were hard, to begin to soften. It gave them an opportunity to say to themselves, *I wonder which of those brothers I'm like.* Even Pharisees could do this because they weren't being pressured.

These stories allowed people time and space to think, circumventing their pride or fear. A story invites reflection, not argument. That's why we need to meditate on the parables. The lessons in the parables are absolutely vital and fundamental, and meditating on them will allow our understanding to grow, blossom, and bear fruit.

GUIDANCE

The Bible was not given to us as a book of instructions independent of the leading of the Holy Spirit. When we try to understand it on our own without God, "the letter kills" (2 Corinthians 3:6). Jesus knew this and thus taught in a way that people would be led and reasoned by the Spirit into a realm of reality—the kingdom of God—because "the Spirit gives life" (2 Corinthians 3:6).

Jesus' method of teaching by parable and paradox elicits in our mind a response to the Spirit of God in such a way that it relies on a *personal* relationship with God. In so doing, we learn to love the guidance of the Holy Spirit in understanding truth. An example of what I mean can be found in Proverbs:

> Do not answer a fool according to his folly,
> Lest you also be like him.
> Answer a fool according to his folly,
> Lest he be wise in his own eyes. (Proverbs 26:4–5)

Do you answer a fool according to his folly or not? The Bible tells you to do both, but you can't do both. So you *rely on the Spirit of God* to guide you into whether you will answer a fool according to his folly or not, depending on the circumstances.

Jesus' parables seek to prompt the same Holy Spirit response. The Parable of the Two Sons—those whose words don't match their actions—may cause us to see ourselves as one or the other son, depending on the situation. It may cause us to wonder why our yes is not always yes or our no is not always no. The parables of Jesus work like yeast in us, changing how we see God, ourselves, and the kingdom.

The illustrations and examples Jesus chose for his parables planted seeds in the minds and souls of the listeners, slowly sprouting and taking form, *bringing listeners into another kingdom* in which a different kind of life prevails. He was and is our wise and practical teacher.

As you prepare to study and meditate on the parables, this helpful list summarizing Jesus' teaching methods can provide tools to help you evaluate and apply the teaching in each parable.

TOOLS FOR REFLECTION AND GROWTH

Jesus was deeply intentional with his methods and helped his listeners *truly hear*, *remember*, *think deeply*, and *embrace* what he said. The parables of Jesus tend to have five aspects that continue to work long after we have heard them:

1. **CULTURALLY RELEVANT.** Jesus sought to challenge and radically change the culture of the fallen world and the prevailing presumptions of the day—things people believed and lived without even thinking about it.

2. **EASILY REMEMBERED.** Jesus' stories were unusual and difficult to forget.

3. **IN THE CONTEXT OF ORDINARY LIFE.** Jesus used everyday objects and activities—things his listeners were familiar with—to help them connect with the story.

4. **LOGICAL.** Jesus used the power of logic, reason, and common sense to get right down into the heart of people's assumptions about where they lived.

5. **MORE MEANINGFUL AS TIME PASSED.** Parables are like yeast that keeps expanding over time. People needed time to fully work out what Jesus said and grow in the truth the parables were communicating.

Parables have two parts—the vessel and the treasure within. Jesus designed the vessel of his parables to be sturdy enough to endure a long journey and to keep the treasure safe and secure. The treasure within the parables is the kingdom of God. As you read this book and study the parables, delight in the ingenuity and intentionality of how they are built, but always remember to seek the treasure within.

But we have this treasure in earthen vessels (2 Corinthians 4:7).

CHAPTER 3

WHY PARABLES?

As you therefore have received Christ Jesus the Lord, so walk in Him, rooted and built up in Him and established in the faith, as you have been taught, abounding in it with thanksgiving.

COLOSSIANS 2:6–7

When Jesus came, he essentially told people to forget what they thought they knew about God, because no one "know(s) the Father except the Son, and the one to whom the Son wills to reveal Him" (Matthew 11:27). This idea is crucial to keep in mind as we study the Bible. To say it a different way, we are not going to understand God or his Word by being clever, intelligent, and scholarly, or even by studying very hard because *the interaction of God with us through his Word is a personal matter. It depends on the condition of our hearts, our minds, and our lives.* As we study the Parable of the Sower, we will see just how important this is.

THE FIRST PARABLE

The three aspects of Jesus' ministry during his earthly life included teaching, preaching, and healing: "Then Jesus went about all the cities and villages, *teaching* in their synagogues, *preaching* the gospel of the kingdom, and *healing* every sickness and every disease among the people" (Matthew 9:35, emphasis added). The flow of Matthew's gospel from chapters 4–12 shows us how this worked.

In Matthew's fourth chapter, we see that when Jesus *preached* and ministered the kingdom of God, saying "Repent, for the kingdom of the heavens is at hand" (Matthew 4:17, paraphrased), he drew in masses of people from all over the area. In Matthew 5–7, Jesus *taught* about the nature of the kingdom of God in the Sermon on the Mount. As soon as he came down from the mount,* he began to *heal*, and we read stories of how he ministered the power of the kingdom of God in his healing (Matthew 8–9).

Chapters 10–12 contain discussions about the continuation of his ministry and how he sent out his followers to do what he did. That is the disciples' way of ministry then and now—to do what Jesus did. This aligns with Luke 10, where Jesus sent out his apprentices two by two, saying, "Now go do what I've been doing." When they came back rejoicing that "even the demons are subject to us in Your name," he responded, "Don't rejoice over that. Rejoice that your names are written in the Book of Life" (Luke 10:17, 20, paraphrased).

An extended record of Jesus' teaching, especially about the kingdom of God, begins in Matthew 13, where the Parable of the Sower appears to be the first recorded parable. That's not to say he never told a parable before, but it does mark a significant change in his teaching ministry.

As Jesus' ministry had progressed to this point, he began to notice people's varied reactions to what he was saying. Not everyone could receive his words, and those who did receive

---

* Editors' note: Dallas believed that Matthew 5–7 are the contents of one sermon, not a collection of Jesus' sayings. See Willard, *Divine Conspiracy*, 132–34.

them received them in different ways. Those whose hearts were set against God and concerned simply to have their own way were hardened by the message of Jesus. He sensed their resistance, and the Parable of the Sower portrays the different reactions to his teaching.

SEEDS EVERYWHERE

As Matthew 13 opens, we see that large crowds followed Jesus because of his teaching, preaching, and healing:

> On the same day Jesus went out of the house and sat by the sea. And great multitudes were gathered together to Him, so that He got into a boat and sat; and the whole multitude stood on the shore.
>
> Then He spoke many things to them in parables, saying: "Behold, a sower went out to sow." (Matthew 13:1–3)

To "sow" seeds meant to scatter them *where they would have a chance to germinate*. It was a common occurrence that his listeners frequently saw. Everyone knew what sowing was. Jesus continued:

> "And as he sowed, some seed fell by the wayside; and the birds came and devoured them. Some fell on stony places, where they did not have much earth; and they immediately sprang up because they had no depth of earth. But when the sun was up they were scorched, and because they had no root they withered away. And some fell among thorns, and the thorns sprang up and choked them." (Matthew 13:4–7)

Jesus may have paused between these descriptions because it was likely people were nodding and saying, "Yes, we know what that is. We've seen that happen." He concluded:

> "But others fell on good ground and yielded a crop: some a hundredfold, some sixty, some thirty. He who has ears to hear, let him hear!" (Matthew 13:8–9)

Now you'll notice there's not one religious word in that story. Jesus didn't read Scripture; he didn't pray; he didn't sing a hymn. He just told them a story in the context of the ordinary life of a farmer who was sowing seed. It appears that his disciples got worried about this. They may have said among themselves, "Uh-oh! What's happening here? He's slipping! Something has gone wrong!" So when they got him alone later, they said, "Jesus, why did you do that? Why did you just tell that story?" (Matthew 13:10, paraphrased). Jesus offered the following explanation.

SEEDS VERSUS WEEDS

The "seed" in this parable is the Word of God:

> "Therefore hear the parable of the sower: When anyone hears the word of the kingdom, and does not understand it, then the wicked one comes and snatches away what was sown in his heart. This is he who received seed by the wayside. But he who received the seed on stony places, this is he who hears the word and immediately receives it with joy." (Matthew 13:18–20)

When the Word of God comes into an individual's life, it begins to feed upon the soil that is there. This is why it's so important to understand the Parable of the Sower. If the person is too busy with other things to receive the Word of God, the Word will not take root. Or if it does take root, it will be starved and anemic.

I'm something of a farm boy myself, and I have done a lot of planting and harvesting. I remember going down into the creek bottoms in South Missouri where we plowed in the spring and planted corn. The dirt was so black; it was like chocolate. It had so much *good stuff* in it. But the weeds seemed to know about that rich soil too, so they came and occupied the same ground. By the middle of July, we could hardly tell the corn stalks from the weeds because the corn stalks were little starved, spindly things. They were not able to produce any good corn. In the fall, we picked the corn, but when we pulled the husks off, there were only three or four grains of corn on each cob because the plants were starving to death. A *lot* of folks are like those starving plants today.

FREE WILL

The Parable of the Sower is one of the most important parables Jesus gave about the kingdom of God because it answered the question, "Why doesn't the Word—the *logos*—have the effect on people we might hope for?" It moves us to ask again why God doesn't just change people.

This does not reflect a lack of power on God's part. In fact, if God wanted to turn me into a helicopter and fly me out the window, he could do it. Please understand that if God wanted to, he could have rewired every one of us to be faithful followers like Job, Hannah, and Daniel.

This is not a question about what God *can* do; it is a question about what God *will* do. It is a question about the precise manner of how God chooses to interact with people to accomplish his purposes. It's true that the God of all the earth can do anything he wants to do, but there are a lot of things he doesn't want to do. If we're going to work with God in the kingdom of God, we have to find the ways he has chosen to work, and then work with him in those ways.

The kingdom of God is a kingdom of love and understanding

and maturity, where people live together under the governance of the most glorious Being in all of reality—God himself. It will never be a kingdom of people who are knocked on the head or rewired to become religious robots. It is a kingdom of God's creatures whom he made to learn and grow freely.

Think back to how God presented himself and his kingdom through the long processes of history and then in the fullness of the Son of God himself. God did so in such a way as to *win the heart and capture the mind*, but also to give those who wished to turn away a chance to do so. When a human being says, "I want to have my way!" God says, "Alright, you can have your way." Sadly, the worst thing that can ever happen to a human being is to have their way when that way does not include God.

HARDENED HEARTS

There is a degree of hardness of heart beyond which God will not go to reach people. At that point, the effect of the Word of God is to harden, blind, and make deaf. That's what happened with Pharaoh. We're told that God *hardened* Pharaoh's heart (Exodus 7–15). How could this be? I suggest that God hardened Pharaoh's heart by showing him his power.

Moses told Pharaoh repeatedly to let the Israelites go or a certain plague would happen. Pharaoh always refused, and then one of the ten plagues would fall on Egypt. Then Pharaoh would say, "Oh, *let up*! Please, I'll give in. The Israelites can leave!" But the moment God *let up*, Pharaoh would say no to Moses and the Israelites. So this went on for a while, until the tenth plague occurred where God took the firstborn males of Egypt. At that point, Pharaoh's heart was broken because he lost his own son. Then he let the Israelites go (Exodus 12:31–32).

We see in this story that goodness (withdrawing the plague each time) does not always soften or break someone's heart. It sometimes hardens the heart. For some people, the Word of God and the gospel message simply harden their hearts.

THE POWER OF THE WORD

With this in mind, let's look at Jesus' explanation of the Parable of the Sower and how it addressed the receptivity of people's hearts. Remember that this parable caused the disciples to come to him and question, "What does this parable mean?" (Luke 8:9). It is the key to understanding all the parables (Mark 4:13). Jesus was teaching to those who "had ears to hear," but also in a way that would hopefully penetrate the other soils.

Jesus began his explanation with these words: "When anyone hears the word" (Matthew 13:19). The Greek word for *word* here is *logos*.[†] Logos is derived from the Greek word *lego*, which is a powerful term referring to the structuring and forming of things. *Logos* conveys that this formation is being done now—present tense. When Jesus said "the word," he used the word *logos* because he was talking about a personal power that was going forth. Jesus was referring to himself as "the *logos*." "In the beginning was the Word," the *Logos*, that was Jesus (John 1:1).

DECIDING TO LISTEN

"When anyone hears the *logos* and *does not understand it . . .*" (Matthew 13:19, paraphrased, emphasis added)

Hearing and understanding the message involves the mind, but also the *will*. The will has very little power in and of itself, and many people overestimate the power of their will and their

---

† This is very different from the Greek word *semeion*, which stands for a mark or sign, like a chalk mark, an ink mark, or even a sound. When people came to Jesus and said, "Master, show us a sign," they were asking for a *semeion*. Instead of talking about a sign (*semeion*) here, Jesus spoke of the *logos*.

mind. They think they can accomplish much more with them than they actually can. Even the brightest mind and most steadfast will are tremendously limited.

When the Word of God comes into our minds, we decide how important it is to hold on to it. That is why the first important question is, "What am I choosing to do with the Word that has come into my mind?" If your will is set against the Word of God, you will get nowhere in understanding it. This parable is about how the will responds to God.

The primary function of the will is to trust God. The set of a person's will is key for how the Word of God affects the mind because the will and mind are deeply integrated. On the one hand, what the mind dwells on determines what the will chooses to act on; on the other hand, the orientation of the will may determine what stays in the mind. It's important to ask ourselves, *What is my mind dwelling on and why is it dwelling there?*

As we mature, we get a deeper sense of the mind's limitations and our reliance on habit. The mind gets clogged with thoughts, ideas, opinions, and notions that are sometimes misleading, false, or wrong. In our fallen condition, our minds are often turned toward the wrong things, and we can't even think the thoughts we need to think, disabling our will from turning to God.

An essential investment of our life with God is to take care of our minds by cultivating our thoughts. The unkempt mind becomes obsessive, and then the will works from those frenzied thoughts.[‡] So you can't let just anything run through your mind. When tempted, you have to say to yourself, *There are some thoughts I will not think!*

---

‡ For a deeper understanding of the will and the way it works with our thoughts, you may want to read "Larger Psychology on the Will," in William James, *The Principles of Psychology* (New York: Holt, 1890).

FIRST THREE SOILS

Wayside Ground

> "Behold, a sower went out to sow. And as he sowed, some seed fell by the wayside; and the birds came and devoured them." (Matthew 13:3–4)

The first thing Jesus pointed out at the beginning of the parable was that an enemy is watching, and, in various ways, he simply snatches the Word out of the mind. This emphasizes why it is important to actively hold on to the Word. We may think we are smart enough that we don't need to study the Bible or memorize Scripture, but these practices are crucial.

Satan finds many ways to keep the Word out of our minds. This may be as simple as believing we have something more important to do. In *The Screwtape Letters*, C. S. Lewis described a man who was working on a line of thought and was just about to conclude that God is real, but then it struck him that it was lunchtime. He didn't pursue the thought any further.[8] That's the way the mind works.

When Jesus described the birds snatching the seeds away, he was explaining that the devil is active in our hearing process and doesn't want people to truly hear the message. Our minds are filled with a steady stream of slogans and ideas that keep us from hearing the Word: "Happiness is being single"; "Have it your way"; "If it feels good, do it!"

Another device of Satan is to distort the Word. For example, if we think the invitation of God means he will provide easy solutions to our problems, we might try to use the message for our purposes—to solve problems, to get what we want. There's no inward turning toward God, no inner turning from self toward others. There's no humility and surrender to the truth. The result is we remain shallow and are simply using God. When a little trouble comes, we complain, "This is not what I had in mind. No, thank you. I'll just leave."

Satan also works through loneliness. Mother Teresa of Calcutta wrote, "In the West there is so much loneliness. . . . The greatest disease in the West today is . . . being unwanted, unloved, and uncared for."[9] The enemy is busily working to keep people apart. In workplaces, families, schools, and even churches, people believe that if they don't get along with certain people, they should simply have nothing to do with them.

Thoughts like these come to us over and over. We're so busy letting feelings run our lives and doing things "our way" that we can't hear any messages of love, unity, forgiveness, and acceptance. Those notions simply get whisked out of our minds.

Stony Ground

> "Some [seeds] fell on stony places, where they did not have much earth; and they immediately sprang up because they had no depth of earth. But when the sun was up they were scorched, and because they had no root they withered away." (Matthew 13:5-6)

In the stony ground, the people hear the Word and say, "Whoopee, this is wonderful!" But they don't receive the Word at the deep level of their soul where it can penetrate the depths of their personality. The seeds don't take root because there is nothing within the person's character to take hold of. A person's character is the internal, overall structure of the self that is revealed by long-running patterns of behavior and from which actions more or less automatically arise. It's what runs our life. It shows itself in our thinking and choices and in our habitual ways of behavior that are built into our bodies and become obvious in our relationships. What we will seriously think about is one of the strongest indications of how our character has grown.

The way our thoughts are directed affects our feelings *before and apart from* the point where they settle into the habits of our body and our social relationships. Receiving good news can make our bodies jump up and down with joy because our feelings are largely determined by our thoughts. That's why people jump up and down when they win the lottery. But then very often their winnings ruin their life because their feelings were one thing and their character was something else.

That's what's happening in this second category of soil. The feelings come in response to the Word of the kingdom, but there is no true repentance—probably because they have other things on their mind. Their faith lasts for a little while, but when trial or persecution arises because of the Word, they are offended. They turn away and say, "Well, I wasn't really looking for *this*!" Without the roots of character, the good news withers.

Thorny Ground

"And some fell among thorns, and the thorns sprang up and choked them." (Matthew 13:7)

Jesus was saying that in the thorny ground, the *logos* actually took root. But other things crowded out the *logos*—"the cares of this world ["the worries of this life" in the NIV] and the deceitfulness of riches" (Matthew 13:22). Mark and Luke added "the desires for other things" and "pleasures of life" (Mark 4:19; Luke 8:14).

In the Lukan telling of this parable, these things choke the seedlings so that they "bring no fruit to maturity" (Luke 8:14). The *thorns*—and how well Jesus named them "thorns"—represent the things that keep us too preoccupied to give thought to the *logos* when it presents itself. The cares of this world—wars, social tension, famine, or pending failures of economic systems—keep us in a worried state.

Riches aren't "thorns" in and of themselves, but their danger is in their deceitfulness, which creates an illusion of a power, security, and merit that belong only to God. Our tendency with riches is to trust in them, think about them, become obsessed with them, and do anything for them. Jesus addressed this in the Sermon on the Mount when he said, "You cannot serve God and mammon" (Matthew 6:24). He was describing how disjointing it is to deeply desire to serve God and to deeply desire wealth. It isn't just that you shouldn't do it; it's that no matter how hard you try, you *can't* do it.

To serve wealth is to be in bondage to material goods. One test for considering whether we're in bondage to material goods, including food and clothing, is to consider how much of our time and our best thinking we give to these things. The mind is often piled so high with treasures and pleasures that we can't focus well (Matthew 6:19–23). When Jesus said, "Do not worry about your life, what you will eat or what you will drink; nor about your body, what you will put on. Is not life more than food and the body more than clothing?" (6:25), he was not saying, "Don't iron your clothes" or, "Don't think about cooking dinner." He was saying, "If thoughts of food, clothing, and material goods are uppermost in your mind, those thoughts will run your life." The desire for pleasures and belongings can create a bondage to material goods that entangles us in a complexity that wears us down and wears us out.

Jesus' sermon went on to discuss how helpless we are in the face of the pursuit of material things: "Which of you by worrying can add a single hour to your span of life?" (Matthew 6:27 NRSVue). He concluded by saying not to worry about what to eat or drink or what to wear. God knows we need these things, and he will provide them. "But seek first the kingdom of God and His righteousness, and all these things shall be added to you" (Matthew 6:33). The thorns of life keep us from bearing the fruit of the good news.

FERTILE SOIL

> "But as for that in the good soil, these are the ones who, when they hear the word, hold it fast in an honest and good heart and bear fruit with endurance." (Luke 8:15 NRSVue)

Receiving the Word with "an honest and good heart" means not only truly hearing the Word but also holding on to it and acting in connection with it. It means we join our *will* with the Word we've received. The same Word goes forth, just as it goes forth while you are reading this book, and it is the difference in the *heart* that makes the difference in the *effects*.

This is one of the ways the will affects how we hear. The will can be set on believing we don't need help or need other people, that we are *doing fine*. But the humble person reaches out for help. As we use our power of choice to turn our *minds* to God, we have greater contact with God throughout our day, developing a conversational relationship with him. We bring the reality of God into our lives by making contact with him through our minds, and then our actions are based on the understanding that results from the fullness of that contact.

There is a kingdom of God we're all being invited to live in, and we can know it by experiencing its reality. We can come to know the presence of the King in our lives with such constancy and power that even when we are suffering great pain or lying down to die, we can feel and know the presence of the kingdom and be blessed.

Our inward turning toward God allows us to turn toward

others. The redemptive fellowship of the body of Christ heals our loneliness in this kingdom where we don't need to carry our burdens alone. It's a wonderful thing to be loved to the point where you'll never feel like you're alone again.

There is nothing mysterious here. This is why *the mind, and what we turn our minds to,* is the key to our lives. This results in an abundant harvest—thirty times more, sixty times more, a hundred times more (Matthew 13:8).

TAKE HEED

Remember that a parable (*parabola*) is characterized by throwing one thing down beside another. Looking at one of the things helps us better understand the thing next to it. So when we look at how seeds grow or don't grow in the Parable of the Sower, we can see why people react the way they do to the Word of the kingdom. Those living like the soils on the wayside, the stony ground, and thorny ground are not able to let the Word work at a deep level in their soul. God puts forth the Word of his kingdom in such a way that those who have ears for the purpose of hearing can hear it. They have the privilege and responsibility of receiving it.

If someone's desire for God resembles any of the first three soils in the parable, that doesn't mean they'll stay there forever. Jesus didn't say the heart never changes. There is good reason to have hope for ourselves and others. What a person couldn't hear yesterday, they may be very open to hear today.

Sometimes this parable is read fatalistically, as if what happens with the seed can't be helped. But that was not Jesus' intent. His next words were, "No one lights a lamp and covers it over with a container" (Luke 8:16 NASB). This shows that the initiative of God comes into play. The sower (God) who comes out to sow the Word of the kingdom of God does not intend for the lamp of the Word to be covered up. It's his intention that it should be lifted up (i.e., set on a lampstand) to give light to everyone in the house. We are to be the light of the world wherever we are. God has appointed each of us a time and place when and where we are the light of the world. That happens as we receive the Word of the kingdom into our lives and live *in* that reality.

Notice how Jesus continued with this wording about taking responsibility: "Therefore take heed how you hear. For whoever has, to him more will be given; and whoever does not have, even what he seems to have will be taken from him" (Luke 8:18). This teaching tells us to pay close attention to *how* we hear. True repentance ("repent, for the kingdom of the heavens is at hand") expresses itself in the humble act of listening. This is how we position ourselves in a place where Jesus can reveal things to us.

I used to listen to an old preacher who once said, "If a dog came to town preaching the gospel of Jesus Christ, I would listen to that dog." He was emphasizing that we cannot be humble before God unless we can be humble before the lowest creature on earth that might speak to us of the kingdom. We could, in fact, be wrong about some things, so we had better listen. Others have been wrong; so yes, *we* could be wrong. Our obsessions may be driving us in the wrong direction. So we must stop, be reflective, and think about it. And above all, we must listen to the Word of God's kingdom, and ask ourselves where our hearts and minds are before him.

As disciples, we need to understand that the Parable of the Sower applies to each of us all the time. The sower is Jesus. And he works with people, of course, speaking through them to sow the Word of the kingdom. What we have been given by others who have sowed in us will be added to greatly as we pursue life in the kingdom of God. But if we don't listen with care, even what we've heard may be lost. The Word of God comes to us in a hearing kind of life, a life lived in the Spirit with a mind attuned to the Trinity. The Word of God comes and fills our lives if we want it, but we have to want it and seek it. And if we don't want it, God will allow us to live the "with me" life—the source of all our troubles—instead of the "with God" life, which is a life of growth and abundance.

ATTUNED TO GOD

When we begin to seek the Word of God, we will become the kind of people who are able to hear God's voice. We shouldn't expect his Word to be only a to-do list. Most of what God will say to us will provide insights that shine a light on what is happening in and around us.

The gentle Word of God, which we increasingly learn to recognize, is something we will not hear if we don't listen with care. We simply won't recognize it. The practices Jesus modeled within the spiritual life are important means for us to grow in this and other areas of our lives. They are ways of listening and desiring to truly *hear*.

Being attuned to hearing God's Word and receiving it into the fertile soil of our lives comes from lives marked by friendship with and confidence in God. The kind of personal relationship between ourselves and God that we find demonstrated in the Bible is a "with God" life, the eternal kind of life lived in conversational relationship with God (John 17:3).§ It is a life of abiding in Jesus Christ where we bear much fruit, shine before men, and where our works give glory to our heavenly Father (John 15:5; Matthew 5:16).

---

§ For more about how we live in a conversational relationship with God and any of the topics on prayer in this book, see my *Hearing God: Developing a Conversational Relationship with God*, rev. ed. (Downers Grove, IL: InterVarsity, 2012).

MAIN POINTS ABOUT
THE KINGDOM OF GOD

- The Parable of the Sower portrays the different reactions to Jesus' teaching by illustrating how our heart is set to respond to God. If we are too busy or distracted with other things, the Word will not take root or it will be starved and anemic.
- The kingdom of God is a kingdom of love, understanding, and maturity, where people can live together in a conversational relationship with the most glorious Being in all of reality.
- God desires that we receive his Word into the good soil of our hearts and live our lives in the reality of his kingdom.
- The Parable of the Sower applies to each of us all the time because every day is a new opportunity to receive the Word of God and tend to the soil of our heart.

CHAPTER 4

THE SECRET
INNER WORKING
OF THE KINGDOM

Now to him who is able to do immeasurably more than all
we ask or imagine, according to his power that is at work
within us, to him be glory in the church and in Christ
Jesus throughout all generations, for ever and ever! Amen.

EPHESIANS 3:20-21 NIV

Jesus had a way of saying the most surprising things. No one
would have thought that the kingdom of God was like an ordinary, tiny seed any more than we would say it is like a soda
bottle. But Jesus needed to correct the mistaken impressions
people had about the nature of God and his kingdom, and, of
course, he used parables such as this one:

> "The kingdom of God is as if a man should scatter seed on
> the ground, and should sleep by night and rise by day, and
> the seed should sprout and grow, he himself does not know

how. For the earth yields crops by itself: first the blade, then the head, after that the full grain in the head. But when the grain ripens, immediately [the farmer, the man looking after his crop] puts in the sickle, because the harvest has come." (Mark 4:26–29)

The kingdom is like seed that a farmer simply threw out in his garden. Jesus didn't say the farmer "planted" them. He threw them out just as someone might toss an old tomato into the backyard and then be surprised to find a tomato plant growing in the spring. Jesus used the image of a seed to indicate that the Word (*logos*) of the kingdom has a power and life of its own. The farmer did nothing to cultivate it; in fact, "he himself [did] not know how" the seed sprouted and grew.

Then He said, "To what shall we liken the kingdom of God? Or with what parable shall we picture it? It is like a mustard seed which, when it is sown on the ground, is smaller than all the seeds on earth; but when it is sown, it grows up and becomes greater than all herbs, and shoots out large branches, so that the birds of the air may nest under its shade." (Mark 4:30–32)

Jesus made a point of saying that this smallest of seeds took root and grew into a large bush big enough for birds to land in it and take up residence in its branches.

In Luke's account, Jesus followed the mustard seed parable with a similar metaphor:

"To what shall I liken the kingdom of God? It is like leaven, which a woman took and hid in three measures of meal till it was all leavened." (Luke 13:20–21)

Yeast kneaded into dough works unseen until the whole mass of the dough has the life in it. You just put the yeast in there, and it grows and takes over. The kingdom of God is a kind of life that keeps growing like a mustard seed and leaven. It grows far beyond what we would call the church, which is often thought of simply as a group of people gathered together in a building on Sunday mornings. But the church is not the kingdom of God. The church is a particular *manifestation* of the kingdom of God, where God is certainly at work, but God is just as involved in all areas of life—business, science, and the arts—as he is in the church.

THE MIGHTY POWERFUL SEED

It's interesting that nothing appears more often in Jesus' parables than a seed. Seeds are wonderful things. As a child I was fascinated by seeds, and I still have a tender spot for nurseries and seed catalogs. I eventually learned I'd never be able to grow things as beautiful as plants pictured in catalogs, but it was such a wonderful and wondrous thing to look at them.

A seed is just a dry little thing, maybe no bigger than your little fingernail. You put that in the ground, and soon a plant springs out of the earth. You water it and fertilize it, and after a little while, you see this marvelous thing—maybe a watermelon—emerging out of that little seed.

The seed is a *power* to organize reality. Please think about that for a moment. When you put that little seed down in the earth, it's already packed with potent substances. The power contained within it cracks the shell of the seed and puts out a little root. That little root starts eating dirt, eventually putting out a little leaf, then more leaves, and then fruit. The seed has *organized reality* in a specific and defined way to make a watermelon out of dirt, water, and sunlight. That's why the *logos* is aptly portrayed as a seed—it is a spiritual power to organize reality.

God designed creation so that when you plant a watermelon seed, you don't get a stalk of corn. Every seed knows exactly what it's supposed to absorb out of the soil and what to leave behind. If it doesn't select the right nutrients, it simply won't function well—and it may not live at all. It also needs water and sunlight. The seed organizes all these things together and produces tasty food and beautiful plants to enjoy. That's why the metaphor of the seed is exactly right and why Jesus returned to it over and over again.

Jesus himself is referred to as "the *seed* of Abraham" (Romans 9:7; 11:1; 2 Corinthians 11:22, emphasis added). Abraham was a man of faith who propagated "after his kind" through the centuries until it came to the *perfect* man of faith—Jesus Christ himself, the Son of God, who was the *seed* of Abraham.

Jesus was a seed in the sense that he was planted in a world God prepared and began to organize reality in order to display the kingdom of God (Galatians 4:4). Jesus did not come right away when Adam sinned, nor in the time of Moses, Joshua, or Isaiah. He came in the *fullness* of time when the ground was right, so that he could be implanted as a seed in the fertile earth of history and bring forth the church of the Lord Jesus Christ. If he had come earlier, the church could not have been formed in the way God had chosen to do it.

DIVIDING SOUL AND SPIRIT

Mark closes this series of parables with these words:

> And with many such parables He spoke the word to them as they were able to hear it. (Mark 4:33)

Their ears were open.

Notice that Jesus spoke *the Word* to them in parables—*one* Word, *many* parables. The Word in question is the Word about the kingdom of God. The Word of God is God speaking, just like your word is *you* speaking. The word of a person is the speaking or writing of *that person*.

Let's take a good look at the Word of God, beginning with Hebrews 4:12—perhaps the most commonly recognized statement about God's Word. This description may be the most *analytical* of any in the Bible, laying out what we *mean* when we talk about the Word of God:

> For the word of God is living and powerful, and sharper than any two-edged sword, piercing even to the division of soul and spirit, and of joints and marrow, and is a discerner of the thoughts and intents of the heart. (Hebrews 4:12)

When God speaks a word, it has a unique quality—it is *living*. Older translations use another word for "living," the word *quick*, like the quick of your thumbnail—the place at the bottom of a fingernail where you have feeling. It's alive. The Word of God is *living*, *personal*, and *powerful*. It is sharp enough to be able to divide the parts of the mind and the personality from one another.

The expression "division of soul and spirit" is one of those delicious phrases that invites further study. The *soul* is fundamentally the life principle that is in the individual person, given to them by God, which makes their body and mind function. The *spirit* is the element that is especially given by God to hold the soul and body together. When Jesus died, he said, "Unto you I surrender my spirit" (Luke 23:46, paraphrased), not "my soul" or "my body," but "my spirit." "God is spirit" (John 4:24 NIV)—not soul, not body; in defining God, he is spirit.

The soul and the spirit don't occupy any space at all. They

are invisible to the naked eye. Even under a microscope set to the highest power, they cannot be seen. Even the sharpest and most intricate knife cannot separate them. But the Word of God can.

Now when the Word of God comes into the midst of a life or group, it is *so sharp* that it can divide, distinguish, and clarify the difference between what is spiritual and what is merely an expression of an individual's own strength and life—a very important truth, but one that may not seem as important to us today as it was in the time of the apostles and of Jesus himself. We are *not as familiar* with the reality and workings of the spirit.

We see a great difference in the condition of the church during the time of the apostles compared to most of church history. And that difference, above all, is seen in the reality of the spirit. It was important for the early church to distinguish what was the work of the soul and the flesh as opposed to what was the work of the spirit. They knew that unless it was the work of the spirit, it amounted to nothing. The Word of God is *able* to distinguish between the two.

The Word of God pierces even to the division of "joints and marrow, and is a discerner of the thoughts and intents of the heart. And there is no creature hidden from His sight, but all things are naked and open to the eyes of Him to whom we must give account" (Hebrews 4:12–13). When the Word of God as God speaking comes into the life of a person or a group, discernment is present and *all things* are open. The world, however, runs away from openness, especially when it comes to sin because they don't know what to do with sin. Those who have been touched by the Spirit of God and have learned of the kindness of God in Jesus Christ know, as Israel's King David said, that they must fall into the hands of the Lord when they do wrong.

When David sinned by numbering the people, he was given a choice: Would he fall into the hands of the Philistines, or would he fall into the hands of the Lord? He replied, "I am in great distress. Please let us fall into the hand of the LORD, for His mercies are great" (2 Samuel 24:14). We don't have to hide from God, even though we are not perfect. Like a child who knows the loving heart of their mother or father when they do what is wrong, we seek reconciliation. All things are open when the Word of God is present.

LIVING AND PURPOSIVE

Along with revealing the thoughts and intents of the heart, the Word of God is a *power* that is present in the world. The Bible contains many eloquent descriptions of this power. Psalm 107 is one record of the ways the Lord dealt with the people of Israel in many of their trials and tribulations. Even though they had drifted away from him in their foolishness and had rebelled, the Lord acted on their behalf, sending his Word:

> Oh, that men would give thanks to the LORD for His
>   goodness,
> And for His wonderful works to the children of men!
> For He has broken the gates of bronze,
> And cut the bars of iron in two.
>
> Fools, because of their transgression,
> And because of their iniquities, were afflicted. . . .
> Then they cried out to the LORD in their trouble,
> And He saved them out of their distresses.
> He *sent His word* and healed them,
> And delivered them from their destructions.
>   (Psalm 107:15–17, 19–20, emphasis added)

Because the Word of God is *living*, it knows what it is doing. It is *purposive*. When "He sent His word and healed them," that was God speaking in his kingdom. And where the word of the king is, there is power (Ecclesiastes 8:4). That's what distinguished the Word of Christ when he came. People were astonished that his Word and his doctrine came with power, saying they had never heard anything like it before (Luke 4:32). They tried to figure it out: "What is this? What new doctrine *is* this? For with authority He commands even the unclean spirits, and they obey Him" (Mark 1:27, paraphrased, emphasis added). God had done it again: he *sent his Word* and he healed them.

The action of the Word of God in the domain of nature is illustrated in the final few psalms in the book of Psalms. Psalm 147 contrasts the work of humanity with the work of God as it tells of the goodness of God, his power, and his creation:

> He heals the brokenhearted
> And binds up their wounds.
> He counts the number of the stars;
> He calls them all by name.
> Great is our Lord, and mighty in power;
> His understanding is infinite.
> The LORD lifts up the humble. (Psalm 147:3–6)

Then it contrasts this with the so-called strength of humans:

> He does not delight in the strength of the horse;

We might say, "He does not delight in new stealth bombers."

> He takes no pleasure in the legs of a man.

He is not impressed by human strength.

> The LORD takes pleasure in those who fear Him,
> In those who hope in His mercy. (Psalm 147:10–11)

Regarding the Word, the psalmist said:

> He sends out His command to the earth;
> His word runs very swiftly.
> He gives snow like wool;
> He scatters the frost like ashes. . . .
> He sends out His word and melts them. . . .
> He declares His word to Jacob,
> His statutes and His judgments to Israel.
> (Psalm 147:15–16, 18–19)

The psalmist said this about his creation in Psalm 148:

> Fire and hail, snow and clouds;
> Stormy wind, fulfilling His word. (Psalm 148:8)

The psalmist saw all of the phenomena of nature as keeping the commandment of the Lord. The commandment of the Lord is God speaking. It is his Word.

WORD AS SUBSTANCE

One final aspect of the Word of God for us to understand is that it is a *substance*. That's why Jesus likened it to a seed. When the Israelites ate manna (a word that means "what is it?") in the desert, that was congealed Word of God. When Jesus was in the wilderness being tempted, Satan came to him and said, in effect, "Why don't you turn these little stones into loaves of bread, just like mother Mary used to bake?" Jesus was hungry, but he replied: "'Man shall not live by bread alone, but by every word that proceeds from the mouth of God'" (Matthew 4:4).

Jesus also referred to the Word as substance when the disciples returned from going into the city of Samaria to get something to eat. They offered him food, but Jesus told them, "I have food to eat of which you do not know" (John 4:32).

God's Word is a substance that offers sustenance, just as food does. We live in two landscapes—the physical and the invisible—and when we fast, we are taking in substance from the invisible landscape. We are learning how to live on the nourishment of the Word of God. We don't fast to prove our goodness to God, to others, or even to ourselves. Jesus said, "When you fast, don't look sad. Don't let it be noticed by others" (Matthew 6:16–18, paraphrased). Instead, get a new haircut, try on new clothes, enjoy your friends. Fasting helps us to learn inwardly what it is like to live on the nourishing, substantial, living, powerful Word of God.

ORGANIZING REALITY

To be "born again" (John 3:3) is to be born of the Word of God. You are born from another realm—the realm of the spirit. That is to say, you are given a new life—a different kind of life. Being born again is commonly mistaken to mean, "I get a new start." No, it's not a new start, but rather a new *life*. This is not a second try at the same old stuff. Something new has been implanted in you.

In the garden of Eden, God told Adam, "Of the tree of the knowledge of good and evil you shall not eat, for in the day that you eat of it you shall surely die" (Genesis 2:17). Did Adam and Eve die when they disobeyed? They were still alive, but they died spiritually. They had a life in them that they lost. That's a death. They were put out of the garden and had to make it on their own. This created a need for a new birth, an additional birth, an animated life from above.

Notice the italicized phrases in the following three passages that show us the availability of this life from above: "As many as received him, to them gave he power to become the sons of God, even to them that believe on his name: which were *born, not of blood, nor of the will of the flesh, nor of the will of man, but of God*" (John 1:12–13 KJV, emphasis added).

Now in order to more fully grasp just how God did that, let's look at 1 Peter 1:22–23: "Since you have purified your souls in obeying the truth through the Spirit in sincere love of the brethren, love one another fervently with a pure heart, having been *born again*, not of corruptible seed but incorruptible, *through the word of God which lives and abides forever*" (emphasis added).

In addition, the Word is embedded and established in us: "Therefore lay aside all filthiness and overflow of wickedness, and *receive with meekness the implanted word*, which is able to save your souls" (James 1:21, emphasis added). The implanted Word is like a seed because it is a power to organize reality. It will take what is in your life and rearrange it.

THE KINGDOM BRINGS POWER

Like the farmer in this chapter's first parable who scattered the seed on the ground and then watched for the harvest, we have to sow the *right* word. The gospel of the kingdom of God is the only word that will have the effect Jesus described as the effect *of the kingdom*.

The Word of God contained in the Bible is the written Word of God.* It is infallible and constantly kept in God's hand to accomplish his purposes, but the *gospel* of the kingdom of God is

---

* I explain and defend my views of biblical inspiration and inerrancy in *The Allure of Gentleness: Defending the Faith in the Manner of Jesus* (San Francisco: HarperOne, 2015), 104-9, and briefly in *The Divine Conspiracy: Rediscovering Our Hidden Life in God* (San Francisco: HarperSanFrancisco, 1998), 4, in a section titled "My Assumptions about the Bible."

not a gospel about the Bible. The Word that brings forth the fruit of the kingdom is not a gospel about your church either. There is a glory in the church, and it will speak for itself, but that's not the gospel we live and teach.

Please read this next part carefully because I don't want you to be offended or confused by it. The gospel of the kingdom of God is also not a gospel *only of the death, burial, and resurrection of Jesus Christ*. That is *part* of the gospel of the kingdom of God, but it is not the *whole* gospel.[†] I remind you that Jesus Christ himself did not preach that historical reality as the whole gospel. The gospel of our Lord Jesus Christ is the present availability of the kingdom of God. This helps us understand what salvation is in the New Testament sense. This salvation includes three things that are available to us:

- *Forgiveness of sins.* Through the work of Christ and his substitutionary stand before God on our behalf, our sins are forgiven through the mercy of God.
- *Transformation of character into the image of Jesus Christ.* We are meant to be conformed to the image of Jesus Christ (Romans 8:29). This is a work of grace just as much as the forgiveness of sins. And there is *nowhere* any indication that this is something that is supposed to happen after we die.
- A *significant degree of power over evil*, both in our own lives and in the life of the church of which we are essentially a part.

The fullness of redemption in the Lord Jesus Christ, as it is presented in the New Testament, is a fullness that comes to

---

† This came to be the gospel of the church because they understood in it the meaning of the gospel of the kingdom of God. Now, if you believe in that, you'll go to heaven when you die. But we have a great deal more to do in this world than to go to heaven when we die. And if we don't understand that the gospel of our Lord Jesus Christ is the gospel of the kingdom of God, we will not be able to understand what salvation is in the New Testament sense.

those who live in his church, which is an outpost of his kingdom in this world.

When we communicate, teach, and preach the right word, we do so with confidence that the kingdom brings power wherever it grows, just as the seed does. We know that we do not live or teach in our own power. The kingdom of God is not something we produce within ourselves. It comes to us through the Word. We have the power that is in the seed, which *is* the Word of God.

Sometimes our work lacks confidence in the gospel of the kingdom of God. We could say we have every reason not to be confident as we see murder, theft, and exploitation around us. Yet in the face of all that, we offer people the kingdom of God. There is no other hope. None. Jesus did not live in a world that was much different from ours. In many ways, it was more brutal than ours. And yet he spoke about the kingdom of God. He lived it out in his person, and he welcomed others to join him in that same life. He had confidence in God. Like the farmer when he sowed the seed, he *abandoned* it to the earth.

HAVE PATIENCE

This emphasis on the power of the seed and the yeast is important because religious organizations sometimes put arduous burdens on people about all the things they're supposed to be doing, both in devotion and in service, as though the kingdom itself had no power. Yes, there are things for us to do, but we have to understand what grace really means. Divine grace is God acting in our lives to accomplish what we cannot do on our own. It infuses us and our actions, making them effective in the wisdom and power of God. In the reality of the kingdom of God, grace means that *God will do the work along with us* if we make the effort to open our hearts and minds to the Word of the kingdom.

Grace doesn't mean we do nothing. The farmer went out and sowed the seed. Grace is not opposed to effort (that's an *action*), but rather to earning (that's an *attitude*). We let the Word of the kingdom come and occupy our minds. We study what Jesus said about the kingdom—the way he expressed it and how he taught about it.

After our farmer scattered his seeds, a few days passed and then a little shoot came up out of the ground. He continued to watch the plant as it grew, going through his days as he normally would, and eventually something edible arose there. Although the farmer didn't know how it all worked, the plant still developed and grew.

This means we don't have to carry the load of making "it" happen. This is one of the most important things to understand. We don't have to try to force people to do anything; we just speak the Word of the gospel, live as a disciple, lovingly teach, and be with people—and the growth will come.

As a child, I tried to make a rosebud open. It seemed like a good idea. I liked roses, so why should I wait? Why not just open it up? But you know what happened: That rose never opened up. Very shortly, it lay in my hand, a disarray of disjointed petals. It *never* blossomed. In the same way, if you dig up a seed to see if the root is growing and then put it back in the ground, it will not continue to grow. You have to *abandon* it to the ground and leave it there.

I tore the rosebud apart when I tried to force it to blossom, and there are people who want nothing to do with Christ and his church because they've had their soul torn apart by well-meaning Christians who pressured them to comply with what they think it means to become a Christian. Their souls have been wounded by, as Paul said, "a zeal for God,‡ but not according

---

‡ In this case, *zeal* refers to misguided or uninformed enthusiasm or energy.

to knowledge" (Romans 10:2). Paul had once been this kind of person—the kind of person who would force compliance. Our enthusiasm must be infused with patience as we wait for the seed to bear fruit.

UTTER CONFIDENCE

As a young "preacher boy," as we were called when I was a Baylor University student, I sensed the Lord saying to me, "Never try to find a place to speak. Try to have something to say." He taught me that I could concentrate on that, simply live with him, and count on him to have the effect he wanted. That can be a source of relief, rest, and power for all of us in our work, our congregations, our communities, and all the places we go as Christ's people.

We are to let the living water flow and to concentrate on taking it in. I would have been out of the business of speaking for Christ decades ago if I had not learned by experience the power of the Word of the kingdom of God. I didn't have to make anything happen. So now I have abandoned trying to get anyone to do anything. It's not my business. It is the Lord who adds daily to the church.

This means we can relax. Jesus was one of the most absolutely relaxed people who ever lived on this earth. He had complete and utter confidence in the power of the Word that he spoke. He never doubted. Like the farmer, he abandoned it to the ground, which is the point of this parable. The results conformed to his faith. Remember, the rule is this: "According to your faith let it be to you" (Matthew 9:29). This is another benefit of having the faith *of* Christ. Like Jesus, we abandon the seed to the ground and let it work.

YOU DON'T HAVE TO MAKE IT HAPPEN

The farmer planting the seed is generally associated with sharing the Christian faith. Many people have been made to feel guilty for not speaking more forcefully to others about what they believe, but it is not our business to *make* things happen. We are told to be witnesses, saying what we have seen and experienced, and we are told to make disciples. The job of the Christian is to witness to the Word of truth, to show forth the kingdom of God in their lives and in their prayers, and to "give an account of the hope that is within them with gentleness and respect" (1 Peter 3:15, paraphrased). They can do these things with complete confidence that the seeds they sow will not be in vain.

Instead of trying to compel people into heaven, we do as the farmer did—sow the seed and then abandon it. You lay the seed down, whether it's what you say to your child or to the students in a class you teach. I have found that if people weren't so anxious about *making* people think a certain way or do a certain thing, they would do a much better job of presenting the gospel of the kingdom of God. Their strained efforts to get people to do these things make it difficult for others to truly hear the Word of God.

And when the harvest comes, you put in the sickle. But if we don't preach, teach, and live the gospel of the kingdom of God with confidence and abandonment, the harvest will either not come or it will be scraggly because it was forced to bear fruit.

Give God the time to work. Speak the Word. In that regard, as Paul said, "Be instant in season, out of season" (2 Timothy 4:2 KJV). There is no time when we should not be speaking the Word in some way. Our witness is constant. And indeed if the Word dwells richly in our hearts, it will be constant: "Do all things without complaining and disputing, that you may become blameless and harmless, children of God without fault in the midst of a crooked and perverse generation, among whom you shine as lights in the world, holding fast the word of life" (Philippians 2:14–16).

MAIN POINTS ABOUT
THE KINGDOM OF GOD

- The Word of the kingdom is brimming with a power like seeds bursting with energy as they emerge from the soil.
- The role of a disciple is to learn from Jesus how to live their life and to share what they have experienced.
- When we share God's kingdom with others, we abandon the seed to the ground and let it work. Patience and confidence in God and his Word are helpful virtues.

CHAPTER 5

THE GREATEST OPPORTUNITY

Behold, I stand at the door and knock. If anyone hears My voice and opens the door, I will come in to him and dine with him, and he with Me. To him who overcomes I will grant to sit with Me on My throne, as I also overcame and sat down with My Father on His throne.

REVELATION 3:20-21

Back on the farm in Missouri, we used to give medicine capsules to the sheep every year to treat intestinal parasites. One of us would grab the sheep, while the other held a scissors-like tool with an extremely long handle and a clamp on the end. Wedged in that clamp was a large capsule that we forced down the sheep's throat as far as physically possible. It wasn't easy for the sheep or for us, but we knew it was good for them.

You can't force something down the throat of a human being and expect it to do much good. That's why Jesus designed his parables to circumvent the resistance of our hard hearts so the truth could go down more easily. He inserted truth in each parable, which would work like a seed in the ground that has a life of its own. That truth—like the seed—is able to initiate growth, organize, and give form to the life until it matures into the fruit of the kingdom of God.

The parables are so rich that they often shower us with a number of truths, but Jesus designed each one to give us a *particular* truth in a special way. In this chapter, we focus on a parable that Jesus used to illustrate how people pass by their true blessings, missing the greatest thing that could possibly happen to them. They miss that which matters most for the sake of small, trivial, but often good things.

The Parable of the Great Supper falls in a sequence of teachings that have to do with feasts, or what we think of as banquets or large formal dinners. A lot of peculiar behavior can go on at banquets, and Jesus pointed to some of that in the Parable of the Wedding Feast that leads up to the Parable of the Great Supper.

PECKING ORDER GAMES

When Jesus was attending a banquet at the home of one of the chief Pharisees on the Sabbath day, he observed how the dinner guests jockeyed for the best seats with the most honor. (We are often so enamored by status that it seems impossible to attend any event without thinking that some seats are better than others.) The best seats indicating the highest social ranking were those closest to the host, such as our "head table," and people would make every arrangement to get as close to the place of dignity and honor as possible.

Jesus cautioned against this:

> "When you are invited by someone to a wedding banquet, do not sit down at the place of honor, in case someone more distinguished than you has been invited by your host, and the host who invited both of you may come and say to you,

Instead, Jesus offered the opposite idea in a tongue-in-cheek
way—a "better" way to be honored:

"But when you are invited, go and sit down in the lowest
place, so that when he who invited you comes he may say
to you, 'What are you doing down here? You're my friend!
C'mon, sit up here closer to me.' Then you will have glory in
the presence of those who sit at the table with you." (Luke
14:10, paraphrased)

Imagine Jesus motioning to John, who was sitting next to
him, and saying, "Get up, and go down there." John would slink
to the folding table in the kitchen. But using the advice in verse
10, John should have started out at the table in the kitchen so
that Jesus would look at the head table and say, "Where's John?"
And the servants would reply, "John's out at the folding table in
the kitchen." Jesus would then exclaim, "He's *where*?" And he'd
head out toward the kitchen, shouting, "John, come up here now!
Sit by me. We need to talk." So John would get up, walk to the
head table, and sit down—and people would think, *This guy
John must be important!*

Does it seem like Jesus would give a formula for being honored at a banquet? Jesus was, of course, using a little humor to
get around the defenses of his hearers, pretending that he agreed
that it's good to want to be honored. Using this playful approach,
Jesus appealed precisely to the kind of "desire to be honored"
that he was confronting. He wasn't recommending this approach
to look important, but rather was revealing something profound.
It's possible that the person who went to the folding table in the

kitchen first was actually *not* humble; they just had a strategy. So Jesus concluded with these words:

> "For whoever exalts himself will be humbled, and he who humbles himself will be exalted." (Luke 14:11)

Everything depends on what is in our hearts.

Jesus took advantage of this very human scene to teach something about the kingdom of God. In the order of the great inversion, the person who is last on the scale of human importance may well be first, and the person who is first on the human scale may well be last. We need to remember this principle concerning the work of God. To exalt one's self is actually to be demeaned. One of the main ways we exalt ourselves is by blatantly or subtly letting our good qualities and our good deeds be made known. It can be a very poisonous thing. This is an area where the discipline of secrecy can be extremely helpful for us.*

UNUSUAL DINNER GUESTS

After his comments about the seating arrangements, Jesus addressed his host, a ruler of the Pharisees:

> "When you give a dinner or a supper, do not ask your friends, your brothers, your relatives, nor rich neighbors, lest they also invite you back, and you be repaid." (Luke 14:12)

No doubt, that's what his host had done.

Be assured you can afford to forego playing games of currying favor. Because you live in the kingdom of God, you will be taken care of. You will not be overlooked. Jesus says instead:

---

* Learn more about the discipline of secrecy in my *The Spirit of the Disciplines: Understanding How God Changes Lives* (San Francisco: HarperSanFrancisco, 1988), 172–74.

"You will be blessed, because they cannot repay you; for you shall be repaid at the resurrection of the just." (Luke 14:14)

Jesus was pointing to a particular truth. He observed that those who made feasts tended to invite people to eat who didn't *need* to eat. They invited people who were well-off enough to pay them back with an invitation to eat at their house on another occasion.

The point of eating is to nourish the body, not to reinforce social distinctions. Sometimes big dinners are ways of getting together to reassure ourselves that we are "the" people—and all those others are not. When you look at the social life in your community, it can easily become a matter of who is invited and who is not. Being one who is invited determines if you're anything at all. If you're not invited, then who are you? Jesus was addressing the way we use essential things such as eating to establish social distinctions that are harmful and hurtful.

Before we continue, notice that this illustration in verse 12 was one that might be turned into a legalistic thing: *Do not invite your relatives for dinner.* (Some of you have been looking for that verse. You may be thinking, *Oh, good! I don't have to invite my sister over now because Jesus said not to.*) Remember, we must read Jesus' illustrations in light of the prevailing cultural presumption he is setting aside. Here Jesus is telling people to break free from the practice of quid pro quo—I do something for you so you will do something for me. You don't need to play that little game. And, by the way, you can invite your relatives too. The point isn't about the relatives; the point is about the practice.

IN THE MIDST OF THE NEEDY

In this brief exchange with the Pharisee, Jesus also corrected the prevailing practice of neglecting those in real need. These were people who didn't have the means to reciprocate the favor—"the poor, the maimed, the lame, the blind" (Luke 14:13). He was saying something very simple: "Feed those who need it."

We very badly need to hear this message of our responsibility for individuals who are in need. Even if we are giving money to charitable organizations, we should never avoid skin-to-skin contact with people who are in need.

I'm saying something quite simple. When we encounter people in need, we should try to help them. Jesus was there to meet their needs, refusing to shrink from walking in the midst of those who were hungry and hurting, and we should be there too. God wants us to enjoy our food and the fellowship of friends and those we love, but also to include those who need it.

A fellow sitting at the table with Jesus was impressed by what Jesus said and responded, "Blessed is he who shall eat bread in the kingdom of God" (Luke 14:15).

I think his heart lit up with joy, as if to say, *What a wonderful thing it would be if the kingdom of God is like that—if God is like that! Won't it be wonderful when that day comes? The day when all the rich and poor, the disabled and the frail, sit down with all the high and the mighty, and everyone lives together in God's world as God's children? Won't that be a wonderful thing?*

Jesus did not disagree with him. Perhaps he was thinking of the kingdom as something occurring in the future (as we often do). The point of the Parable of the Great Supper is exactly what this man perceived—how blessed the feast in that kingdom will be. Beyond the blessed nature of the kingdom, Jesus also wanted to teach him something about why people don't come to the feast.

Many people have paid a great price to move from one country to another in search of freedom, abundance, and opportunity. The kingdom of God is an even greater country. Those in the hall of faith in Hebrews 11 had a vision of the reality of the "country" of God's kingdom.

These all died in faith, not having received the promises, but having seen them afar off were assured of them, embraced them and confessed that they were strangers and pilgrims on the earth. For those who say such things declare plainly that they seek a homeland. And truly if they had called to mind that country from which they had come out, they would have had opportunity to return. But now they desire a better, that is, a heavenly country. Therefore God is not ashamed to be called their God, for He has prepared a city for them. (Hebrews 11:13–16)

The people in the Parable of the Great Supper didn't have that kind of compelling vision of the kingdom of God. They didn't understand that the city of God is now available. It's going to have more glorious moments later, but it's available now. The message goes out: "Come and live *in* the kingdom of God."

Jesus was aware that many people have something they think is more important than to enter and live in the kingdom of God. That's the point of this parable. Let's look at it in detail and think about its application to our lives.

POOR EXCUSES

Then He said to him, "A certain man gave a great supper and invited many, and sent his servant at supper time to say to those who were invited, 'Come, for all things are now ready.' But they all with one accord began to make excuses. The first said to him, 'I have bought a piece of ground, and I must go and see it. I ask you to have me excused.' And another said, 'I have bought five yoke of oxen, and I am going to test them. I ask you to have me excused.' Still another said, 'I have married a wife, and therefore I cannot come.' So that servant came and reported these things to his master. Then

> the master of the house, being angry, said to his servant, 'Go out quickly into the streets and lanes of the city, and bring in here the poor and the maimed and the lame and the blind.' And the servant said, 'Master, it is done as you commanded, and still there is room.' Then the master said to the servant, 'Go out into the highways and hedges, and compel them to come in, that my house may be filled. For I say to you that none of those men who were invited shall taste my supper.'" (Luke 14:16–24)

Notice, if you will, that the people who said no had received the invitation some time before. Apparently, they had not yet given any indication they would not attend. A formal supper in those days lasted much longer than today's dinner party. It was not an eat-and-run affair; it lasted a long period of time, perhaps even a few days.

The guests who had been invited ahead of time were the kind of people the supper's host would expect to come, such as friends and relatives. Jesus was alluding to the way the message of the kingdom went out first to the Jews as God's chosen people because the Jews were "the right sort of people"—those who observed the right traditions and exhibited the right habits. As we study other parables, we will see how Jesus returned over and over to this theme that the Jews, who were the ones primarily invited to the great supper, found something else to do when the time came to sit down and eat.

Notice the illogical nature of the excuses the guests had for not coming. The first excuse ("I have bought a piece of ground, and I must go and see it") makes us wonder why the person didn't go and see the land *before* he bought it. Or if he meant he couldn't come because he had plans to plant a crop (surely he could have waited a day or two for that). So this excuse would have sounded dubious.

Another potential guest said, "I bought five yoke of oxen, and I am going to test them." The same sort of problem arises here. Why would you wait until *after* you bought them to test the animals? You're stuck with them. If it's good news, it can wait—and if it's bad news, you had probably better let it go as long as you can. So what's the hurry?

Still another offered this excuse: "I have married a wife, and therefore I cannot come." That might pose some difficulty, but the question could be asked, "Why don't you just bring your wife with you?" That was something that could have been done. This was a banquet, and the important host would have had room for her. In fact, perhaps they could have honeymooned at his establishment.

These excuses don't seem like reasons; they look like dodges. In all of these cases, these folks offered *small, questionable obstacles*, easily remedied, in order to say no to a great opportunity. It appears that each of them had something they thought was more important to do. What you can see, above all, is that they didn't care about the person who was inviting them.

This brings us to the basic question of fundamental importance: Do we love God and the kingdom of God?

It may be that we haven't been taught enough about life in the kingdom of God to answer this question with a yes or a no. So it leads to this soul-searching query: Do we love the kind of day-by-day interaction with God we see in the life of Jesus, in the early church, and perhaps have experienced in our own lives? Or do we love something else more? God will not force the kingdom down our throats.

TRIVIAL PURSUITS

If we don't have a heartfelt love for God and God's kingdom, many trivial things can prevent us from entering into the *present* reality of the kingdom of God with a free and enthusiastic heart. Certainly, some trivial things can be rather good things. After all, it's not bad to buy land and survey it, to buy oxen and try them out, to get married and stay home with our new spouse. These are all wonderful things. The excuse givers in the parable weren't saying, "I can't come because I have to go rob a bank."

Jean-Joseph Surin, a distinguished seventeenth-century minister, was once asked, "Why is it that when so many people undertake to give their direct and full service to God, there are so few Christlike persons?" And he replied, "The chief reason is that they give too big a place in life to indifferent things."[10] It's all too easy to give too much time and energy to things that are not central and then let them fill up our lives.

This is not to say we should not have times of recreation and relaxation. Sometimes it's just wonderful to be a little silly. I think Jesus was a man who was enjoyable to be around and had a lot of fun. Otherwise, little children would not have loved him so much. He was universally loved by people in many different settings. He caused their hearts to rejoice because he knew what it was like to live happily in the kingdom of God. That's because he had a center there, and he attended to that center. He didn't let the little things—even *good* little things—distract him. One of the main things this parable is saying is that it's the small but good things that defeat us.

THE ONE THING

This parable about not missing out on the kingdom is as much for those inside the church as those outside it. When Jesus knocked at the door of the church, saying, "Behold, I stand at the door and knock" (Revelation 3:20), he was inviting the people in the church to let him in. But those in the church may be so busy doing good things that they miss that *one thing* that is necessary.

Mary and her sister Martha had a little altercation because Martha was busy doing good things while Mary simply sat at the feet of Jesus. You can imagine Martha resenting Mary and saying to Jesus, "Why don't you tell this lazy sister of mine to get up and help me? The biscuits are burning, the dressing isn't made yet, and we're all going to starve to death before everything is ready!" Jesus saw that her heart was "troubled about many things," and redirected her: "One thing is necessary. And Mary has chosen that *good* thing" (Luke 10:40–42, paraphrased, emphasis added).

Even the Old Testament patriarchs made this mistake. In Genesis 25:29–34, we read that Esau was out in the field hunting and became hungry. He came home, flopped down on the couch, and said something like this: "I'm going to die of starvation! I've never been this hungry before in my life."

Meanwhile, Jacob kept stirring his delicious red stew. Esau could smell the aroma and begged for some stew.

When Jacob demanded Esau's birthright as payment, Esau gave it up easily, saying, "I'm going to die from hunger anyway. What good is my birthright?" (Genesis 25:32, paraphrased). But Esau wasn't going to die. He was the kind of person who *became obsessed with what he wanted in the moment*, so he was unable to stand before a little hunger. Our inability to stand before our momentary pangs, pains, and problems can ultimately cause us even greater suffering. So Esau traded away a precious possession of unlimited value—his birthright as the firstborn. And he traded it for stew.

There is a finality in our choices. At a certain point, we can become worshipers of something as minor as soup. We may not even think the soup is very good, but we think about it until minutes have become hours, then days and weeks and months and years, until we've spent a lifetime serving our appetites.

SEEK FIRST

Sometimes we meet individuals who may not seem likely to be invited to the feast of the kingdom, who don't know Jesus Christ yet. Nevertheless, they see the value and beauty of life with God and walk right in, saying, "Yes, I'll take the invitation." And they give themselves to the kingdom of God. They seek it first, last, and always; it is their whole life. And that is the attitude that places a person in the position to become a disciple of Jesus.

After presenting the Parable of the Great Supper, Jesus illustrated the serious commitment required for a life of discipleship. This is quite a contrast to the attitude of those who turned down the invitation to the feast:

> Now great multitudes went with Him. And He turned and said to them, "If anyone comes to Me and does not hate his father and mother, wife and children, brothers and sisters, yes, and his own life also, he cannot be My disciple. And whoever does not bear his cross and come after Me cannot be My disciple. For which of you, intending to build a tower, does not sit down first and count the cost, whether he has enough to finish it—lest, after he has laid the foundation, and is not able to finish, all who see it begin to mock him, saying, 'This man began to build and was not able to finish'? Or what king, going to make war against another king, does not sit down first and consider whether he is able with ten thousand to meet him who comes against him with twenty thousand? Or else, while the other is still a great way off, he sends a delegation and asks conditions of peace. So likewise, whoever of you does not forsake all that he has cannot be My disciple." (Luke 14:25–33)

When Jesus said, "If anyone comes to Me and does not hate his father and mother, wife and children, brothers and sisters, yes, and his own life also, he cannot be My disciple" (Luke 14:26), he was not saying, "I won't *let* him be my disciple." He said that person could not be his disciple. He was *unable* to be

Jesus' disciple. It's just logical, like saying, "Truly, truly, I say to you, he that cannot run cannot play football." No one's going to *stop* the person from playing football if he can't run. He simply *can't* play football because he can't run.

Those who put such great value on the new oxen or the bowl of stew don't have the necessary *inward* attitude expressed by "hate . . . his own life also," "bear his cross," and "forsake all that he has" (Luke 14:26–27, 33). That attitude of surrender is what enables an individual to become a disciple of Jesus Christ and receive the life of the kingdom. Without surrender, Jesus says, that person "cannot be My disciple" (14:33). Without it, you just can't make contact with the kingdom of God. "Seek *first* the kingdom of God and His righteousness" (Matthew 6:33, emphasis added).

WHY ARE YOU A DISCIPLE OF JESUS?

Jesus illustrated this with two other parables in Matthew 13:44–46.

> "Again, the kingdom of heaven is like treasure hidden in a field, which a man found and hid; and for joy over it he goes and sells all that he has and buys that field." (Matthew 13:44)

Imagine someone finding a treasure in a field—maybe even oil or gold. He or she gathers all their resources to buy it, thinking it's the best opportunity ever presented. They are ready to do whatever they can to possess it because they understand this as an investment.

> "Again, the kingdom of heaven is like a merchant seeking beautiful pearls, who, when he had found one pearl of great price, went and sold all that he had and bought it." (Matthew 13:45–46)

The pearl merchant may have owned a lot of little pearls, but they kept searching for the best and most beautiful one. When they found it, they gathered up every single resource (including all their other pearls) and bought that pearl. Now do you think they were saying, *Oh no! I have to give up my little pearls—my precious little pearls?* No, because they knew this pearl was worth everything they had. They were glad to give up those other things.

Once we understand who Jesus is and what knowing him means for our lives, we realize that discipleship to Jesus is the greatest opportunity we will ever have in life. We gain perspective about the little good things in our lives, and we happily give them up in order to gain possession of the priceless treasure of the kingdom of God. It's no sacrifice at all.

People who profess the name of Christ often do not comprehend the greatness of the invitation to life in the kingdom of God. The apostle Paul understood this: "To me, who am less than the least of all the saints, this grace was given, that I should preach among the Gentiles the *unsearchable* riches of Christ" (Ephesians 3:8, emphasis added). Other translations use the word *unfathomable*, *incalculable*, *incomprehensible*, or *inexhaustible*. If you can't fathom something, it means you never reach the bottom. No matter how far you go, there's still more!

If we present Christ correctly, the effect will be to ravish people—to delight, even to overwhelm them—with the reality of the kingdom. They will think they have nothing better to do! That's how you make a disciple.

Our problem is that we don't truly see the greatness of Christ. In his book *Your God Is Too Small*, J. B. Phillips laid his finger on the chronic problem of failing to grasp how big God is and our failure to understand the greatness of Christ.[11] When Christians talk about Jesus, they struggle because they have a tiny Christ, a puny Christ who doesn't compare well with others.

My University of Southern California students have occasionally asked, "Why are you a disciple of Jesus?" My answer has been to ask, "Who else did you have in mind?" And I mean this seriously. They've wanted to talk about Buddha, Gandhi, or even their favorite musician or politician, but none of them compare to Christ on close examination.

The reality is that everyone is following somebody. But people are typically not thinking about what is guiding their lives. Good questions for each of us to ask are, *Who am I really following? Who do I look up to? Who are my role models?* No matter who that might be, that person's goodness is finite and even limited. But the goodness of God available through following Jesus is so unfathomable you will never see the end of it.

CHOOSING TO BE A DISCIPLE

Are you a disciple of Jesus Christ?

It may be that you've never had this question asked of you in just this way. Many who profess to know Christ have not intentionally *chosen* to be a disciple of Jesus. Do you even *want* to be a disciple?

Have you consciously chosen *not* to be a disciple? Some people have. They may be eager to know they will go to heaven when they die, but they have chosen not to live a life of discipleship now. God, in his gentleness, will not force this decision on you, no matter how good it is for you.

To be Jesus' disciple means learning from him how to lead my life as he would lead it if he were I—in my vocation, relationships, health, and status. It is a continuing relationship through which all dimensions of our personality come to love God. It really *is* the greatest opportunity life offers. In becoming a disciple of Jesus, we learn to live as Jesus taught us to live. We discover how to handle the ordinary events of daily life in cooperative action with God. We grow in learning how to act in God's power.

Discipleship to Jesus is not supposed to be miserable. Everything he commanded us to do is good for us and brings a good return for us. Yes, there are things we will have to give up, but remember the other side of the Parable of the Pearl of Great Price: we benefit immensely from the relationship. To "count the cost" doesn't mean we just look at what we pay; we also look at what we gain. We won't know how much a new car is going to cost until we also count the cost of not buying it. We have to evaluate what we get and what we pay, and that's what Jesus is talking about when he talks about counting the cost.

While Dietrich Bonhoeffer's great book was called *The Cost of Discipleship*, I think someone needs to write one called *The Cost of Non-Discipleship*.[†] We can never measure the cost of discipleship unless we have measured the higher cost of non-discipleship, which includes the likelihood of spending the rest of our lives being dominated by hatred, resentment, and other afflictions. Discipleship allows us to live lives full of love, joy, hope, peace, and confidence in God instead.

Opportunities present themselves throughout our lives, but we must have enough initiative to choose to take them. The feast awaits us if we've said, "Yes, I will be a disciple of Jesus Christ on *his* terms."

[†] I address this concept in *The Spirit of the Disciplines: Understanding How God Changes Lives* (San Francisco: HarperSanFrancisco, 1988) in a section called "The Cost of Non-Discipleship" (pp. 262–63).

MAIN POINTS ABOUT THE KINGDOM OF GOD

- To exalt one's self is, in reality, to be demeaned. We are children of God, and our place in his heart and kingdom is secure.
- There are so many good things in our lives, like oxen and little pearls, but these can often distract us from the most important thing.
- The great opportunity to be a disciple of Jesus requires us to choose him over everything else. Understanding and weighing the costs of discipleship and the costs of non-discipleship will help us with this important decision.

CHAPTER 6

GROWING TOGETHER IN THE KINGDOM

Go easy on those who hesitate in the faith. Go after those who take the wrong way. Be tender with sinners, but not soft on sin. The sin itself stinks to high heaven.

JUDE 1:22-23 MSG

Where I grew up, farmers had to contend with a plant they called "cheat," a type of grass that looked like oats and could take over an oat field. When the heads of the cheat were opened at the harvest, they would only find a tiny bit of stuff that wasn't even enough to make an oatmeal cookie.

In the Parable of the Wheat and the Tares, the farmer had a similar problem—with tares masquerading as wheat:

> Another parable He put forth to them, saying: "The kingdom of heaven is like a man who sowed good seed in his field; but while men slept, his enemy came and sowed tares among the

wheat and went his way. But when the grain had sprouted and produced a crop, then the tares also appeared. So the servants of the owner came and said to him, 'Sir, did you not sow good seed in your field? How then does it have tares?'" (Matthew 13:24–27)

In this parable, the servant caught the problem of weeds intermingling with the wheat and asked the farmer about it. The farmer answered:

"'An enemy has done this.' The servants said to him, 'Do you want us then to go and gather them up?'" (Matthew 13:28)

No doubt you have some idea of what happens when you pull weeds out of a garden. But a wheat field is not like an average garden. You can't tell where the wheat stops and where the weeds begin. If you try to pull the weeds during the growing season, you'll destroy the wheat. So the farmer said:

"No, [don't do that] lest while you gather up the tares you also uproot the wheat with them. Let both grow together until the harvest, and at the time of harvest I will say to the reapers, 'First gather together the tares and bind them in bundles to burn them, but gather the wheat into my barn.'" (Matthew 13:29–30)

At harvest time, no one will be concerned about destroying the wheat because it will have matured. At that point, a separation can be made.

SEEDS FOR THE WORLD

The disciples requested clarification about this parable when they were alone with Jesus later that day:

His disciples came to Him, saying, "Explain to us the parable of the tares of the field."

He answered and said to them: "He who sows the good seed is the Son of Man." (Matthew 13:36–37)

The seeds are sowed by the Son of Man, who is also "the Word" (John 1:14). Just as the physical seed in this parable grew and became wheat, the sons of the kingdom were sowed by Jesus. This sowing comes after they have received the Word of God as described in the Parable of the Sower. These people gather together wherever the Son of Man has sowed them, and they mature so that they can "shine forth as the sun in the kingdom of their Father" (Matthew 13:43).

"The field is the world, the good seeds are the sons of the kingdom, but the tares are the sons of the wicked one. The enemy who sowed them is the devil, the harvest is the end of the age, and the reapers are the angels." (Matthew 13:38–39)

In the Parable of the Sower, the field is the soil of our life, but the field in this parable is the world. Notice in this parable the seeds are described as people—"sons of the kingdom" or "sons of the wicked one"*—who have either received the Word of God and are maturing or are still of the world that "lies in the power of the evil one" (1 John 5:19 ESV).

When James spoke of the "implanted word, which is able to save your souls" (James 1:21), this is what he meant. The spiritual life, through the Word of God, comes into the natural person and organizes all of that life—the vitality and energy given by nature at birth in the person's body and social setting.

---

* In the Parable of the Sower, the seed was the Word of God. In the Parable of the Growing Seed, the seed was the kingdom of God.

Out of this comes the fruit of the Word of God, which is our life as a son or daughter of the kingdom.

When we are commanded to put off the old person and put on the new, we do that by putting all of the natural power that runs through us—physical and psychological—through Christ. In this way, we put on Christ (Romans 13:14; Ephesians 4:24). We become seeds planted in the world to renew and redeem it through the fruit we bear (John 15:2).

> "Therefore as the tares are gathered and burned in the fire, so it will be at the end of this age. The Son of Man will send out His angels, and they will gather out of His kingdom all things that offend, and those who practice lawlessness, and will cast them into the furnace of fire. There will be wailing and gnashing of teeth. Then the righteous will shine forth as the sun in the kingdom of their Father. He who has ears to hear, let him hear!" (Matthew 13:40–43)

When the Word of God was sown in the heart of the natural person (seed), it germinated and brought forth spiritual life born of the Spirit of God. This renewed person becomes the good seed that is planted in the world, which then begins to organize the world around it in kingdom ways. The inclusiveness of the kingdom means we will also have people in the same field who are of the world (tares) and who still need to receive the Word of God in the soil of their lives and become sons and daughters of the kingdom. Allowing the wheat and tares to grow together provides time and opportunity for the tares to become wheat through the power of God's Word.

WHY GOD ALLOWS WEEDS

The key phrase in this parable is "the field is the world," which clarifies that the field is not the church (Matthew 13:38). In the

Parable of the Great Supper, all kinds of people were invited into the kingdom (Luke 14:21). No one was excluded, except those who excluded themselves with their own excuses. In the Parable of the Wheat and the Tares, we see two different types of people who have accepted the invitation—those who are both *in* the kingdom and *of* the kingdom (wheat), and those who are *in* the kingdom but their thoughts and actions are not *of* the kingdom (tares). Once again, the use of these two small prepositions, *in* and *of*, creates an important distinction.

Living for Christ in the world today means being *in* the world but not *of* the world. *In* but not *of*. Christians can live squarely in the world but with a Christlike character. But right next to them, just as the tares grew in the wheat fields, there are people who are *in* God's kingdom who are offensive and lawless. They may be involved in kingdom activities, but their nature (character) remains *of* the world. They are not *of* the kingdom, and they will be gathered *out* of his kingdom (Matthew 13:41).

This parable puts forth an idea that many find difficult: God allows the good wheat and the weeds to grow together in the kingdom of God's world until the harvest. We may share the mentality of the servant who said, "Well, if there are weeds out there, let's pull them up. Just get rid of them!" (Matthew 13:28, paraphrased). But we must be careful about judging others.

NOT THE NET AGAIN!

The folks to whom Jesus spoke were basically fishermen, farmers, or businesspeople, so his parables were normally drawn from that circle of people. Jesus chose to illustrate this same inclusive dynamic with a parable for the fishermen:

> "Again, the kingdom of heaven is like a dragnet that was cast into the sea and gathered some of every kind, which, when

> it was full, they drew to shore; and they sat down and gathered the good into vessels, but threw the bad away." (Matthew 13:47–48)

Jesus' audience saw people doing this whenever they walked along the Sea of Galilee. They had watched fishermen throw their nets in the water, wait for the fish to fill it, and haul into their boats whatever was caught in the net. No sorting was done in the net. The kingdom of the heavens is like that. Only after pulling the net into the boat did the fishermen sit down, collect the fish they could use, and throw the others back. Maybe some of the discarded fish had been through the net fifty times and when caught again, thought, *Oh no, not the net again!*

> "So it will be at the end of the age. The angels will come forth, separate the wicked from among the just, and cast them into the furnace of fire." (Matthew 13:49–50)

These parables and the teachings of Scripture generally divide people in the kingdom into two groups: those who are *in* the kingdom but whose character is *of* the world, and those who are *in* the kingdom of God and whose character is *of* the kingdom (1 John 2:19).

Jesus also made this distinction of being either "of the kingdom" or "of the world" in what is commonly called the high priestly prayer for his followers:

> "I have given them Your word; and the world has hated them because they are not *of* the world, just as I am not *of* the world. I do not pray that You should take them out of the world, but that You should keep them from the evil one. They are not *of* the world, just as I am not *of* the world. Sanctify them by Your truth. Your word is truth. As You sent Me *into*

the world, I also have sent them *into* the world." (John 17:14–18, emphasis added)

Jesus said the disciples were *in* the world but not *of* the world. Indeed, this applies to everyone who makes contact with Jesus Christ and draws life from him.

OASIS IN THE DESERT

Being *in* the world is not a bad thing; it's a good thing. This world is God's creation. It is the place where God has appointed us to live. Our birth and life to this point haven't taken God by surprise; he prepared this time and place for each of us with a specific purpose. We, like Jesus, interact with all kinds and any class of people in this world—both the wheat and the tares. This includes those who follow God and those who don't, even those who participate in less-than-desirable activities. Remember that Jesus was criticized for associating with the latter (Luke 15:1–2). When we mingle with those who are *of* the world—those who "offend"—that doesn't mean we are *of* the world. We are *of* a completely different kind of character, radiating love, joy, and peace.

But is this possible? How are we to think about *in* but not *of*? Picture a desert landscape with dust and dryness as far as the eye can see. Right in the middle of it, a spring of water bubbles up, forming a pool of refreshment for all who pass by. The spring and the pool are *in* the desert, but they are not *of* it. They do not *originate* in the desert, but rather come from rain and snow and limpid streams on faraway mountains that feed the springs through hidden passageways in the earth. The stream and pool are not of the same *nature* as the desert and, in fact, seem unnatural in the desert.

You can be *in* something without being *of* it. A person can fall down into a hog pen without being a hog. A person can be *in* a university without being an educated person. Someone can be *in* an art museum without being an artist. And someone can be *in* a church without even wanting to be a disciple of Jesus. Being *in* something is a much more superficial thing than being *of* it.

KINGDOM LIKENESS

What does it mean to be *of* something? When Jesus described James and John as "Sons of Thunder" (Mark 3:17), he was identifying their nature. When we say that someone is *of* something, we refer to their *origin* and their *nature* (*character*). We may say of a person regarding their family, "He is one of the Longs" or, "She is one of the Kims." Because a son originated from Mr. and Mrs. Long, he likely resembles the nature of the Longs. Because a daughter originated from Mr. and Mrs. Kim, she likely shares the character and attitudes of the Kims. No matter what circumstances they may be *in*, they are *of* that family.

Someone who is *of* the kingdom of God has their origin and their nature *of* or *from* that kingdom. That is what Jesus talked about with Nicodemus (John 3:1–21). A new origin and nature require a new birth, and so we are *born* of the Word of God. That Word is the spiritual agency by which people are brought into the kingdom of God. Like the wind, the Spirit comes and moves in the lives of individuals so that they become *of* or *from* the kingdom of God. People see the results, but they can't see what causes the results. This is abundant life in its fullest sense—life lived from hidden sources that come into the soul from God and his kingdom. Such abundant life is possible no matter where you are or what you happen to be doing.

Those who are concerned about their standing in the kingdom can be sure in their own heart, if they will simply stand and walk as disciples of Christ, that they can find the reality that assures them and makes clear that they are both *in* the kingdom of God and *of* the kingdom of God. Being *of* the kingdom means praying, "For thine is the kingdom, and the power, and the glory, for ever. Amen" (Matthew 6:13 KJV). We can *know* the power of the risen Christ. He who raised Christ from the dead can give life also to our earthly bodies through Christ Jesus. We can know that power if we *choose* to know it.

The old song that says, "Lord, I want to be a Christian in my heart,"[12] gets at this issue of *wanting* to be a disciple of Jesus. Disciples of Jesus Christ wish to be like him, and they arrange and rearrange the details of their lives so they may be like him.

NEITHER PART NOR PORTION

That wide casting of the net means many people are *in* the kingdom of God, but their character is not *of* it. Their thoughts and desires come from the world, and their *nature* is restricted to the world. They have probably seen people being healed and being transformed. They have seen supernatural evidences of God's presence all around. Although they may be sitting in the middle of it, they are not *of* the kingdom of God. This may seem strange to you, but it is possible to be in the scope of the divine power and not be *of* that power.

The writer of Hebrews tells us:

> For it is impossible to restore again to repentance those who have once been enlightened and have tasted the heavenly gift and have shared in the Holy Spirit and have tasted the good word of God and the powers of the age to come and then have fallen away, since they are crucifying again the Son of God to their own harm and are holding him up to contempt. (Hebrews 6:4–6 NRSVue)

This passage refers to persons who *have* been told. They have *felt* the powers of a world to come. They have tasted the good Word of God and had a touch of the Holy Spirit upon them.

Yet in their hearts, they have said, *No, it is not the most important thing in this world for me to be like Jesus Christ.* They have turned away and put Christ to open shame because what they're saying is, *You didn't do enough for me, Lord.* They looked at it, fully sensed it, and said, *No, thank you. Not for me.* Such people are impossible to bring to repentance.

You may remember Simon the magician of Samaria (Acts 8:9–24). When he heard about Jesus from Philip, he was baptized. Later, when Peter and John arrived and began doing the works of the Holy Spirit, Simon tried to buy the gift of the Holy Spirit. This is how Peter replied:

> "Your money perish with you, because you thought that the gift of God could be purchased with money! You have neither part nor portion in this matter, for your heart is not right in the sight of God. Repent therefore of this your wickedness, and pray God if perhaps the thought of your heart may be forgiven you. For I see that you are poisoned by bitterness and bound by iniquity." (Acts 8:20–23)

Simon had seen that the kingdom of God was the greatest thing that has ever happened to this earth. Many people have enough sense to see that, but not all have a heart that is right in the sight of God.

A lot of folks sitting in range of the kingdom are not there for the purpose of discipleship. Often it's because they haven't been challenged or even taught how to be a disciple. Other times, they've had it explained and have turned away. Even in the Western world, many people have never heard anything about life in the kingdom of God. They think the church is the building on the corner instead of a *people* who are infiltrating the whole world. This will continue until people realize the solution to human problems is not a human solution. It is learning to live in the kingdom of God through apprenticeship to Jesus Christ and increasingly becoming like him and *of* his kingdom.

WHO'S REALLY IN CHARGE?

Being *of* the kingdom of God has nothing to do with being from a certain cultural group, religious background, racial makeup, or cultural or economic strata. The Old Testament passages of Psalm 145 and Daniel 4 give us a fresh impression of the *far-reaching extent* of the kingdom and help fix this idea in our minds.

The kingdom of God is a concept that originated late in the history of Israel, which is why we first begin to see discussion of the kingdom of God and the kingdom of the heavens in the late psalms, the book of Daniel, the book of Nehemiah, and the later historical books. The term was very clear by the time Psalm 145 was written. Notice the repetition of the word *all*.

> The LORD is good to *all*,
> And His tender mercies are over *all* His works.
>
> *All* Your works shall praise You, O LORD,
> And Your saints shall bless You.
> They shall speak of the glory of Your kingdom,
> And talk of Your power,
> To make known to the sons of men His mighty acts,
> And the glorious majesty of His kingdom.
> Your kingdom is an everlasting kingdom,
> And Your dominion endures throughout *all* generations.
> (Psalm 145:9–13, emphasis added)

"The LORD is good to *all*." That leaves out no one. Just like the net.

In the book of Daniel, we are introduced to King Nebuchadnezzar of Babylon, who had become the ruling power in as much of the world as was known to him. It was clear that Nebuchadnezzar's elevated position had become a problem in his thinking, so God took the time to help him come to a more realistic understanding and to remind him that God's kingdom and authority are above that of all human kings.

Nebuchadnezzar was sitting in his throne room one day and started thinking what a great fellow he was, and the next moment, he was out eating grass and walking on all fours. He had lost his mind. The Bible then records these words of Nebuchadnezzar:

> "At the end of the time I, Nebuchadnezzar, lifted my eyes to heaven, and my understanding returned to me" (Daniel 4:34).

Notice that, first, Nebuchadnezzar lifted up his eyes to heaven and then his understanding returned to him. Most of the insanity of the world in which we live is due to the fact that eyes are not lifted to heaven. That's what puts everything into the perspective of reality, and when Nebuchadnezzar finally got his eyes to look up to heaven, his mind returned to a state of order:

> And I blessed the Most High and praised and honored Him who lives forever:
>
> For His dominion is an everlasting dominion,
> And His kingdom is from generation to generation.
> All the inhabitants of the earth are reputed as nothing;
> He does according to His will in the army of heaven
> And among the inhabitants of the earth.
> No one can restrain His hand
> Or say to Him, "What have You done?" (Daniel 4:34–35)

Some churches today have a problem of attracting good,

sensible, thoughtful people who aren't particularly interested in having God be in charge. These people are not mean, and they're not trying to do anything wrong. They say, "I want to be a good person. I believe in God. I want to associate with a church that is dynamic." So they come to church, and because they are hardworking, intelligent, highly motivated people, they soon carry the burdens of leading the church. As they gradually start to take over and run the show, they forget who's in charge, just like Nebuchadnezzar did. And the church continues to grow and prosper. But if God were to die, they might never know it because the church is simply functioning on good organizational principles and effective means of socialization. That's why so many churches tend to get in trouble when they grow larger, they split, they lose the spirit of Christ, and they refuse to forgive and get along with one another.

The graduate course in the spiritual life is not failure; it's success. As the kingdom of God succeeded, the emperor Constantine said, "My interests would be best served if I were a Christian. Why don't we rename our establishment the Holy Roman Empire?" Or someone says, "I really need friends" or "I'm looking for a spouse," so "Why don't I try going to church?" They come and say, "This is a good place to be. These people are so friendly!" And so they warm themselves by the fire because they're lonely.

There is nothing wrong with Christians being warm and friendly. But you want to remember that people come into your fellowship for many reasons. I'm not saying you should pull them up and throw them out. But recognize that this challenge exists.

The church consists basically of those who have been called out by God to join together to become outposts of his kingdom. It is first and foremost the calling of human beings to God that constitutes the church, and the Lord adds daily to the church, as we're told in the book of Acts. The people of God are to be a touchpoint between heaven and earth, where the healing of the cross and the resurrection can save the lost and grow them into the fullness of human beings in Christ.

BRING THEM ALL

So you see, the kingdom of God in its most inclusive sense is simply the rule of God over everything. There isn't a single thing or person left out. The old song "He's Got the Whole World in His Hands" is the teaching of the kingdom of God.[13] In that sense, there's nothing outside of it. The devil himself is not outside of the kingdom of God. *Evil* is not outside of the kingdom of God. *Every*thing is *in* the kingdom of God *in that sense*.

But there's another sense of the kingdom of God in which it is given to people for them to participate in. The story of the Old and New Testaments is basically the story of the kingdom rule of God being given to people. God invited Moses to partner in kingdom leadership as Moses exercised the power of God. The whole nation of Israel was given a set of institutions and rituals in which they participated and by which they received the power of God. The call of the Hebrew people was to *be* precisely a light to the entire earth to show it how to live for God (Isaiah 49:6). They didn't succeed. And that job was handed to the church as outposts of this inclusive kingdom that included Jews and Gentiles of all kinds. We shall later study in more detail exactly how Jesus taught about this, and how, as he said, the kingdom of God would be taken from leaders of the nation of Israel and given to those who bring forth the fruit of the kingdom (Matthew 21:43).

When thinking about being *in* the kingdom of God, I want to emphasize the liberality of the invitation. In the Parable of the Great Supper, when those who were invited did not come, the Lord simply said, "Then go out into the highways and byways and bring them in. Bring in the lame and the blind. Bring in anybody!" (Luke 14:23, paraphrased). He didn't inspect the people or test them in any way.

God does not say, "Get ready, and then come." He simply says, "Come." When the invitation is given, as the old hymn says, "Whosoever will may come." The openness and bigheartedness of the message bring people in. As in the parable, the net is cast widely! All that is required is the willingness to come. And as we grow in our life in the kingdom, we cooperate with God in that life.

MANY KINDS OF PEOPLE

God casts a very wide net, and it draws in all kinds of people. It is the very power of the kingdom of God that gathers within it *many* kinds of people, just as the mustard seed grows into a huge tree that supports "the birds of the air" that find shelter in it and build nests (Luke 13:19). Sometimes when we look at our church's fellowship, we may wonder how all these different kinds of birds have landed there. That's what the Parable of the Great Supper and the Parable of the Net are saying. God is not saying this is *wrong*. This is what we should expect.

The most striking example might be one of Jesus' own followers, Judas, who followed him for the wrong reasons. We aren't doing justice to the facts when we just suppose that somehow Judas temporarily got off track when he decided to betray Jesus. He was there to embezzle funds (John 12:6) and probably to force a political uprising.

Jesus attracted a huge following of people, ministering to them with bread and with truth. One day he asked them, "Why are you following me? Do you know, if you follow me, you're going to have to eat my flesh and drink my blood?" (John 6:53, paraphrased). Many people turned away and deserted him when he said that, even some who were considered disciples (6:66). Perhaps they figured Jesus was about to go over the edge. All kinds of people followed Jesus with wrong motivations. That situation still exists today.

KINGDOM OUTPOSTS

Churches are a primary expression of the presence of the kingdom among us. When Jesus gave the Great Commission to his followers, he didn't tell them to go start churches. He sent them out to establish beachheads of the kingdom of God. A beachhead is a piece of the beach that an army captures so they can establish a base of operation.

How did the disciples establish these advance outposts? That's where Jesus' authority comes in: "I have been given say over all things in heaven and on earth" (Matthew 28:18, paraphrased). This is what happened in the book of Acts. What we call churches were a spin-off of those outposts because they grew up where the disciples established beachheads. These churches drew all kinds of people out of the world and formed them into a peculiar kind of group that stood out in their community. Their task was to penetrate the surrounding territory and extend the beachhead, which they did successfully, and we now continue their work.

Because of God's wide net, the world and our local gatherings often have a mixture of "wheat and tares" growing up together. Our shared identification with Christ in our communities is intended to become our new and positive reality. The accessibility of the kingdom means our outposts will have weak and needy people and will most likely include some distressing events in the process, but we must always trust God with the outcome.

BLESSED ASSURANCE

The psalms offer vivid pictures of God's ability and desire to seek and save his own. Psalm 126 tells a story about Zion in its weakness. The people of Zion had puffed themselves up, thinking they were the greatest kingdom that ever lived. They thought they'd *never* be wiped out or destroyed. Then after the temple was burned and they were led away to Babylon as prisoners in shackles, they began to learn what the kingdom of God is really like and how it really works. The Lord finally redeemed the Jews from captivity, and this song memorialized that event:

> When the LORD brought back [those of] the captivity
> > of Zion,
> We were like those who dream.
> Then our mouth was filled with laughter,
> And our tongue with singing.
> Then they said among the nations,
> "The LORD has done great things for them."
> The LORD has done great things for us,
> And we are glad.
>
> Bring back our captivity, O LORD,
> As the streams in the South. (Psalm 126:1–4)

This image of "the streams in the South" refers to how dry creek beds in the desert become torrents after a thunderstorm. This illustrates how all of the power of Zion as a human institution was destroyed, yet God took their side. They didn't bring themselves back from captivity; God brought them back. They had learned this deep truth and rejoiced:

> Those who sow in tears
> Shall reap in joy.
> He who continually goes forth weeping,
> Bearing seed for sowing,
> Shall doubtless come again with rejoicing,
> Bringing his sheaves with him. (Psalm 126:5–6)

A STEADY GLEAM

Our local groups of disciples generally contain people at all stages of the journey and some who might still be in captivity. A church should be like a hospital with people in all of the different stages of healing and health, receiving treatment and progressively getting better. Some are in intensive care and others are getting well and going out into the world with the steady gleam of "a better country" (Hebrews 11:16 ESV) in their eyes. It isn't a place of perfection, as people might think about it; rather it is a place where people live with one another in healing love under the power of God. So we would expect and receive people as they are, and that was Jesus' way, wasn't it? As the old hymn puts it, "Christ receiveth sinful men,"[14] and he takes these broken, hurting people into the local congregation.†

Our coming to understand that tares are growing along with the wheat may seem discouraging. Knowing that some folks are there for wrong reasons might trouble us, but we must remember that our confidence is "through Christ toward God" (2 Corinthians 3:4). And then out of the abundance of that confidence, we act. We do not act out of scarcity, fear, or weakness; we act out of strength, fullness, and confidence. And by doing that, we enter into a power that is so great that we can speak of the kingdom advancing among human beings.

---

† For a more in-depth exploration of these ideas, see my *Renovation of the Heart: Putting on the Character of Christ* (Colorado Springs: NavPress, 2002), chapter 13.

MAIN POINTS ABOUT THE KINGDOM OF GOD

- The kingdom draws all kinds of people, both wheat and tares. God casts a wide net—a very, very wide net.
- God allows the wheat and the tares to grow together, and the power of his Word in and through us can help transform tares into fruitful wheat.
- A church should be like a hospital with people in all of the different stages of healing and health, receiving treatment and progressively getting better.
- Everyone is invited into the kingdom of God; no one is excluded, except for those who exclude themselves.

CHAPTER 7

GROWTH AND RESPONSIBILITY*

So God created man in His own image; in the image of God He created him; male and female He created them. Then God blessed them, and God said to them, "Be fruitful and multiply; fill the earth and subdue it; have dominion over the fish of the sea, over the birds of the air, and over every living thing that moves on the earth."

GENESIS 1:27–28

As humans, we were made to take charge of a certain amount of things around us, even to control these things. Each of us has a domain, our little kingdom, over which we have say, where things are done in the way we have decided they should be done. God

---

*   Dallas chose not to include the Parable of the Talents in his 1983 series on the parables because its point is taught so frequently. Thankfully, he offered in-depth teaching about the talents (minas) on two other occasions: "Finding Our Place in What God Is Doing Now Where We Are" (1996), "Who You Are and Why You Are Here" (1994).

gave humanity dominion over everything on the earth when he created us (Genesis 1:26, 28). He did not set that aside when Adam and Eve fell, even though human beings continued to sin. We still have the job of managing the earth, to rule over and care for it, but we were never meant to do this in isolation from God. Our sin and separation from God lead toward corruption and death, just as a cabbage will degrade and die if you pull it out of the ground and let it languish on the sidewalk. This is a constant struggle and creates a terrible mess because we're uprooted from God.

God expects us to step into governing this domain in partnership with him. He has given each of us a realm that is uniquely our own, but this became terribly distorted when sin entered the world.

INTENDED TO RULE

To understand who we are includes understanding that we were made to rule, to have say over things. If you don't think people are intended to rule, just try to get in the way of what they are planning to do. You can't interfere that way and expect it to go well. And of course, the larger problem of negotiating the differing rules of humanity in a fallen world is horrendous. This conflict explains much of the trouble we see between social groups, within families, and among warring nations.

When Jesus came announcing the availability of the kingdom of God, that included an invitation for us to harmonize all of our individual domains (kingdoms) so that we can live together without antagonism and isolation. God did not intend our present kingdoms on earth to be in conflict with one another. We are invited to live together under the two great commandments: "'You shall love the LORD your God with all your heart, with all your soul, with all your strength, and with all your mind,' and 'your neighbor as yourself'" (Luke 10:27).

FAITHFULNESS

You and I are unceasing spiritual beings with an eternal destiny in God's great universe. That eternal destiny is one in which "they shall live with his face in view, and the truth that they belong to him will show on their faces. Darkness will no longer be. They will have no need of lamps or sunlight because God the Lord will be radiant in their midst. And they will reign through the ages of ages" (Revelation 22:4–5, paraphrased). Reigning creatively with God in his universe is the eternal destiny for which we were meant.

After our physical death, we are going to receive a quality similar to the nature of the angels. Jesus described this: "Neither can they die any more: for they are equal unto the angels; and are the children of God, being the children of the resurrection" (Luke 20:36 KJV). He was pointing to the endless life into which we will enter. It's hard to imagine this or to understand it because we now exist in a world that is turned against God. We see little in our visible landscape that we can truly identify with the power of God.

Sometimes, even in Christian work, it seems like people are pushing and pulling, using purely human energy. This happens when we have not learned how to place ourselves at God's disposal, living and acting in faith. As we learn faithfulness *in the small things* that make up our lives, God teaches us more and more about the invisible landscape of his kingdom and brings us deeper into our eternal destiny. This is our training for reigning forever and ever with him.

UTILIZE YOUR TALENTS

The way this works out practically is that God expects us to take charge over the things around us, including our bodies, and use them *in reliance on him* to create the greatest good we can to the glory of God. Money is a primary part of this responsibility as a way of extending our rule and reign because it enables us to do things we can't do without it. Jesus understood this and addressed it. He knew that money becomes important because it gives power.

The parable Jesus told about the talents is a teaching about our responsibility. It is not about death or final judgment, but speaks directly to contemporary life. Talents in the time of Jesus were money, so this might be better called "the Power Parable of the Dollar." In this story, a nobleman gave various people some money and then went on a journey. He left them to invest it and be responsible for it. In Luke 19, it's called the Parable of the Minas, and I prefer that version to the one found in Matthew 25:14–30.

Jesus told this parable near the end of his final trip to Jerusalem just after he and the disciples had dined at the home of Zacchaeus.

> At this point, the crowd was listening to how the Son of Man came to seek and to save those who were lost. Because they were near Jerusalem, many supposed the kingdom of God was going to appear immediately. (Luke 19:10–11, paraphrased)

Jesus' followers were always thinking, *Are we there yet?*

> Therefore He said: "A certain nobleman went into a far country to receive for himself a kingdom and to return. So he called ten of his servants, delivered to them ten minas, and said to them, 'Do business till I come.'" (Luke 19:12–13)

It often happened that a person went to Rome and returned having been made king over a city or a territory. Before the nobleman left, he gave each of the ten servants one mina, which was worth roughly 100 days wages. So that was a good bit of money.

> "But his citizens hated him, and sent a delegation after him, saying, 'We will not have this man to reign over us.'" (Luke 19:14)

The nobleman's subjects made an end run around him and went to Rome, saying, "Don't make this guy our king!" They tried to keep him from gaining power to reign over them.

> "And so it was that when he returned, having received the kingdom, he then commanded these servants, to whom he had given the money, to be called to him, that he might know how much every man had gained by trading. Then came the first, saying, 'Master, your mina has earned ten minas.'" (Luke 19:15–16)

That's 1,000 percent earnings. This servant was told to "do business," to take charge of it and use it, but not specifically how to do that. He wasn't told what to do with the money; he took the initiative. In the same way, we need to be involved in God's business. This gives us something to talk with God about. It helps us understand the unique purpose he has given to each of us and builds our relationship with him.

> "And he said to him, 'Well done, good servant; because you were faithful in a very little.'" (Luke 19:17)

Notice the phrase "very little." One of the main ideas Jesus was addressing in this parable is how people are misled because they believe they have very little. They don't understand that their body and their place in life is where they are meant to reign. It's that simple.

Think about yourself for a moment—your body, your intellect, your talents. Few people are satisfied with these traits about themselves, but our first question needs to be, "Can we be faithful with these basic gifts God has given us?"

To the one who was "faithful in a very little," the nobleman said, "Have authority over ten cities" (Luke 19:17). Since he had been made king, he had cities to give out.

Being in charge of ten cities would be quite a challenge. People constantly complain about the government, but suppose *you* were in charge of the government. What would you do? You can sense the demands the role would place on your character. But many aspects of our life are about being in charge of things and whether or not we can be trusted with any authority.

The second servant who had been given a mina put it to use and earned five more (Luke 19:18). Not everyone can handle the same load, but he did well enough to be given five cities to rule (19:19).

I think this nobleman deserved to be reigning as a king. He was smart. He left town thinking, *I want to see how these servants do, because when I get back, I'm going to need people to put in charge of my cities.*

THE JOY OF THE LORD

In the Matthew 25 version, Jesus had the master say these words:

> "Well done, good and faithful servant; you were faithful over a few things, I will make you ruler over many things. Enter into the joy of your lord." (Matthew 25:21)

To enter into the joy of the Lord is to create good and rule for good. That's what God does. His joy is to create, and to create good. Isn't that what we all like to do? God has infinite creative will. His design for us is to learn how to use what we are in charge of to create good. As we learn to be responsible for "little" before God, we are put in charge of more. Advancing in the kingdom of God is never a matter of egoism; it's a matter of growth and gaining responsibility because we have been responsible with our very little.

If we're to grow spiritually, we have to understand that we already are in charge of some things. So find what you have say over and use it to become the kind of person who can manage ten cities. The physical universe isn't going to disappear; it's here to stay. And there will always be a need for people to supervise it. We were made to be in charge.

THE ONE-TALENT MAN

In both versions of this story, the condition of the third fellow who comes to the master is very instructive. In the Matthew account, he said, "I knew you . . ." But the problem was that he had the wrong view of his master. Many people have the wrong view of God and do not know him—although they *think* they do.

> "'Lord, I knew you to be a hard man, reaping where you have not sown, and gathering where you have not scattered seed. And I was afraid, and went and hid your talent in the ground. Look, there you have what is yours.'" (Matthew 25:24–25)

This poor, frightened, little one-talent man was playing a quid pro quo game: you gave me that, I'll give you this. But God doesn't work in those terms. This servant was playing it safe and seemed to be thinking, *Well, I didn't do anything wrong.* But trying not to do anything wrong was the biggest wrong of all. He did not venture out with what he had, invest it, and count on the kingdom of God to multiply it. We can be on the wrong side of life when we are on the wrong side of knowing God's character.

Many people are frightened by God, finding him threatening. Perhaps they haven't heard the gospel accurately, so they've never been exposed to the tenderness and gentleness that is in

Jesus. Or perhaps they had the misfortune of an upbringing with unkind caregivers and have the deep but common problem of thinking of God in terms of those bad examples. So they're hiding from God.

Sometimes they're frightened because they're thinking in human terms. We have to understand that God's greatness is not like human greatness. Humans who are "great" have layers of people who keep others from getting to them so they won't have to speak to them. We really do have to understand that God is not like executives at huge corporations or in high-level positions of government.

God's greatness is seen precisely in his lowliness. He is ready, willing, and able to deal with the smallest of things. His care and love go out to every person, no matter how insignificant people might say they are.

This servant was going nowhere with God. He exhibited the attitude of many people today who do not move forward in the kingdom because they don't know how good God is. They have not absorbed the truth of what the love of God in Jesus Christ toward human beings is, and the dignity that human beings were given in creation. The Lukan account portrays the servant this way:

> "Then another servant came and said, 'Sir, here is your mina; I have kept it laid away in a piece of cloth. I was afraid of you, because you are a hard man. You take out what you did not put in and reap what you did not sow.'" (Luke 19:20–21 NIV)

Sometimes our basic motivation in our interaction with God is fear. It drives us to hide, not to trust God and let ourselves open up to him. Fear drives us into a corner and makes us lonely, frightened, and untrusting. Fear is, in many ways, the worst thing that happens to people.

As Jesus crafted this parable, he chose an interesting response to the frightened servant who thought he was playing it safe:

> "The master said, 'Out of your own mouth will I judge you. You believe that about me? That's just what I'm going to be to you.'" (Luke 19:22, paraphrased)

The one mina he had was taken away from him because he was afraid of his master. And in both accounts, the mina (or the talent) is given to the other servant who had ten.

This servant did not do justice to the generosity of his master. He didn't regard himself as seriously as his master did. The most important thing to take away from this passage is that you must take yourself seriously as God's creature. You must believe that you are worth God's investment in you.

We do not need to be afraid of God. We identify our "minas" (money, mental and physical capacities, family, work), take responsibility for them, and invest them for his glory. Then, like the servant who made ten minas from one, we can use these things to prepare for a fuller life in which we step into the purposes God has for our lives, including responsibility over our own version of ten cities (Luke 19:16–17). And as our trust in Christ grows, we come into the kingdom that God appointed for us from the foundation of the world.

LET'S MAKE A DEAL

This theme of taking responsibility and investing in the future was a crucial part of the message of Jesus. He emphasized this idea in the Parable of the Unjust Steward (Luke 16:1–12). The steward was in charge of the financial affairs of his master and was probably not doing a good job. So he got put under the microscope, and the boss fired him.

"'Now what am I going to do?' he said. 'I'm unemployed. I'm not physically able to go out and dig ditches. . . . I know what I'll do so that when I'm removed from the stewardship they will receive me into their homes.'" (Luke 16:3–4, paraphrased)

Apparently, his boss had given him time to clear up his work. So he called in each creditor, discounting the debt they owed to his master. For example, he said:

"You still owe my boss $100. Give me $50, and I'll mark it paid." (Luke 16:6, paraphrased)

Now, this was standard business practice. To say that the steward was unjust was not to say his behavior was crooked; it was to say that he did not meet the standards of being a good steward. But he was being very wise. He deliberated and made a choice. This way, at least his master got *something*. If the man had just run away, his master wouldn't have gotten anything because he didn't know how to run the business. The master was dependent on his steward's wisdom to make something good out of this for both of them, and he praised the steward for acting so shrewdly. Jesus went on to say this:

"The sons of this age are more shrewd in relationship to their own kind, than the sons of light. And I say to you, make friends for yourself by means of the mammon of unrighteousness, that when it fails, those friends may receive you into the eternal dwellings." (Luke 16:8–9, paraphrased)

What is the mammon of unrighteousness? Mammon includes the things we have say over—possessions, money, and goods of various kinds. There's nothing wrong with those things in and of themselves, but they are often used in unrighteous ways. And when Jesus said, "That when it fails, those friends may receive you into the eternal dwellings," he was talking about banking on heaven. Jesus concluded by saying these words:

> "If, therefore, you have not been faithful in the use of unrighteous mammon, who will entrust the true riches to you? If you've not been faithful in the use of that which is another's, who would give you that which is your own?" (Luke 16:11–12, paraphrased)

All of us have whole realms in our lives that we are challenged to bring under the rule of God. This includes mental and physical capacities, talents, and financial resources. God has put all those things in your kingdom. When you bring all the details of your life under the rule of God, the outcome is that you are able to do the things he said.

Just as Jesus said, "I've been given say over all things in heaven and on earth" (Matthew 28:18, paraphrased), we've been given say over a few things. This is part of learning how to live with Jesus in such a way that when we do our jobs, care for our families, buy a car, or go to a football game, we do it as Jesus would do it. We're able to handle ordinary events of life in the way he would.

The important thing is the kind of person we become, not our income or accomplishments. After the nobleman found that one servant had expanded his money a thousandfold, he didn't say, "Oh, good, now I get more money!" Instead, he said to the servant, "I'm impressed with you!" (Luke 19:17, paraphrased). The nobleman was interested in who that servant was as a person. That's what God is always working for. God's treasures are not the output of our work. What God is going to get out of my life, whatever I may do otherwise, is the person I become.

Notice that the nobleman began by putting his servants in charge of a little thing. This is wisdom. Willingness to put others in charge of little things plays itself out well in raising children and dealing with employees. It's only when we are willing to release responsibility to others that we begin to know who they are. The other side is that *they* don't know who they are until they've been given dominion over something.

Some people spend their lives dreaming about what they would do if they were put in charge. Sometimes they do much better than people expect. Jesus said that the person who is faithful in very little is also faithful in much (Luke 16:10). Learning to live in the kingdom of God is a matter of being responsible, and being responsible means making judgments about what is good and what is not. Many folks are bothered about the "smallness" of what they're doing. The person who is faithful in little realizes that what is important is *the faithfulness*, not *the size* of what's going on. But some are unfaithful in little things because they are thinking, *This is so little that it doesn't matter whether I'm faithful or not!* It's the faithfulness that matters.

STRETCH OUT YOUR HAND

What is in your kingdom? What have you been given say over? You're in charge of your body, and you are here to use that body as the place of God's glory—of honoring God and blessing others. Think in terms of your work, your family, and your community as well. Your work is not just your job but the total amount of good you will accomplish in your lifetime. If you have children or grandchildren, you're in charge of your side of your relationship to them. You can determine what that will look like, and your commitment can have incredible effects.

Some of us have a deep investment in our congregation and our fellowship with others. Don't minimize simple things such as helping out in the sound booth, serving coffee, or teaching children. All of this is part of the creative good you produce in *your kingdom*.

Your kingdom is not limited to religious things. Dorcas made clothes and gave them to people who needed them (Acts 9:36–43). Your kingdom may include anything from artwork to political activity, from business organization to evangelization or prayer ministries. All these things are places where you might decide, *Yes, this is for me to do*.

There may be things you have only partial say over or areas where you're questioning your abilities or where you're not trusting God with them. These issues need to be addressed. We can be like the man with the withered hand who obeyed Jesus when he said, "Stretch out your hand" (Mark 3:5). He did so, but we may think that even that small thing is beyond us. We feel more like Moses, who complained that he couldn't talk but then God answered, "Who gave human beings their mouths?" (Exodus 4:11 NIV). God will help us.

How can you cultivate these aspects of your life in the kingdom of God now? One of the chief things to do is to recognize that you are in charge of them. We each have a purpose, and we are put here to make a difference. You might want to look at what you invest yourself in and say, "These are my minas. This is my little piece of mammon that has been given to me. I'm going to take it and invest it; I'm going to put myself behind it." So, first of all, *accept* it, and say, "This is what I'm in charge of."

You may decide *not* to be in charge of some things. For example, it's better not to be in charge of your neighbors and the way they behave. In a world saturated with busyness, we usually find ourselves with too many distractions and not deeply invested in the crucial things. You may want to look for clarity about one or two important things in which you can partner with God, walk with him in those things, and see them through.

Secondly, be definite about what you want to see happen. Many times in our prayers, we don't get anywhere because we haven't made a specific request. We pray, "Bless them!" and God answers, "Well, how? What do you want?" We need to understand the importance of being intentional and definite.

Finally, make sure your desired outcomes are of God. If you're looking for a certain kind of house or teaching a class or developing investment banking or working as a lawyer, let your expectation be *of God*. Try big things you know you can't do by yourself—things you're fairly certain you'll fail at—and you'll be expectant of God because you know the desired result is not within your power to accomplish. *It is important to attempt to do more than we can expect to accomplish ourselves.* Evidence of the presence of the Spirit of God is the incommensurability of the outcome with the effort. When you see that tremendous difference in outcome, you know that God is on the scene. That is what we really have to do to cultivate the kingdom of God in our lives.

Consider the band of semi-outlaws in the upper room after Jesus ascended. Jesus had been thoroughly rejected and then crucified. The disciples had run into a corner to hide. In their minds, Jesus had bailed out and gone to heaven. But as Pentecost approached, this band was still together. Suddenly an enormous racket from heaven descended upon the house, and signs and wonders occurred. Then Peter spoke, and thousands of people believed (Acts 1:13; 2:1–47). That's incommensurability.

Most of us are not going to see fireworks when we put ourselves on the line. God often works so quietly we may not experience something extra. The everyday investment of our faith in what we are put in charge of will show up brilliantly when we look back on things: "Thus far the LORD has helped us" (1 Samuel 7:12). Noticing how God has worked in our kingdom is crucial to our training. God wants to see what we do when there are no fireworks. But he will work, and you will see the incommensurability standing out.

GOD ACTS WITH US

For now, focus on taking responsibility for things uniquely your own—where your choice determines what happens. You can *practice faith* in the kingdom of God: see how it works, move with it, and know that it's real. God invites us, "You do it. You know I'm there, but you do it. And I'll act with you." You may not see it in the moment, but you will know it when you look back.

An example of someone who acted with God within her "kingdom"—the range of her effective will—was Rachel Saint. Her brother was one of the five missionaries killed by the Auca Indians in Ecuador. Rachel lived among the tribe who killed her brother and dedicated the remainder of her life to being with them.

Before she died, she told her nephew, "Stevie Boy, when I came to serve the Lord, I really didn't have much to offer him. I was never much of a linguist. I was pretty old when I came to work with the Huaorani tribe. I couldn't teach and preach nearly as well as other people. I was no theologian." Then her nephew asked her, "What do you think it was that the Lord honored in you?" She thought for a moment and said, "Well, I loved the Lord with all my heart, and I trusted him completely. And I was willing to obey him, because I trusted that he wanted me to do what I was doing and that it was best for me if I did it." And then she paused and said, "I guess I just learned to persevere. I just learned to keep on going with whatever he gave me to do."

And then Rachel Saint's nephew reflected wisely, "When an ordinary man or woman commits their life to Christ, God does uncanny supernatural things with them. That's the story about Rachel."[15]

When we look back over our lives, we see the loving hand

of God. It's real. It's the biggest thing in the world. And it's what makes Jesus look forward to saying to us, "You have been faithful over a few things. Be ruler over ten cities."

MAIN POINTS ABOUT THE KINGDOM OF GOD

- Life in the kingdom involves reigning creatively with God in his universe. This is the eternal destiny for which we were meant.
- The Parable of the Talents teaches us about our responsibility for the things God has given us (our kingdom). He wants us to take charge over those things, even small things, using them in reliance on him to create the greatest good we can to the glory of God.
- One of the key ideas Jesus addresses in the Parable of the Talents is how people are misled because they believe they have very little. We must take ourselves seriously as God's creature. We must believe we are worth God's investment in giving us the life we have.
- God is able to accomplish abundantly more than all we can ask or imagine (Ephesians 3:20). We can step into this reality of the kingdom by choosing to do something with God that we can't possibly accomplish in only our own power.

CHAPTER 8

REVOLUTIONIZING LEADERSHIP

"Even so, every good tree bears good fruit, but a bad tree bears bad fruit. A good tree cannot bear bad fruit, nor can a bad tree bear good fruit. Every tree that does not bear good fruit is cut down and thrown into the fire. Therefore by their fruits you will know them."

MATTHEW 7:17–20

God gave the nation of Israel the exercise of his kingly power. But as Israel exercised that power, it developed institutions and leaders who led against God. The point of the Parable of the Workers in the Vineyard is to bring out that simple fact. It also points out what happens to those who lead—*even with God's power*—but are not with God in their hearts. This situation can still be found today.

I want to make it clear that I do really mean leaders *inside* the kingdom of God. We're not talking about people who are outside of the kingdom. As we learned from the Parable of the Net and the Parable of the Wheat and the Tares, the kingdom of

God attracts and gathers all sorts of people. We can expect this to include leaders, but I find that it's difficult for us to accept the idea that people can exercise God's power, yet not be with him in their hearts. So I want to try to help our understanding by looking at a few verses from the end of the Sermon on the Mount (Matthew 7).

BY THEIR FRUITS

Near the end of the sermon, Jesus said some striking things about everyday fruit trees. He pointed out that some bring forth good fruit, while others produce bad fruit:

> "By their fruits you will know them." (Matthew 7:20)

Back in Missouri, we would occasionally see a tree that "said" it was an apple tree. But the fruit it bore were knotty little things you couldn't even make applesauce out of. It was a bad tree, and it bore bad fruit.

After this, Jesus cautioned listeners about false prophets, explaining that their fruit revealed the kind of prophets they were. This contrast between the inner and outer person is absolutely fundamental. Christianity is a religion of the heart. By no means does that mean external behavior is unchanged. What it means is that the root of Christian faith *and behavior* is found in the heart. No matter how much good behavior you may have, you haven't got the real thing if you don't have a good heart. A necessary and unbreakable connection exists between the nature of the tree and the nature of the fruit.

EATING SHEEP

Leading up to his discussion of good and bad fruit, Jesus warned against those who mislead others. They may appear to be very good, but inwardly they are governed by their own desires:

> "Beware of false prophets, who come to you in sheep's clothing, but inwardly they are ravenous wolves. You will know them by their fruits." (Matthew 7:15–16)

Outwardly they look like sheep, but inwardly they are only thinking about *eating* sheep.

Jesus continued:

> "Not everyone who says to Me, 'Lord, Lord,' shall enter the kingdom of the heavens, but he who does the will of My Father in heaven." (Matthew 7:21, paraphrased)

Verbal acknowledgment of Jesus as Lord is not enough. Anyone can *call* Jesus Lord. But to *have* Jesus as your Lord is a different thing.

We think that if someone is exercising God's power, certainly they must be with God in their hearts. That is not always true. Recall from chapter 6 that those who have tasted of the good Word of God and the powers of the age that is to come may still not be right with God. Repentance may be beyond them. It is possible to be in the kingdom of God—even a Christian leading a church or a business—but not have a right heart with God.

To have our hearts turned toward Christ, to think his commands are wise, and to do them goes much deeper. It requires a special kind of life with Christ where there is loving communication as we do the will of the Father. The *will* of the Father is acting and living as Jesus taught and becoming increasingly loving, humble, kind, forgiving, and gracious—all of the things laid out in 1 Corinthians 13. *That's the will of the Father.*

Jesus explained "doing God's will" even further:

> "Many will say to Me in that day, 'Lord, Lord, have we not prophesied in Your name, cast out demons in Your name, and

> done many wonders in Your name?' And then I will declare to them, 'I never knew you; depart from Me, you who practice lawlessness!'" (Matthew 7:22–23)

These people didn't do God's will, even though they believed they did many wonderful works. People may be able to do many wonderful works without being known by the Lord.

Knowing and being known are important realities in our with-God life. Biblically speaking, knowledge is a friend of faith. It is essential to faith and to our relationship with God in our spiritual life. Knowledge is interactive relationship. George Eldon Ladd said it well: "Knowledge in the Bible is far more than intellectual apprehension. Knowledge means experience. Knowledge means personal relationships. Knowledge means fellowship."[16]

Notice that Jesus didn't say, "*You* don't know *me*." He said, "*I* never knew *you*," which is a significant phrase that is both troubling and revealing. Do we allow the Lord to know us, or have we remained hidden? For example, we may say we know a famous person or somebody we recognize, but they don't know us because we are not a part of their lives in such a way that they would know us. In the same way, it matters whether we have an interactive life with God or only know about God.

ABILITY-DERIVED AUTHORITY

According to Luke, Jesus told the Parable of the Workers in the Vineyard during the early part of the final week of his life. The context was the joyous way the common people and many of the leaders received Jesus. Some leaders, such as Joseph of Arimathea, Nicodemus, and others, saw Jesus as the promised Messiah who had come to deliver the people of Israel. But for the most part, the power structure of Israel was set against him.

They opposed him on a simple point: *he threatened to undermine their authority.* They had their own authority structure, and

Jesus was not a part of it; yet he had authority that they did not give to him. They brought up the issue of his qualifications, with this kind of thinking underlying their opposition: *Did this man really graduate from Hebrew University? Did he have legitimate credentials? How could he possibly know what he was talking about?*

The leaders couldn't question that he knew more than they did. That was obvious, but what lay behind their questions and tests was a criticism based on the idea that Jesus didn't have proper credentials. He didn't study under any rabbi, nor did he study under John the Baptist. He had no human qualifications.

Many groups, religious and otherwise, hold tightly to their authority. For example, organizations issue certificates to indicate that someone has the authority and ability to act on behalf of the organization. Generally speaking, you can't fix a Toyota or teach math or preach in a church without a related certificate. But even if you have one, you may still not be able to *actually* do it.

There is another kind of authority that comes from *ability*. There can be a tremendous gap between authority and ability, between *certification* and *enablement*. You may not be authorized to make the most delicious cheesecake in town or to set up a computer system, but you still may be able to do it, and do it quite well. If you are one of those people, others rely on you and see you as an authority. The people of Israel had long suffered under leaders who had certificates but not the authority that comes from ability.

Take a moment to think about the idea of authority and its associated word *author*. An author in the broadest sense is someone who can create something or accomplish certain tasks. You "author" something when you produce it, when you bring ideas into reality—a plan or a book. Jesus was the *author* of teaching that rang so true that the common people said:

> "Where does this man get this? He speaks with authority; not like the scribes." (Matthew 7:29; Mark 1:27, paraphrased)

They recognized his abilities as a teacher because he was someone who could not only bring truth into reality, but also heal, cast out demons, and raise the dead.

Because Jesus was not certified by the religious leaders, they questioned him:

> Now it happened on one of those days, as He taught the people in the temple and preached the gospel, *that* the chief priests and the scribes, together with the elders, confronted *Him* and spoke to Him, saying, "Tell us, by what authority are You doing these things? Or who is he who gave You this authority?" (Luke 20:1–2)

They were looking for a certificate with the stamp of the high priest on it. That's like a person coming to your favorite piano-playing friend and saying, "Where did you get the authority to make such great music?" Your friend would probably laugh and say, "You don't need authority to make music. You just need to know *how to do it*." Perhaps you've noticed that the religious leaders never said to Jesus, "You don't have any authority," but rather, "Where did you get your authority from?" They could not deny that he had it.

Jesus, the master of the soul, came to the nation of Israel, which had been appointed by God to be a light to the world, a people who would show the entire world how to live (Isaiah 49:6). Within Israel, some people were prepared to listen to God, but they were not the ones in authority. And this was the heart-breaking thing he found.

SPIN DOCTORS

There are two sources of authority—God and humans. Human authority can be obtained by jumping through whatever hoops are required to receive certification, but we can't get authority from God that way. God looks much deeper; he looks into the heart. God knows I may jump through the hoops, which may not match the reality of my inner life. And so Jesus said to the religious leaders:

> "I also will ask you one thing, and answer Me: The baptism of John—was it from heaven or from men?" (Luke 20:3–4)

Jesus wasn't trying to trick them but was simply being logical. If they *really didn't know* where John's authority to baptize came from, then any answer Jesus gave them wouldn't make sense to them; it wouldn't be reasonable or useful. The source of his and John's authority was God.

It's the same issue as with those who find multiplication and division baffling because they don't have the foundational skills of addition or subtraction. Jesus' reasoning behind his response was something like, *It's not going to do them any good. Maybe the Lord will lead them into something that will help them understand as time goes by.*

Besides, the leaders were boxed in by their own political strategies. They couldn't say what they really thought, so they lied and said they didn't know where John's authority came from. They were not being honest and authentic, which is a necessary virtue for persons who will lead for God. They knew that those who had witnessed the fire and power of John the Baptist were certain he was from God. But the leaders couldn't say that about John, because if they did, they would be saying that Jesus was from God.

Everyone knew John the Baptist had authorized Jesus, in effect, by baptizing him. You could say that Jesus was "certified" by John. John had even protested that Jesus should be the one baptizing him because he recognized Jesus' authority. If the leaders had said John the Baptist was from God, then Jesus could have said, "The same person—God—who authorized John authorized me." Jesus knew a power struggle was coming, and that God had sent John the Baptist *to stand as an authority from heaven* in the nation of Israel.

The leaders had to spin their response. They had come out of the security of the temple and found themselves standing in this mob of people who thought Jesus was, at the very least, a great prophet. So they deliberated:

> They discussed it with one another, saying, "If we say, 'From heaven,' he will say, 'Why did you not believe him?' But if we say, 'Of human origin,' all the people will stone us; for they are convinced that John was a prophet." So they answered that they did not know where it came from. Since the leaders couldn't give Jesus a straight answer, he replied, "Neither will I tell you by what authority I am doing these things." (Luke 20:5–8, paraphrased)

JESUS IS THAT STONE

Jesus was not unresponsive to the leaders or their question. He offered a parable to help them think.

> "A certain man planted a vineyard, leased it to vinedressers, and went into a far country for a long time. Now at vintage-time he sent a servant to the vinedressers, that they might give him some of the fruit of the vineyard. But the vinedressers beat him and sent him away empty-handed." (Luke 20:9–10)

The owner planted the vineyard and then leased it to tenants to take care of the vines. The owner was not nearby so the tenant-vinedressers apparently thought it would be possible to do whatever they wanted with the property and whatever fruit it produced.

"Again he sent another servant; and they beat him also, treated him shamefully, and sent him away empty-handed. And again he sent a third; and they wounded him also and cast him out.

"Then the owner of the vineyard said, 'What shall I do? I will send my beloved son. Probably they will respect him when they see him.' But when the vinedressers saw him, they reasoned among themselves, saying, 'This is the heir. Come, let us kill him, that the inheritance may be ours.' So they cast him out of the vineyard and killed him. Therefore what will the owner of the vineyard do to them? He will come and destroy those vinedressers and give the vineyard to others."

And when they heard it they said, "Certainly not!"

Then He looked at them and said, "What then is this that is written:

'The stone which the builders rejected
Has become the chief cornerstone'?" (Luke 20:11–17)

Jesus was quoting the mention of the cornerstone in Psalm 118:22, describing exactly what was going to happen to him. He was the stone about which the people in charge would say, "That one will not do. Let's throw that one away. We cannot build our kingdom on Jesus Christ and his principles and his way of life." Jesus is that stone, the one "cut out of the mountain without hands" that fills the entire earth (Daniel 2:45).

Jesus' path crossed with the path of Israel's leaders, but their paths never merged. So the leaders threw him out, just as the corrupt tenants threw out the son. The leaders saw what he did; they saw the healings, and *even after experiencing the presence of his resurrection in their midst*, they said, "No. That won't do. That's not good enough. That's not what we want."

The leaders rejected Jesus even though he was "the stone

which the builders rejected, the same is become the head of the corner" (Luke 20:17 KJV). That stone is the part that holds the building together—the keystone. Even though Jesus was rejected in that moment, he became the cornerstone who holds the building together.

> "Whoever falls on that stone will be broken; but on whomever it falls, it will grind him to powder." And the chief priests and the scribes that very hour sought to lay hands on Him, but they feared the people—for they knew He had spoken this parable against them. (Luke 20:18–19)

BATTLE OF GREAT PROPORTION

Through the vineyard parable, Jesus was saying to the leaders, "You've got the certificate, but you don't have the right heart. You cannot lead the people for God." The prophets whom Israel's leadership had killed were like the servants who went to the vineyard and said, "Give me the fruit of the vineyard," but were sent away in one form or another.

Jesus later delivered a stinging message to this same group of scribes and Pharisees, describing their offenses: "For they bind heavy burdens, hard to bear, and lay them on men's shoulders; but they themselves will not move them with one of their fingers" (Matthew 23:4).

These leaders were people who say but do not do. Their insides didn't match their outsides. They talked, but they didn't have the power. And Jesus said, "Do what they say; just don't do what they do" (Matthew 23:3, paraphrased). Then he named what they were doing to mislead people and how they had killed the prophets. Jesus was emphasizing the contrast between words and actions.

I believe this message to the Jewish leaders became a standard one that was delivered over and over to the nation of Israel after Jesus' death. In the book of Acts, Stephen's sermon to the religious council was an example of Jesus' message recorded in Matthew 23. He recapped Israelite history stage by stage from Abraham to Moses to Stephen's own time, echoing Jesus' words about how Israel killed their prophets. Stephen's closing message was such a stunning and terrible indictment that the leaders killed him in rage:

> "You stiff-necked and uncircumcised in heart and ears! You always resist the Holy Spirit; as your fathers did, so do you. Which of the prophets did your fathers not persecute? And they killed those who foretold the coming of the Just One, of whom you now have become the betrayers and murderers, who have received the law by the direction of angels and have not kept it." When they heard these things they were cut to the heart, and they gnashed at him with their teeth. (Acts 7:51–54)

What was happening here was a battle of great proportion between very powerful forces. The coming of Jesus and his death did not stop this battle. It is still going on today. So it is crucial for us to understand just where the failure of these leaders came from, so that we might understand ourselves better and guard our own hearts and pray in an effective way for those who lead us.

MIND GAMES

The Pharisees did not react kindly to the Parable of the Workers in the Vineyard:

> When the scribes and chief priests realized that he had told this parable against them, they wanted to lay hands on him at that very hour, but they feared the people. So they watched him and sent spies who pretended to be honest, in order to trap him by what he said, so as to hand him over to the

> jurisdiction and authority of the governor. (Luke 20:19–20, paraphrased)

After this, they pretended to defer to him but were actually trying to trap him. First, they challenged him about giving taxes to Caesar, to which he replied:

> "Render therefore to Caesar the things that are Caesar's, [and here was the sting] and to God the things that are God's." (Luke 20:25)

The leaders knew they weren't doing that. They had wanted to trap him, but they caught themselves instead.

Then the Sadducees tried to trap him about the resurrection. Jesus was, in this regard, aligned with the Pharisees in Israel, believing in the reality of angels, believing that God continued to speak to people, and believing in the resurrection. Since the Sadducees did not believe in the resurrection, they thought up cute little stories to try to tie up those who did believe.

They devised a test about a man who had been married but died childless. His brother had a duty to marry that woman and raise up children in his older brother's name (a custom instructed by Deuteronomy 25:5–6). But then the second brother died as well, and this continued so that she sequentially married seven brothers. Last of all the woman died. (And many people would say, "No wonder," after all that.)

The leaders tested Jesus with this question:

> "Therefore, in the resurrection, whose wife does she become? For all seven had her as wife." (Luke 20:33)

Jesus replied that in the resurrection, people "neither marry nor are given in marriage" (Luke 20:35). Jesus clearly taught that what we know as marriage will not exist in heaven, but there *will* clearly be a resurrection and heaven. God is not the God of the dead; he is the God of the living for "all live to Him" (20:38).

These attacks were clever. It's as if these leaders had PhDs and MDivs and were playing intellectual games. Maybe they huddled each time and said, "Let's try this one on him. Let's mix him up this time." But with every attack, they were themselves burnt in the game. No matter how tricky they got, he surpassed them in logic and wit. They found that when they were face-to-face with the Son of God in an intellectual game, they were beaten every time.

PRIDE AND ARROGANCE

Jesus profoundly embarrassed the Pharisees in front of the whole crowd. In the last verses of Luke 20, Jesus explained that their problem wasn't intellectual but that it involved deeper issues—the motives and intentions of the hearts of the leaders.

> Then, in the hearing of all the people, He said to His disciples, "Beware of the scribes, who desire to go around in long robes, love greetings in the marketplaces, the best seats in the synagogues, and the best places at feasts, who devour widows' houses, and for a pretense make long prayers. These will receive greater condemnation." (Luke 20:45–47)

These "greetings in the marketplaces" were no ordinary greetings. They involved meeting someone and then with a loud voice trying to one-up them with all sorts of clever compliments and phraseology that would, at the same time, reflect glory on themselves. They also sat in the highest seats in the synagogue where everyone would notice them.

To "devour widows' houses" referred to the many clever ways they found to take ownership of the possessions and support of poor people and justify their actions in the name of God. It was the duty of every child to support their parents, but the leaders had worked out a little arrangement in which people could give a certain amount to the synagogue and be free from such obligations (Mark 7:11–13). Jesus knew these widows had no one to stand up for them.

These people were greedy and dishonest; they were filled with the fear of men and with pride and arrogance. They were enslaved to receiving honor from the people they feared. That was their problem. They were smart, well-dressed, and well-spoken, but they were bad trees bearing bad fruit. Their problem was they had rotten hearts. The decayed hearts of these leaders in the nation of Israel blinded them to the goodness of God. Jesus pointed this out to them:

> "Blind guides, who strain out a gnat and swallow a camel!
> "Woe to you, scribes and Pharisees, hypocrites! For you cleanse the outside of the cup and dish, but inside they are full of extortion and self-indulgence." (Matthew 23:24–25)

Jesus painted these instances of hypocrisy as someone seeing a little gnat in their drink and almost vomiting, but then casually opening their mouth to let a camel walk right in. Here's a person who takes a cup and just scrubs and polishes the outside, while the inside is still full of filth and rotten food. This is the issue of the inside versus the outside.

Jesus continued to warn them:

> "Woe to you, scribes and Pharisees, hypocrites! For you are like whitewashed tombs which indeed appear beautiful outwardly, but inside are full of dead men's bones and all uncleanness. Even so you also *outwardly* appear righteous to men, but *inside* you are full of hypocrisy and lawlessness.

> "Woe to you, scribes and Pharisees, hypocrites! Because you build the tombs of the prophets and adorn the monuments of the righteous, and say, 'If we had lived in the days of our fathers, we would not have been partakers with them in the blood of the prophets.'" (Matthew 23:27–30, emphasis added)

The leaders decorated the graves of good persons and said, "Oh, if we had just lived in the time of Isaiah or Jeremiah, *we* would have been nice to them. *We* wouldn't have killed them!"

Jesus summed this up by saying:

> "Therefore you are witnesses against yourselves that you are sons of those who murdered the prophets. Fill up, then, the measure of your fathers' guilt. Serpents, brood of vipers! How can you escape the condemnation of hell?" (Matthew 23:31–33)

These are troubling words. The religious leaders' failure was one of the heart. We need to keep this in mind as we think about ourselves and as we think about our leaders. We have quite unrealistic expectations of our leaders most of the time. We tend to think that if they would just stay out of trouble when it comes to sex and money, they would be fine. Consider that King David was in spiritual trouble long before he looked out from the roof of his house and saw Bathsheba.

Sex and money make it into the newspapers. Pride, arrogance, and hardness of heart do not. The problem with some leaders of religious organizations who may never get in trouble is that they have hard hearts. They have no trust in God. They are people-pleasers. They do not seek the honor that comes from God, and they have put their faith in making people happy.

TOUGH LOVE

Very early in his ministry, Jesus was concerned about the gap between the inner heart and the outer actions, pointing out how the leaders of Israel searched the Scriptures to justify themselves: "You search the Scriptures because you think that in them you have eternal life; and it is they that testify on my behalf. Yet you refuse to come to me to have life" (John 5:39–40, paraphrased).

Eternal life does not come from the Scriptures apart from Jesus Christ, to whom the Scriptures point. It doesn't matter how high your view is of inspiration—how firmly you believe that the Bible is the Word of God—you can go to hell hugging it to your chest if you don't find the Christ of the Scriptures.

Jesus was able to say hard things to people when he believed it would help them because he wasn't concerned with being honored and liked:

> "I do not receive honor from men. But I know you, that you do not have the love of God in you. I have come in My Father's name, and you do not receive Me; if another comes in his own name, him you will receive. How can you believe, who receive honor from one another, and do not seek the honor that comes from the only God? Do not think that I shall accuse you to the Father; there is one who accuses you—Moses, in whom you trust. For if you believed Moses, you would believe Me; for he wrote about Me. But if you do not believe his writings, how will you believe My words?" (John 5:41–47)

No one can believe when they are trapped in the fear of people or when they seek honor from others. They can't believe because they are putting themselves in God's place. Anyone who is concerned about the strength of their faith may need to seek

God's grace in rooting out any desire to be honored by people. It is a struggle we all share; this was true for Israel and its leadership, and it is true for the church and its leadership today.

MAGNIFY YOUR OFFICE

Leadership as God intends is a major element in the structure of love and care for one another and is imperative for those living in community. He has created specific roles to support our being together as loving communities, which require leadership that promotes direction, cooperation, and exemplary motivation (1 Peter 5:2–3). As I address some important qualities of Christian leaders and how those qualities can be developed, keep in mind that all leaders are really just people, and these are virtues all disciples of Christ should strive to develop.

Some of the main qualities necessary for leaders include intelligence, creativity, energy, and strong moral character. These are required for the specific activities of the leader, as well as to inspire confidence in those who work with them. These qualities grow as we "become participants of the divine nature" (2 Peter 1:4 NRSVue) and discover God has "given us everything needed for life and godliness, through the knowledge of him who called us by his own glory and excellence" (2 Peter 1:3 NRSVue).

Christian leaders must act with the understanding that God is acting *with* them. It needs to be clear that leaders are under Christ, that he is their head. When we remember that we should "not be called leaders; for only One is your Leader, that is, Christ" (Matthew 23:10 NASB), it will transform everything and change the entire character of everyone's work.

Paul used that wonderful phrase, "I magnify my office" (Romans 11:13, paraphrased) and described himself as "a slave of Christ Jesus" (1:1 NLT). We can think of our office as our purpose and responsibilities under God. There is no non-Christian work for the slave of Jesus Christ and for those willing to see that the effects of their actions are not things they accomplish by their own abilities. This especially needs to be clear to the leaders themselves. Those who follow these leaders will also be confident that, in reality, they are working under God and with God.

This quality of leadership depends on the interior life of the individual. That is, what is in their heart or will, in their thoughts and emotions, in their body and soul, and in the automatic responses of their social relations. This may all be summarized as their character. It is who they really are, as distinct from how they manage to appear. Indeed, one of the greatest burdens a leader may come to bear is that of keeping up appearances. Christian leaders must learn not to carry that burden, but to resign it to the Lord and live lives of authenticity and truthfulness.

It is important to know that the person we are becoming is more important to God than the work we do. "To obey is better than sacrifice" is a profound statement that character is what counts before God and before people (1 Samuel 15:22). Those we live with and lead will forget almost everything we say, but they will always remember the kind of person we were.

The character required of Christian leaders never comes merely as the result of the natural course of life and special acts of grace. They must assume responsibility for the development of their own character and the maintenance of it at the level that pleases God. Paul wrote to Timothy, "Train yourself in godliness, for, while physical training is of some value, godliness is valuable in every way, holding promise for both the present life and the life to come. . . . Put these things into practice, devote yourself to them, so that all may see your progress. Pay close attention to yourself and to your teaching; continue in these things, for in doing this you will save both yourself and your hearers" (1 Timothy 4:7–8, 15–16 NRSVue). Of course, we do this in partnership with God.

The general description of practices for training ourselves in godliness, that is, for shaping the inner dimensions of life, is spiritual disciplines, or better, disciplines for life in the Spirit. These are training activities that enable us to do what we cannot do without that training, such as controlling our anger, our lusts, or our tongue. Spiritual disciplines are a means of drawing grace into our souls and bodies and transforming our habits (what we are ready to do without thinking) into godly character. They are not righteousness or law, but wisdom. A few that are especially helpful for those in positions of leadership are the following:

- *Solitude and silence.* Being alone and quiet and not speaking or hearing are disciplines that are especially useful to break the habit of being in charge, of carrying the world on our shoulders. Leaders need some extensive time each week when they do nothing. As people grow in these practices, they will rediscover their soul, learn that God is here, and know that his world is in good hands, as Jesus repeatedly said.
- *Secrecy.* This is the practice of not letting one's good deeds be known. (For bad deeds, the discipline is openness.) This establishes the posture of living for the audience of One. This is especially important for leaders, but Jesus made plain its importance for everyone (Matthew 6:1–15). Practicing secrecy breaks the power of praise addiction. It results in peacefulness and being strong in the face of criticism.
- *Scripture memorization.* Memorizing long passages, such as 1 Corinthians 13, Colossians 3:1–17, or John 14–15, restructures a person's thoughts and thereby their feelings, spreading to their whole life.
- *Fasting.* Those who fast affirm the Word of God and its

sufficiency to their bodily being. They align themselves more closely with God's action with them. As with all disciplines, this is hard at first and has to be learned in order to do it profitably. It is a primary exercise in taking up the cross, and through it those who fast learn to remain sweet and strong when they do not get what they want.

LIVING A LIFE WORTHY OF THE LORD

What do people who lead in this way for Christ do? They bring the life of the kingdom to other people by opening their lives to it themselves. This is the calling of every follower of Christ. That's what Jesus himself said, and that's what he did. When he said, "Repent, for the kingdom of the heavens is at hand" (Matthew 4:17, paraphrased), what was at hand? The kingdom that was *in him*. As people looked at him and listened to him, they realized that the kingdom of God was there and that it was available to them, and as a result, they became his disciples.

Disciples of Jesus exemplify eternal living and bring it to bear on everything around them because their lives are caught up in God's life as they steward his kingdom on earth. What Jesus is doing is a part of what they are doing, and what they are doing is a part of what he is doing. Taking the easy yoke on oneself (Matthew 11:29) means to use his strength and ours together, to bear our load and his.

As Jesus' apprentices, we will "discipline ourselves for the purpose of godliness," as Paul said (1 Timothy 4:7, paraphrased), and lead others into the same way of life so that they increasingly become good trees bearing good fruit for the glory of their heavenly Father. We will "walk worthy of the Lord, fully pleasing to him" and will "bear fruit in every good work and as you grow in the knowledge of God" (Colossians 1:10 NRSVue).

MAIN POINTS ABOUT
THE KINGDOM OF GOD

- The Parable of the Workers in the Vineyard brings out the tragic fact that leaders in God's kingdom, past and present, sometimes have hard hearts and develop institutions that lead against God.
- Disciples of Jesus exemplify eternal living and bring it to bear on everything around them because their lives are caught up in God's life as they steward his kingdom on earth.
- Leadership as God intends is a major element in the structure of love and care for each other, and this type of leadership is imperative for those living in community.
- Doing God's will is about having the faith of Jesus and living as Jesus taught, becoming more and more like him in our character and habits.
- Christian leaders must act with the understanding that God is acting with them.

CHAPTER 9

LOST AND FOUND

"But love your enemies, do good to them, and lend to them without expecting to get anything back. Then your reward will be great, and you will be children of the Most High, because he is kind to the ungrateful and wicked. Be merciful, just as your Father is merciful.

"Do not judge, and you will not be judged. Do not condemn, and you will not be condemned. Forgive, and you will be forgiven. Give, and it will be given to you. A good measure, pressed down, shaken together and running over, will be poured into your lap. For with the measure you use, it will be measured to you."

LUKE 6:35-38 NIV

Jesus told three stories that highlight three different ways of being lost and three dimensions of the generous heart of God who yearns and waits for our return. Something that is lost is not where it is supposed to be, and therefore cannot be integrated into the life of the one to whom it belongs and to whom it is lost (God). This state of being out of place means we are disconnected from God. This makes us useless to God and ourselves,

143

just as a lost set of keys is useless to its owner. We may be fully aware that we are lost, or we may be lost while sincerely believing we are in the right place. No matter what our lostness looks like, the heart of God relentlessly pursues those who are lost and is always giving, forgiving, and reconciling. He helps us find our way back to him because his heart is full of kindness and mercy and is never condemning.

As we look at these stories that exemplify the attitude of our generous Father and the attitudes of our own hearts, it's important to keep in mind that some folks can't be found because *they've never been lost.* You may want to reply, "Well, yes, they *have* actually been lost, but they didn't know it. They didn't understand. They've never seen themselves in that way." And you would be right.

SINCERELY LOST

The first group of lost people have never come to see themselves as lost or beyond hope. Maybe they were raised in a family which guided them along so nicely that they always succeeded. Their parents loved them and provided a good home. Maybe everything went well in the church or synagogue where they were involved. They got married, had children, and lived happily ever after. They never failed, felt out of place, or suffered the kinds of things that put them at the end of their rope.

Some of these folks come to church and recognize it as a good thing. They are intelligent people who "have it all together," so they pitch in and do good work. Many of them give themselves entirely to helping God do his work and believe God *needs* them to help him. They haven't yet realized that they are lost and need to be found by God. Jesus warned his disciples about some people in their day who saw themselves as "God's helpers," saying, "There will come a day when they will give you up to death and think they are doing God a favor" (Matthew 24:9; Mark 13:11; Luke 21:12, paraphrased).

Jesus wasn't saying such people were insincere. Saul was very sincere as he persecuted the Christians (Acts 9:4), and the people who crucified Jesus believed they were doing a good thing. When the chief priest, Caiaphas, said, "It is more important that we save the nation of Israel by sacrificing one man, than that we let this one person live and bring trouble on the whole nation" (John 18:14, paraphrased), he believed he was simply *doing his job*.

As we study the Parable of the Two Sons, we'll meet a second type of lost individual—those who *say* the right thing but don't do it. Both sons in this parable were insincere. This same behavior prompted Jesus to say about the scribes and the Pharisees, "Do what they *say*, but don't do what they *do*," (Matthew 23:3, paraphrased, emphasis added).

We'll also meet a third kind of lost person—those who have failed and know it. Their biggest failures are not the tragedies that entered their lives, but the failures that came from their own choices to turn away from God and refuse to do as he asked. These people do not blame others, saying, "Someone did this to me." Instead, they confess, "It was *I* who did it. I was the one who was lost. My failure is *mine*, and mine alone."

SHAMELESS ADORATION

The heart of those who are forgiven and know what it is like to live in God's grace was beautifully played out when Jesus was anointed by a sinful woman (Luke 7:36–50). A number of things happened to Jesus at a meal with a man who sincerely thought he'd never been lost and a woman who knew she had been. Put yourself in this story and remember that Jesus was a rabbi respected by many people. He could easily have been concerned about managing his reputation as a righteous man.

> Then one of the Pharisees asked Him to eat with him. And
> He went to the Pharisee's house, and sat down to eat. (Luke
> 7:36)

Inviting Jesus was bold and risky for the Pharisee because Jesus ate with (that is, slummed around with) all those *other* people. It turns out that this Pharisee was watching to see what would happen. He had his suspicions about Jesus—suspicions that were *fully* confirmed.

> And behold, a woman in the city who was a sinner, when
> she knew that Jesus sat at the table in the Pharisee's house,
> brought an alabaster flask of fragrant oil, and stood at His feet
> behind Him weeping. (Luke 7:37–38)

She was a woman who *knew* what it was like to be lost. She approached Jesus as he talked and ate, reclining with his feet behind him.

> She began to wash His feet with her tears, and wiped them
> with the hair of her head; and she kissed His feet and
> anointed them with the fragrant oil. (Luke 7:38)

Imagine inviting your pastor to your home for dinner, and a woman whom everyone knows to be guilty of a flagrant sin shows up wanting to see him. As she comes in, she starts to cry and then kneels down and takes off your pastor's shoes, wipes his feet with a cloth, pours oil over them, and gives him a foot massage. Not many pastors' reputations could handle that. If your pastor is really a good person (not to mention a person with dignity), this kind of thing would *never* happen! I put it this way because we should be a little sympathetic with this fellow who invited Jesus.

> Now when the Pharisee who had invited Him saw this, he spoke to himself, saying, "This Man, if He were a prophet, would know who and what manner of woman this is who is touching Him, for she is a sinner." (Luke 7:39)

This Pharisee may have been one of the many good folks who believed their goodness consisted of doing everything right. He evaluated the actions of those around him and judged whether each person was of God. This Pharisee knew that anyone who was a prophet would not let this woman do *that* to his feet. Jesus didn't deny this, but chose to tell a story.

> And Jesus answered and said to him, "Simon, I have something to say to you."
>
> So he said, "Teacher, say it."
>
> "There was a certain creditor who had two debtors. One owed five hundred denarii, and the other fifty. And when they had nothing with which to repay, he freely forgave them both. Tell Me, therefore, which of them will love him more?"
>
> Simon answered and said, "I suppose the one whom he forgave more." (Luke 7:40–43)

You see, Simon only owed fifty denarii, but this woman owed five hundred. Simon had probably been around Jesus enough to know what was coming next, so he said, "Well, I *suppose . . .*"

> And He said to him, "You have rightly judged." Then He turned to the woman and said to Simon, "Do you see this woman? I entered your house; you gave Me no water for My feet, but she has washed My feet with her tears and wiped them with the hair of her head. You gave Me no kiss, but this woman has not ceased to kiss My feet since the time I came

> in. You did not anoint My head with oil, but this woman has anointed My feet with fragrant oil." (Luke 7:43–46)

Simon's withholding of these common courtesies like washing Jesus' feet and other traditional greetings seems to have been based on Simon's suspicions about Jesus. Perhaps Simon guessed something like this would happen and didn't want to have to tell his friends that he had actually washed this guy's feet.

> "Therefore I say to you, her sins, which are many, are forgiven, for she loved much. But to whom little is forgiven, the same loves little." (Luke 7:47)

Jesus was not saying that her sins were forgiven because she loved much, but the opposite: *because* her sins were forgiven, she loved much. Her love was an expression of the forgiveness received. "For the Son of Man came to seek out and to save the lost" (Luke 19:10 NRSVue).

We see a profound and important truth here: when people don't love the Lord very much, it's often because they lack a sense of how much forgiveness they have needed. Maybe they have a small sense of it, but not very much. Perhaps no one has really walked them through what it means to be forgiven.

> Then He said to her, "Your sins are forgiven."
>
> And those who sat at the table with Him began to say to themselves, "Who is this who even forgives sins?"
>
> Then He said to the woman, "Your faith has saved you. Go in peace." (Luke 7:48–50)

The guests caught up in their love of propriety couldn't resist passing judgment on this scandalous situation and said, in effect,

"Check this guy out! What does he think he's doing? *He's forgiving sins?*"

There are those who have never stood as lost and condemned before God and the whole world. They've never been driven aimlessly across the events of life, not knowing which way to go or which things were right, feeling completely worthless, and then found themselves in the arms of a loving Father. They may say and do the right things and be happy to be God's helpers, but the heart of the one who is forgiven—who has been lost and fully *knows* it—truly can say, echoing Romans 8:33–35, "Who is the one that condemns me? Jesus Christ died for me, and I'm not going to get upset because someone doesn't like something I did—even if it was wrong—when Jesus himself died for me."

TURNING BACK

Our second story, a parable, began this way:

> "But what do you think? A man had two sons, and he came to the first and said, 'Son, go, work today in my vineyard.'
>
> "He answered and said, 'I will not,' but afterward he regretted it and went." (Matthew 21:28–29)

Think about how this might have happened. The son would have answered, "No, Dad, I'm not gonna do it." But while lazing around in the house, his heart turned toward his dad as he thought about him out there working in the vineyard: *Well, look at him, he's working so hard.* So he would have gone out and said to his dad, "Aw, Dad, please go sit in the shade and let me work here for you."

Jesus' parables were stories about the kind of things that would actually happen in normal life. Sometimes children refuse to do what their parents ask but then change their minds because they can't stand the thought of their father or mother being stuck doing it. The truth is that they love their mom and dad, and their hearts turn toward their parents.

The key point is that in the middle of their disobedience, they decide to go. They had said no, planning to disobey. But from somewhere inside, the thought comes, *You know, I want to please my father.*

Jesus continued:

> "Then he came to the second and said likewise. And he answered and said, 'I go, sir,' but he did not go." (Matthew 21:30)

This second son said: "I go, sir." The first son hadn't even called his father "sir," but this second son did. The word actually means *Lord.* This son was even showing respect while he disobeyed.

Jesus then asked a question of the good people around him who themselves had said, "I go, sir," and yet hadn't gone:

> "Which of the two did the will of his father?"
> They said to Him, "The first."
> Jesus said to them, "Assuredly I say to you that tax collectors and harlots enter the kingdom of God before you." (Matthew 21:31)

UNFETTERED ACCEPTANCE

The people listening may have wanted to hide their faces because this was so stinging. It's as if Jesus were saying to us today, "Truly I say to you that the gangsters, prostitutes, and dishonest politicians will enter the kingdom of God before you do." Jesus said this not as a list of kingdom qualifications, but rather to teach that the heart of God is open to forgive.

Jesus stunned them by saying, in effect, "Some of you nice

folks who are first in the human order will watch these 'sinners' go into the kingdom of God before you do because you said, 'I go, sir,' and you did not go. Whereas they said, 'No!' but repented."

A heart of indifference and even rebellion may exist beneath the appearance of a nice religious person. And the heart of the prostitute or gangster may know what it's like to live daily without God and finally say, "I have said no to my father, but I will return. I will do the works of the kingdom of God by the grace of God."

Jesus gave the chief priests and elders this parable to show that the heart of God is completely open and ready to receive those who said, "I won't go," and then repented. They knew they were lost. But people who have never seen themselves as lost find God's openness undignified, saying, "You think God is just going to *forgive* people? Just like *that*?"

THE FATHER'S GIVING HEART

The story we know as "the prodigal son" is another story of two brothers with different attitudes toward their father. The older brother appeared to be concerned about pleasing his father and did everything he could to help him. But it turned out that his heart was quite unlike his father's. He did not forgive and was not generous. He had a heart that sought to exact and separate, divide and punish. He was jealous of the love the father gave to the other son.

The younger son had assessed the situation at home and decided it was time to fend for himself. That is where our story begins:

> "A man had two sons. When the younger told his father, 'I want my share of your estate now, instead of waiting until you die,' his father agreed to divide his wealth between his sons. A few days later, the younger son packed all of his belongings and took a trip to a distant land." (Luke 15:11–13, paraphrased)

This story strikingly illustrates the heart of God, the kind of merciful heart that is available to each of us. We won't truly understand love until we understand the father's kind of love where the last word is *mercy*.

The father's heart was a giving heart. We sometimes forget that being a younger son in those days was not a good position to be in. When a father died, everything went to the eldest son, who then gave the other children whatever it pleased him to give.

So this younger son was not necessarily acting unreasonably when he said, "Father, divide your property and give me the part that you want to come to me now, before you die." Perhaps he knew he might not get anything from his older brother, who was right and just but didn't know much about giving, *for*giving, or mercy.

When the younger son made this request, it would have been easy for the father to look into his son's eyes and say, "I know what you're going to do with it, and I'm not going to give it to you. I know how unreliable you are and how easily you are swayed." But the father didn't say that. He gave the younger son what he asked for because the heart of the father is one that gives.

I'm sure this father had grounds to worry about his son, but most children eventually mature enough that the parents' role in their lives becomes one of helping them do what they want to do. You may say, "But that's dangerous!" But it is the giving, helping heart of the father and mother that will win the child, not the condemning heart that says, "No, I don't trust you. I have no confidence in you."

A time comes when the mercy we have received leads us to show mercy. We say, "Here, I'll help you. You want to dye your hair green or purple? Sit down right here. I'll help you."

Our children were given to us to love, not to sit on. And while we often feel responsible for their behavior, there comes a moment when we have to turn them loose and say, "I'll help you." We need to have confidence in them because we have confidence in God. The father in the parable understood the difficulty his son was facing, and he chose to help his son.

LIVIN' HIGH ON THE HOG

I'm sure the father's heart troubled him as he watched his son walk out the door, suitcase in hand. He must have prayed, "God, help me. God, help him." As it turned out, the young man took his money, went to another country, and experienced hard times. Everything his father may have feared came true. Jesus described it this way:

> "And there he wasted all of his money on parties and prostitutes. And about the time his money was gone, a famine swept over the land and he began to starve. He persuaded a local farmer to allow him to feed his pigs. But the boy became so hungry that even the husks he was feeding the swine looked good to him. And no one gave anything to him." (Luke 15:13–16, paraphrased)

He had a lot of friends when he had money, but not so many when he was down and out. Taking care of pigs was about as low as a Jewish man could get. And not only was he taking care of them; he was prepared *to eat what they ate.*

Many people have found themselves in this place. They've been reduced to eating what the pigs eat and maybe even what they *wouldn't* eat. In most cases, they were acting in rebellion against what they knew was best as they continued justifying what they were doing. This whole business of justification is very important. They probably sat on the fence around the hog pen and sang songs about what a wonderful time they were having. They chose to sit there on the edge of an increasingly ruined life rather than give in and say, "I *blew* it. I'm lost."

Eventually, this younger son had eaten one too many meals out of the hog trough and discovered he was lost.

> "When he finally came to his senses, he said to himself, 'You know, the servants in my father's house eat better than this, and here I am, dying of hunger. I'm gonna go back and ask Dad for a job. I'm gonna say, "Now, look, Dad, I know I have no claim on you. You have given me everything you owe me. All I want is just a job. I know that you need workers, and so you might as well hire me. So here I am."'" (Luke 15:17–19, paraphrased)

We can imagine what the father had been doing during the many days he waited to hear from his son. He may have sent a servant to check on him. Maybe the servant followed the son as he lost all his money, and perhaps he even knew that the son was down in the pigpen.

But the moment came when the father saw his son coming from a long way off because the father was out there looking. Probably he had looked down that road day after day with a yearning, broken heart. He didn't sit in his living room righteously judging his foolish son. He was *hoping* his son would come home.

> "And while he was still a long distance away, his father saw him coming and was filled with loving pity, and ran to meet him." (Luke 15:20, paraphrased)

And he didn't say, "Now, when you get cleaned up and get the hog smell off you, I will come and give you a hug and a kiss." Instead, the father ran down the road, took him in his arms, and said, "Come here, son. The bath comes later." He was lost and had been found. Whosoever will may come.

It was the father's generosity toward the son that turned the heart of the son toward home. I like to think that the son understood the kindness of his father's heart and knew the father would be kind to him. It's this kindness of God that leads to repentance (Romans 2:4). "[God] is kind to the unthankful and evil" (Luke 6:35). Yes, God is kind even to people who actually prefer to sin.

WHISPERS AND SCANDAL

I was raised with that old human attitude that forgiveness should be hard to obtain. The role of forgiveness in human affairs was to allow one person to grind away at another, holding their offense over their head. But when someone in our family has done foolish things—a spouse, a child, a relative—it isn't our job to make sure they know what fools they've been. The forgiving heart of the father is one that yearns and waits for the lost child to come back.

The prophet Hosea illustrated this in his own life. He was a righteous man, a prophet and teacher in Israel, somewhat like a pastor today. To give a message to the nation of Israel, God told Hosea to marry a woman who would be unfaithful to him. His obedience meant he had to endure the whispers, the scandal, and the questions as to whether the little children running around his house were his own.

When Hosea's wife, Gomer, became so degraded that she sold herself into slavery, the Lord came to him and said, "You go down to the auction block—she's being sold down there today— and you buy her back." Hosea went down and brought her back, took her to himself, and loved her once again (Hosea 3:1–3, paraphrased).

It's out of that story of a broken heart that we have the wonderful words Jesus quoted from the Old Testament as he tried to help people understand the merciful, forgiving heart of

God: "For I desire mercy and not sacrifice, and the knowledge of God more than burnt offerings" (Hosea 6:6; see also Matthew 9:13; 12:7).

THE POWER OF MERCY

As the prodigal son returned home, the father who ran toward him had probably forgiven him long before that day. This father so loved his son that forgiveness was his only course of action.

> "His son began to say to him, 'Father, I've sinned against heaven and against you and I'm not worthy of being called your son.' But his father interrupted his story and said to the servants, 'Quick, bring the finest robe in the house and put it on him! And a jeweled ring for his finger, and shoes for his feet. And kill the calf we've been fattening. We must celebrate with a feast. For this son of mine was dead and has returned to life. He was lost, and now he is found.' And so the party began." (Luke 15:21–24, paraphrased)

The son didn't even get to *ask* for forgiveness! He didn't get to perform the song and dance he had so carefully prepared while he was in the pigpen. *He didn't have to go through it!* Maybe he felt disappointed since he had rehearsed it so well, but he couldn't do any of that with this joyful, sobbing hulk of a father hanging on his neck. Oh, the joy of that meeting after the previous agony for both the father and the son!

However, the older brother could not enter into that joy. That's the saddest thing about this story. A great deal can be said for the older son. He probably loved his brother and watched with tears in his eyes as he left. He worked hard for his father and may even have taken on the younger brother's work while he was gone. But the older brother never knew the depths of his father's love.

"Meanwhile, the older son was in the fields working. And when he returned home, he heard dance music coming from the house and he asked one of the servants what was going on.

"'Oh, your brother is back,' he told him. 'And your father has killed the calf we were fattening and has prepared a great feast to celebrate his coming home again unharmed.'

"But the older brother was angry and wouldn't go in the house. Finally, his father came out and begged him. But he replied, 'All of these years I've worked hard for you and never once refused to do a single thing you told me to. And in all that time, you never gave me even one little goat for a feast with my friends. Yet when this son of *yours* comes back after spending *your* money on prostitutes, you celebrate by killing the finest calf we have on the place.'

"'Look, my dear son,' his father said to him, 'You and I are very close. Everything I have is yours. But it is right to celebrate. For he is your brother. And he was dead, and he's come back to life. He was lost, and he is found.'" (Luke 15:25–32, paraphrased, emphasis added)

Just as the father had gone out to meet the younger son, he also went out to the older brother who scorned the party for the younger son. The father did not say, "You're in trouble with me because your heart isn't right." Instead, he said, "Son, you are always with me, and all that I have is yours" (Luke 15:31).

The father *begged* his older son to have mercy on his brother. This is where we see that the heart of the father is a *reconciling* heart. This father not only forgives, but he also goes out to the one who doesn't think he needs forgiveness and begs him to understand mercy.

In a sense, this parable is more about the older brother than the younger one. By addressing it to the grumbling scribes and Pharisees, Jesus illustrated the response of people who prefer sacrifice to mercy and who prefer burnt offerings or religious rituals to living with a merciful heart. Even though one of the beatitudes is, "Blessed are the merciful, for they will receive mercy," many people don't believe it is blessed or beneficial to show mercy (Matthew 5:7 NASB). The older son certainly didn't believe it. His father was being *merciful*, and he thought his father was anything but blessed.

Many who insist on standing up for their rights believe that justice is the final word and do not like to see mercy extended to those who need it. Even in our churches, we find people who are rigid in their belief that extending mercy is wrong. It undermines their sense of security because the human systems we live in work by forcing, condemning, and managing people rather than simply showing mercy. But the father shows mercy because he knows the *power* of mercy.

At the very heart of all we profess as Christians stands the cross. The cross is the merciful heart of God. We cannot comprehend the cross if we don't understand that God's mercy and his justice are not opposed; they are expressions of the same love. On the cross, Jesus died for us. Out of his mercy, he gave. He was kind to us who were unthankful and evil. And that kindness is the key to understanding God's mercy.

CONDEMNATION CONTROL

The surest way to lead someone in the path of goodness is to be merciful to them. The surest way to drive them into wrongdoing and anger is to be *un*merciful. It is the power of mercy that conquers the hardened heart.

You may think, *It's all right for God to be merciful, but what's going to happen if I'm merciful? Won't they just do it again? God can afford mercy, but I don't think I can.*

It's only when we step into the path of mercy that we begin to live in the power of God. It is in the stream of mercy we begin to live without holding anything against anyone—forgiving, giving, and reconciling—and truly know the abundance of God that can meet all of our needs.

On the cross, Jesus' death was sufficient for the forgiveness of all of our sins. When we take Jesus' spirit upon us, we find the power to live giving, forgiving, reconciling lives in every relationship in which we stand. We will know the power of God's kingdom in our lives.

One of the biggest battles when a loved one goes astray is that someone wants to be merciful but other family members refuse. They're worried that mercy will be perceived as *condoning* the wrong the person has done. Or perhaps they think the way to control people is to be unmerciful to them.

Jesus taught about this condemnation, saying, "Judge not, that you be not judged" (Matthew 7:1). He was dealing with people who believed they could *control other people by condemning them*—that if they were to stop condemning them, the offender would keep doing evil things. Even today, people are convinced it's important to keep the condemnation coming thick and fast so everyone will know exactly what to do. And the truth is, they *will* know exactly what to do, which is to condemn *us* in return. And that's what Jesus knew. If you aim a campaign of condemning at someone, you are sure to receive condemnation in return.

The prodigal son probably regretted what he had done for the rest of his life. He would have looked at his dad's gray hair and wrinkles and thought, *I've shortened my father's life by what I've put him through.* Yet the younger son knew how lost he had become and what it was like to be forgiven, what it was like to enter into the kingdom of God and walk in it by the grace of God.

When we live in the kingdom of God, we can have the loving, giving, forgiving, merciful, reconciling heart of God in everything we do, in our relationships with our families, our neighbors, and people who are very different from us. The abundance of life, grace, and mercy we find in the kingdom of God can be extended to anyone and everyone.

MAIN POINTS ABOUT THE KINGDOM OF GOD

- The kingdom of God is a place where mercy and reconciliation take place, where there is always a celebration whenever anyone who is lost is found.
- God relentlessly pursues those who are lost. He is always giving, forgiving, and reconciling because the heart of God is open to forgive and ready to receive those who repent.
- We won't truly understand love until we understand the father's kind of love where the last word is *mercy*. It is the power of mercy that conquers the hardened heart.
- We cannot comprehend the cross if we don't understand that God's mercy and his justice are not opposed; they are expressions of the same love.

CHAPTER 10

PREPARE THE WAY

I wait for the Lord; *my soul waits,*
and in his word I hope;
my soul waits for the Lord
more than those who watch for the morning,
more than those who watch for the morning.

PSALM 130:5-6 NRSVUE

We come now to a serious turning point in the earthly ministry of Jesus. The leaders of Israel had rejected him, and he accepted their rejection. Jesus turned away from the leaders, the temple, and the nation's institutions. Israel as a nation would never have the kingdom again. Jesus turned his back on Jerusalem because, as far as he was concerned, it had become only the place where he was going to be crucified. He no longer spoke to the crowds or addressed the leaders.

To prepare his disciples for his imminent death and physical absence, Jesus told them three parables—the Parables of the Talents, the Faithful and Unfaithful Servant, and the Ten

Virgins, followed by a metaphor of the Lord separating the sheep and the goats.

This dramatic series of events begins in Matthew 23, which records Jesus' final message to Israel as a people and his turning away from them and their institutions. Jesus, grieved over the hypocrisy of the Pharisees, turned his back on Jerusalem:

> "O Jerusalem, Jerusalem, the one who kills the prophets and stones those who are sent to her! How often I wanted to gather your children together, as a hen gathers her chicks under her wings, but you were not willing! See! Your house is left to you desolate; for I say to you, you shall see Me no more till you say, 'Blessed is He who comes in the name of the Lord!'" (Matthew 23:37–39)

This was the moment in the history of God's redemptive act when the king took the kingdom away from the people of Israel. The next event was eloquently portrayed at the beginning of Matthew 24:

> Then Jesus went out and departed from the temple, and His disciples came up to show Him the buildings of the temple. (Matthew 24:1)

Picture the scene in your mind as Jesus and his disciples gazed at the temple. Perhaps his disciples said, "Look at these wonderful buildings! Oh, isn't this marvelous what God has done!" And Jesus said to them:

> "Do you not see all these things? Assuredly, I say to you, not one stone shall be left here upon another, that shall not be thrown down." (Matthew 24:2)

The nation of Israel had become entirely caught up in its temple and its rituals. Jesus was not being vengeful; he knew that in roughly forty years, the Romans would reclaim Jerusalem after a revolt and destroy the Second Temple (AD 70). Jesus was not mad at the people for rejecting him. That was something he wouldn't even have thought of. *He was teaching about what was eternal reality and what was only appearance.*

Jesus was echoing that marvelous Old Testament passage about the foundations of heaven and earth being shaken so that the things that were truly of God could remain (Haggai 2:6, 21). He was telling his disciples that the foundations were going to be shaken and not one of those stones would be left on top of another.

PREPARING HIS DISCIPLES

The gospel of John reflects this same period when Jesus gathered his little band and taught them (John 14–17). He was teaching about what was going to happen but also interceding with his Father in prayer for his friends: "Not only do I pray for these, but also for all who believe" (John 17:20, paraphrased). You and I were prayed for in that time by Jesus.

Jesus taught the disciples in ways that would help them understand the time when they would no longer have the temple to look at, just as he said to the woman at the well, "Woman, believe Me, the hour is coming when you will neither on this mountain, nor in Jerusalem, worship the Father. . . . God is Spirit, and those who worship Him must worship in spirit and truth" (John 4:21, 24).

Jesus understood that we all hunger and reach out for visible things to hold on to. He was intent on teaching about how things were going to be during his physical absence and how people should prepare themselves and keep their hearts open to him in anticipation of his return.

These parables occur at the end of a continuous discourse recorded in Matthew 14–25. Afterward, Jesus began to talk about his death: "Now it came to pass, when Jesus had finished all these sayings, that He said to His disciples, 'You know that after two days is the Passover, and the Son of Man will be delivered up to be crucified'" (Matthew 26:1–2).

The disciples had not been able to accept this. They just couldn't. Their minds were on things like impressive buildings and how to rid Israel of Roman domination. They couldn't even imagine Jesus' death, and we probably wouldn't have either without having two thousand years of church history to help us understand it.

So Jesus gave them these teachings to help them understand how their hearts had to be kept and cultivated in the period of the church, which is the period in which we now live. He used these parables and metaphor we're about to look at to prepare them for how things were going to be.

WHERE YOUR HEART IS

The Parable of the Faithful and Unfaithful Servant appears in both Matthew and Luke. The Lukan version occurs in a slightly different context, which helps us understand the point of this parable. It is possible to lose much of the substance of these parables if we don't understand their point.

This is often assumed to be about the future return of Jesus, but the concern here is *much greater* than just the second coming. The concern is with where our treasure is today. What is our heart really set on?

In Luke 12:31–34, Jesus laid out what we truly need in life:

> "But seek the kingdom of God, and all these things shall be added to you.
>
> "Do not fear, little flock, for it is your Father's good

pleasure to give you the kingdom. Sell what you have and give alms; provide yourselves money bags which do not grow old, a treasure in the heavens that does not fail, where no thief approaches nor moth destroys. For where your treasure is, there your heart will be also." (Luke 12:31–34)

In the Parable of the Faithful and Unfaithful Servant, the unfaithful one was a person whose treasure was in the wrong place. That's what the title is about:

"Be dressed for action and have your lamps lit; be like those who are waiting for their master to return from the wedding banquet, so that they may open the door for him as soon as he comes and knocks." (Luke 12:35–36 NRSVue)

The phrase "from the wedding" means the master has left his house in the hands of his servants and gone off to get married. But now he was coming back. Remember they didn't have clocks that told them the time. Scheduling was entirely different than it is now. It was common for people to agree to meet on a given day and then wait all day for the meeting to occur. And no one got mad.

This means the servants would've had to be ready for the master and his bride to return on a certain day and *remain* ready to greet him. This included preparing lamps if the couple came at night and making sure they had enough oil for the lamps. This business of having a light ready was an important part of this parable and the Parable of the Ten Virgins. If the master came back at night, it wasn't very welcoming to allow him and his bride to stumble up to the door in the dark.

To avoid this, the servants would create a well-lit area and go out to meet the master. One of the servants probably would have gone two or three miles down the road to watch for the master and give the signal that he was coming. No doubt the entire household would have been awake, carrying torches to meet the master and his bride and escort them in. This was the custom of the day.

> "Blessed are those servants whom the master, when he comes, will find watching. Assuredly, I say to you that he will gird himself and have them sit down to eat, and will come and serve them. And if [the master] should come in the second watch, or come in the third watch, and find them so, blessed are those servants." (Luke 12:37–38)

In this case, the master greeted the hospitality of his faithful servants with gratitude and kindness: "He will fasten his belt and have them sit down to eat, and he will come and serve them" (Luke 12:37 NRSVue). It was highly unusual for a master to serve his servants.

WAITING UNTIL THE LAST MINUTE

On the other hand, if the master were to come home and find everyone sleeping and no lights lit so that he might have banged his shins getting in the door, he wouldn't have been very grateful.

> "Therefore you also be ready, for the Son of Man is coming at an hour you do not expect." (Luke 12:40)

"Be ready." Jesus didn't say, "Be experts at predicting when the master will arrive so you can delay getting ready for as long as possible." That attitude is similar to that of those who have made extremely fine-pointed estimates as to when Jesus will return. All of them have been wrong. Jesus didn't ask us to know when he was returning; he was teaching us to joyfully anticipate and prepare for his return.

There is something profound to understand about the Parables of the Faithful and Unfaithful Servant, the Ten Virgins, and the Talents, which appear consecutively in Matthew 24 and 25. These parables were meant to reveal our heart and show how our actions demonstrate the degree to which Jesus is our treasure. For all these servants, *their actions revealed what was in their hearts.* This was true of the one-talent man in the Parable of the Talents, who said to his master, "I knew you were hard" (Matthew 25:24, paraphrased). That revealed the heart of that servant. He didn't know the master at all, and in the master's absence, the servant's heart became known. The heart that loves the Lord does not try to calculate how much it can get away with and still please him. We don't try to cut it close, because our whole heart and life goes out to him.

I heard a story many years ago about a wealthy man who was looking for a driver for his coach. He tested the candidates by taking them to a section of a road that ran along a cliff and instructing them to see how close they could drive to the edge. Most applicants were attracted by the challenge to prove their expertise. But one driver refused to drive closely to the edge. And that's who got the job—the one who had enough concern about the well-being of his passenger that he would never use the situation to show off his driving skills. Those whose hearts are given up in love to the Lord have the Lord on their mind continually, and that is never a burden.

We find the opposite heart in the unfaithful servant who began to beat and mistreat his fellow servants. He simply did not set his mind upon the Lord at all.

> "But if that servant says in his heart, 'My master is delaying his coming' . . . the master of that servant will come on a day when he is not looking for him." (Luke 12:45–46)

That servant was *calculating* how much he could do without getting in trouble with his master. He wasn't saying, "Well, now

I am in charge of my master's house. I must take good care of it for the sake of my master." No, he was saying, "Well, I wonder how much I can do and not get in trouble." His character and his treasure were unveiled.

People can do good things and appear to be very good, but when opportunity arises, they may do whatever it takes to get what they want, even if they have to sin to do so. Character is not about what people do, but rather about what they would or could do given the opportunity. The opportunity reveals where their heart has been aimed all along.

X MARKS THE SPOT

Each of us needs to ask, "What do we treasure? What do we spend our time worrying about, thinking about, and being concerned about? What do we pour our life into?" That's our treasure. As Jesus said, "Where a person's treasure is, there will their heart be also" (Luke 12:34, paraphrased).

When we think about the Lord's coming, we shouldn't imagine that at the last minute we will perform some game-changing trick to sneak in before the door closes. The fullness of our life isn't found in that *moment* but rather in *the entire orientation* of our life. Will Jesus say to us, "I never knew you," or will he invite us to "enter into the joy of your master" (Matthew 7:23; 25:23 ESV)?

In his study of the parables, G. Campbell Morgan's comments about the unfaithful servant discuss how sad it is that people mistreat others and "are not behaving as they ought to do to their brethren," thinking of the church and their own household as a place of profit and "excess of living on the earthly plane."* This is a far cry from the attitude of the faithful and wise servant, who is focused on "caring for all the other members

---

* G. Campbell Morgan, *The Parables and Metaphors of Our Lord* (Old Tappan, NJ: Revell, 1948), 146.

of the household during the Lord's absence, for the sake of the absent Lord."[†]

This is still true. It's sad and unfortunate. When we add this characteristic to those found in the parables about the tares and the net, we recognize that in the kingdom of God in its present form on earth, some folks simply aren't thinking rightly. They are not disciples of the Lord; they are *disciples of themselves*. They are not grateful for the forgiveness of their sins. They don't understand the love that can and should flow from those who have been forgiven much.

The big question from the Parable of the Faithful and Unfaithful Servant is this: Is our faith in Jesus or perhaps in ourselves?

ALWAYS BE PREPARED

The Parable of the Ten Virgins is a revelation of the heart of a different kind. G. Campbell Morgan explains that the Parable of the Faithful and Unfaithful Servant reveals our heart toward the church community, while the Parable of the Ten Virgins reveals our heart toward our individual responsibilities, and the Parable of the Talents then reveals our heart in the context of the world.[‡] These three parables are designed to show us something about ourselves while the Lord is away—where our heart is in relationship to our service in all those settings.

Many folks consider this parable to be about the second coming of Jesus because we know that one day Jesus is coming back for his bride, the church. But this parable, much like the Parable of the Faithful and Unfaithful Servant, is a story not only of the bridegroom coming *for* his bride, but also of him *returning home with* his bride. We must not force the parables to fit our agenda.

[†] G. Campbell Morgan, *The Gospel according to Matthew* (Eugene, OR: Wipf & Stock Publishers, 2017), 288.

[‡] Morgan, *Parables and Metaphors*, chapter 26, particularly p. 148.

This is a familiar story about a rich person who has gone away. Remember that distances meant different things in Jesus' day. People couldn't hop on a plane or a train. To go forty miles was quite an operation.

Jesus began this way:

> "Then the kingdom of the heavens shall be likened to ten virgins who took their lamps and went out to meet the bridegroom." (Matthew 25:1, paraphrased)

These bridesmaids were the outriders of the group. Imagine this story occurring on a large estate with a big house and several barns behind it. Apparently, these young women were members of the household, which in that time was more like a little village with a lot of people associated with it.

These young women were given the job of waiting down the lane with their lamps burning in order to light the path for the bridegroom and the bride when they came back. When it began to get dark and the wedding party had not yet arrived, the bridesmaids went down the lane and took their positions.

Of the ten women, five wisely took extra oil with them in a little jug or flask so they could refill the lamp with oil when it ran out. The other five foolishly didn't bring those provisions. They may have thought, *I have enough oil in the lamp. I'm not going to bother with carrying extra. Besides, oil is messy. It will get on my clothes and make me smell funny. I'll be fine. He's going to get here soon.*

> "But while the bridegroom was delayed, they all slumbered and slept." (Matthew 25:5)

They had found a comfortable place to wait and eventually

had become so relaxed that they nodded off. "Slumbering" is different from "sleeping"; it's what we'd call "dozing."

> "And at midnight a cry was heard: 'Behold, the bridegroom is coming; go out to meet him!'" (Matthew 25:6)

When the servant stationed down the road shouted to them, the bridesmaids shook themselves awake. They quickly fixed their lamps, trimming off part of the wick so the lamp would give the greatest amount of light. That's when the five unwise bridesmaids said, "Uh-oh!"

> "'Give us some of your oil, for our lamps are going out.' But the wise answered, saying, 'No, lest there should not be enough for us and you; but go rather to those who sell, and buy for yourselves.'" (Matthew 25:8–9)

We shouldn't assume the five wise women were stingy or mean. They were just being sensible. They were confronted with a real problem. If they gave oil to the others, there wouldn't be enough for any light at all. They suggested to these unwise bridesmaids that they go buy some oil and come back. And so the unwise bridesmaids hustled off to get their oil.

> "And while they went to buy, the bridegroom came, and those who were ready went in with him to the wedding; and the door was shut." (Matthew 25:10)

"Those who were ready" is the phrase I want to stress. They formed the wedding party and got to go to the wedding. Since the organizers didn't want people coming into the wedding in the middle of the ceremony, the door was shut.

In those days, shutting the door wasn't a simple matter. Jesus once told a story about prayer, where a neighbor came at midnight asking for bread to feed his friend who had just arrived from a journey. The man replied, "Do not trouble me; the door is now shut, and my children are with me in bed; I cannot rise and give to you" (Luke 11:7). You see, those doors were quite large and shutting them was not a simple operation. So behind the closed doors they had a little world that continued to go on where they were all together.

> "Afterward the other virgins came also, saying, 'Lord, Lord, open to us!' But he answered and said, 'Assuredly, I say to you, I do not know you.'" (Matthew 25:11–12)

This is the second time the phrase "I don't know you" has come up. We looked at the other one in chapter 8, where some people said, "'Lord, we have cast out demons. We have done many wonderful works in your name.' And he will say, 'I don't know you'" (Matthew 7:22–23, paraphrased). The deep question is, "Does the Lord know us? Are we a factor in his life?"

The wise servants and bridesmaids had made preparations to be a factor in their master's life. The master knew them. He met them when the time was right. But these others did not make the preparations, and he did not know them.

WATCH WITH ME

> "Watch therefore." (Matthew 25:13)

The image of "watching" comes up repeatedly in Scripture and plays a significant role in the New Testament. It often means "alert readiness." It occurs in the Old Testament with the use of the term *watchman* (Job 27:18; Psalm 127:1; Isaiah 21:5,

6, 11, 12; Ezekiel 3:17; 33:1–7; Hosea 9:8; Micah 7:4). Watchmen were familiar figures in those days. They observed diligently and called out when attention was needed.

When Jesus went into Gethsemane with his disciples to pray, he took three of the disciples—Peter, James, and John—near to the place where he prayed. In his sorrow and distress, he instructed them, saying, "My soul is exceedingly sorrowful, even to death. Stay here and watch with Me" (Matthew 26:38). Shortly thereafter, he found them asleep, and he said to Peter: "What! Could you not watch with Me one hour? Watch and pray, lest you enter into temptation. The spirit indeed is willing, but the flesh is weak" (vv. 40–41). When they kept falling asleep, he said to them, "Watch and pray." To watch means to take the necessary steps so that when the time of opportunity comes, we're ready.

Jesus advised his friends to keep vigil combined with prayer. Doing so would have provided them with a level of responsiveness and power that would be impossible to achieve without it. They were not able to stand with Jesus when his enemies confronted him because they had not watched and prayed.§

THE LEAST OF THESE

The Parable of the Ten Virgins is not just about the second coming of the Lord; it is also about spiritual opportunity. It is about our readiness to seize the day because the present moment, this day, is the only place where you and I live. Scripture tells us that *today* is the day of salvation (2 Corinthians 6:2) and since we cannot live in the past and we cannot live in the future, we have to live *today*.

Salvation is, biblically speaking, deliverance. It is a new order of life (much more than just forgiveness of sins), which means

---

§ For more on this, see my *The Spirit of the Disciplines: Understanding How God Changes Lives* (San Francisco: HarperSanFrancisco, 1988), 151.

we are "delivered from the power of darkness and translated into the kingdom of his dear Son" (Colossians 1:13, paraphrased). We are to have a *different order of life*. We are to live in and from a different "world."

And so we watch for the Lord throughout the day. Would we know him? He may come to us in the form of a neighbor, a little child, a pastor or teacher, a friend, or even an enemy.

To watch means we encounter people with anticipation that this may be an opportunity to meet the Lord, to serve the Lord, to work with the Lord. In the metaphor of the sheep and the goats, Jesus said:

> "I was hungry and you gave Me food; I was thirsty and you gave Me drink; I was a stranger and you took Me in; I was naked and you clothed Me; I was sick and you visited Me; I was in prison and you came to Me." (Matthew 25:35–36)

The righteous were puzzled:

> "Well, Lord, when did we see you hungry? When did we see you in prison and didn't visit you? When did we see you naked and not clothe you?" And then Jesus said, "Whatever you've done [or haven't done] for one of the least of these my brothers and sisters, you have done [or haven't done] it for me." (Matthew 25:37–40, paraphrased)

You see, we often have our hearts in the wrong places. We are distracted and think about everything else. Our lamps have gone out, and we are not dressed for action. The opportunity comes and goes, and the door is shut. And that's all there is to it. This will certainly be the case for many when the Lord returns. But it also happens to people every day in other ways. Be ready. Watch. Pray.

CARPE DIEM

The kingdom of God is here. The King is coming, but the King is also here. The opportunities are now. Today is the day of salvation. When the people of Israel first came up to the land of promise, they were not ready to enter. They sent spies into the promised land, who came back and said, "These guys are like monsters. They'll eat us and step on us like grasshoppers!" (Numbers 13:33, paraphrased).

None of the adults involved entered the promised land except Joshua and Caleb. They all turned back, missing their chance. After God decided to send them into the wilderness, they opted to try to take the land on their own. They engaged in a great battle and got beat to pieces (Numbers 14:41–45). They had missed the day. They didn't seize the opportunity. They didn't go when the Lord was on the move.

By comparison, a powerful passage in the life of David tells of the time he fought against the Philistines, and God told him how to set the battle:

> Therefore David inquired again of God, and God said to him, "You shall not go up after them; circle around them, and come upon them in front of the mulberry trees. And it shall be, when you hear a sound of marching in the tops of the mulberry trees, then you shall go out to battle, for God has gone out before you to strike the camp of the Philistines." So David did as God commanded him, and they drove back the army of the Philistines from Gibeon as far as Gezer. (1 Chronicles 14:14–16)

David's heart was for the Lord. He watched, was dressed for action, and then seized the opportunity when the Lord was moving.

THE CHILDREN OF LIGHT

It is God's intent that the disciples of Christ should be, in him, the light of the world, and should teach all people what the kingdom of God is and how to live in it now. Our destiny and opportunity remain the same today as in Jesus' time on earth. We are to be children of light and the glory of God's love and help for the whole human race. This is the natural outflow of the life of the faithful servant—heart, soul, mind, and strength—as it is indwelt by God.

From our innermost parts will flow the living waters (John 7:38). Here is our treasure and the ultimate glory—humanity in dominion and stewardship over the earth in union with God. We are the light of the world, an outpost of heaven where the angels of grace come and go in the midst of the busy life of humanity. In union with God, we accomplish great things, watching for the opportunities where we give our best, secure in the confidence that he who appointed us will also give his best.

MAIN POINTS ABOUT
THE KINGDOM OF GOD

- The stories in this chapter teach us that life in the kingdom includes joyful anticipation, intentional preparation, and paying attention to always being ready to do God's will.
- When we treasure God, we notice who God notices—including the least of our brothers and sisters—even if others do not.
- The kingdom heart loves the Lord and does not try to calculate how much it can get away with, but eagerly and wholeheartedly follows God.

CHAPTER 11

THE MIRACLE OF FORGIVENESS

Therefore, as the elect of God, holy and beloved, put
on tender mercies, kindness, humility, meekness,
longsuffering; bearing with one another, and forgiving one
another, if anyone has a complaint against another; even
as Christ forgave you, so you also must do. But above all
these things put on love, which is the bond of perfection.
And let the peace of God rule in your hearts, to which also
you were called in one body; and be thankful.

COLOSSIANS 3:12-15

To be hurt is unavoidable in this world, and we have choices
to make as to how we will handle it. To raise the very topic of
forgiveness seems to many people to be unwise, troubling, and
deeply personal. But we need to talk about it. God forgives. We
just can't imagine *how* God forgives. Forgiveness is a miracle.
It's a tremendous act of grace that introduces us into the whole
world of God.

The Parable of the Unforgiving Servant is about the generosity of God's forgiveness toward us. Jesus decided to tell this parable after Peter came to him and said, "Lord, how often shall my brother sin against me, and I forgive him? Up to seven times?" (Matthew 18:21). I suspect Peter must have been thinking, *Oh, seven times is a lot.*

> Jesus said to him, "I do not say to you, up to seven times, but up to seventy times seven." (Matthew 18:22)

When Jesus said, "Seventy times seven," it's possible Peter could have fainted. He thought his suggestion of seven times was already way beyond generous, but Jesus countered, perhaps with a smile, "Seventy times that!" (I assure you he was not saying we can stop forgiving when we reach the 491st offense.)

Jesus was getting at the *legalistic way* of defining righteousness and forgiveness by saying, in essence, "Counting the number of times won't work. You have to cultivate a forgiving heart." The heart of the kingdom is not a heart focused on grievance over past issues, but one that is forgiven and forgiving.

However, the way of human nature in its fallen condition is to be unforgiving. If you were to remove unforgiveness from human life, human history would be transformed beyond recognition. But the way of life in the kingdom of God is to forgive routinely and easily, as illustrated by the king in this parable:

> "Therefore the kingdom of heaven is like a certain king who wanted to settle accounts with his servants. And when he had begun to settle accounts, one was brought to him who owed him ten thousand talents. But as he was not able to pay, his master commanded that he be sold, with his wife and children and all that he had, and that payment be made." (Matthew 18:23–25)

This response may seem unusual today, but it was common at the time. Debtors' prisons were in use throughout history, even in the United States and England, until the early 1800s.

THE POWER OF REQUEST

> "The servant therefore fell down before him, saying, 'Master, have patience with me, and I will pay you all.' Then the master of that servant was moved with compassion, released him, and forgave him the debt." (Matthew 18:26–27)

The servant's approach was met by *astounding* generosity. The master did not just postpone the debt; he released the servant from the debt and forgave him. This response is typical of God and is reminiscent of the father in the Prodigal Son story who refused to see his wayward son as a slave but accepted him fully as a son. The force at work here is the power of asking.[*] God answers prayers simply because we ask, and the king forgave simply because the servant asked. It's as though the king said, "I forgave you everything because *you wanted me to.*"

> "But that servant went out and found one of his fellow servants who owed him a hundred denarii; and he laid hands on him and took him by the throat, saying, 'Pay me what you owe!' So his fellow servant fell down at his feet and begged him, saying, 'Have patience with me, and I will pay you all.'" (Matthew 18:28–29)

Note the extreme contrast in the size of the debts. His fellow slave owed him a tiny fraction of what he had just been forgiven.[†]

---

[*] I will discuss this important principle in greater detail in chapter 14.
[†] One denarii was worth one day's wage. One talent was estimated to be worth twenty years of a day laborer's wage.

Both servants used the same language when their debts were called to account: "Have patience with me, and I will pay you all."

> "And he would not, but went and threw him into prison till he should pay the debt. So when his fellow servants saw what had been done, they were very grieved, and came and told their master all that had been done. Then his master, after he had called him, said to him, 'You wicked servant! I forgave you all that debt because you begged me. Should you not also have had compassion on your fellow servant, just as I had pity on you?' And his master was angry, and delivered him to the torturers until he should pay all that was due to him.
>
> "So My heavenly Father also will do to you if each of you, from his heart, does not forgive his brother his trespasses." (Matthew 18:30–35)

Unforgiveness is the way of normal, ordinary human life. It is so embedded in our thinking that people often do not consider themselves unforgiving when they hold on to past wounds. We tend to accept it and think, *Oh, that's just the way it is.* Certain nations are expected to be enemies of others. People have at times carried unforgiveness down through multiple generations: "Your grandfather did something to my grandfather, and I'm going to get back at you!"

The plots of countless novels and movies focus on revenge, on getting even. But no one ever really gets even because one person will not count as "even" anything but what the other person counts as "beyond." It seems to be built into the human condition that getting even *never* works. For example, when children fight, that last punch or insult is what matters. Whatever was done last is somehow bigger than anything that came before it. No one ever tries to get even by letting someone else have the last word or the last blow.

The gospel of the Lord Jesus Christ declares an end to that battle. It announces from the heights of heaven that *God doesn't want to even the score*, but rather he invites you and me into a life where *we* no longer need to either. This is an expression of the nature of the gospel of Jesus. One of the great spiritual practices is not having the last word. We cease trying to get back at others, catch up, or get ahead.

This is the *only* way peace can come to the human heart and then spread into the world. International negotiations and courts often fail because they focus on trying to make people and nations "even" when they will never be even. Until people rise above getting even, peace will never reign.

It's the same in relationships between brothers and sisters and between spouses. There's no peace as long as we're *trying* to get even. One sibling or spouse may deeply offend another, and the one who was injured may be peaceable for a while, but the offense takes up residence in the heart and eats away. And before long, getting even looks like a good idea. Sometimes spouses enter marriage with an unevenness in social skills, family wealth, or intellect, and when these apparent inequities cause friction, marriage partners become intent on finding the same level of evenness. In that case, a union of souls such as God intended cannot exist.

Forgiving persons lay down all plans to get even for wrongs done, even in small ways. They also let go of requiring compensation, no longer saying, "You must make it up to me!" Getting even is a tremendous burden, and it's a great relief to let it go.

FORWARD-GIVING

Try thinking about forgiveness by playing with the combined wording *forward-giving*. Forgiveness is forward-giving because it looks forward, envisioning future plans to be generous and giving. Forgiveness does not hold on to the past, making the other person suffer because of past wrongs.

In our *actions* toward those who wrong us, we no longer hold them responsible or base our behavior toward them on what they've done. We lay down the grudge. The *inward* side of forgiving means we no longer brood, dwelling on the hurt or wrong. We have come to some degree of liberty from the hurt because we have *chosen* to look to the future.

There must be *readiness* to forgive, even toward a person who is unable to receive forgiveness from us. This works at the level of the will. Pain generally is like that. We have at least some degree of choice as to whether we will soak our minds in the pain or focus on moving forward with our life in Christ. Forgiveness means we are not obsessed by it. We are not dominated by it.

Some wounds are so deep you may be hurt for the rest of your life. We need to understand that the pain is not always entirely bad. As it mixes with our experience of life in the kingdom of God, we remember the pain but are not consumed by it, just as Joseph was not consumed by the harm his brothers intended and was able to see how God used it for good (Genesis 50:20). We find we can still be content and find joy in the eternal life God offers us.

I've seen people crushed by the burden of thinking that if they don't manage to forget the harm done, they haven't truly forgiven the other person. You may not be able to completely forget. God can help you with that, and maybe someday you will forget. But if you've been deeply injured by someone, you're not going to forget it, and I don't recommend you try. But you *can* forgive them.

Someone who has harmed you may say, "If you haven't stopped hurting, you haven't forgiven me." Please don't believe that. To forgive does not mean to forget. People who say that are trying to manipulate you to make it easier on themselves because they're struggling to come to terms with what they've done.

If you're trying to stop hurting when you forgive, this may confuse you so much that you will not be able to forgive. Your hurt may go on, even though you've let the person off the hook and released your intention to get even with them. The mark of forgiveness is *not* that you no longer hurt; it is that you are no longer preoccupied with the hurt.

GROWING IN GOD'S FORGIVENESS

It's important to understand *what* forgiveness is and *how* to forgive. People experience a lot of grief because they feel they *should* forgive; they feel obligated to do so. They would even *like* to forgive, but it isn't clear to them how to go about doing that. You can do several things to help yourself grow into a person who forgives more easily and naturally.

First, as with many things in the spiritual life, approaching forgiveness too directly may cause you to fail. It's the same way with temptation. If you're being strongly tempted by something and decide to confront it head-on, you will probably fail. If you're tempted to eat candy from a bowl on the table, you had better find something else to do other than think about how you're not going to eat the candy. If you dwell on it, it will conquer you. It will just reach up, grab your mouth, and climb right in. And you will say, "That terrible candy! Look what it did!" *You must focus your mind on something else.*‡

Second, be mindful that *forgiveness is not a simple act of will*. You cannot handle forgiveness the way you would normally handle many other things. Forgiveness involves the will, but it is not an act of the will alone. I suggest you approach it this way: If someone has hurt you badly, don't just try to *not pay them back*, but fill your mind with Jesus Christ and how he responded to

---

‡   For deeper insight, see my *Renovation of the Heart: Putting on the Character of Christ* (Colorado Springs: NavPress, 2002), chapter 7, particularly pp. 118, 122, 137.

those who hurt him. Look at Jesus. Set him before your mind. Dwell on stories of his life. Consider how he must have felt when he was wronged. Doing so will immediately take you away from yourself and your woundedness and put your mind in the right place to receive the grace of forgiveness.

Third, *pray, acknowledging to God that you cannot forgive another person without his help.* Ask for the grace of God to enter your heart and mind to help you forgive. Forgiveness is one of those things in our life through which God teaches us how dependent we are on him. If we say to the Lord, "I can't forgive," he will say to us, "Of course you can't forgive *without my help.*" You have to accept forgiveness as something that comes from God through you to others. And then, because Christ is living in you, you will be able to forgive those you thought you could never forgive.

Forgiving is not quick, and it does not mean the relationship can or should be fully restored. Suppose you've been betrayed by a business partner. Not only were you hurt deeply, but you may also never recover financially. You anticipate that your children won't be able to attend the school you had planned they would attend, and you won't be able to live where you had hoped to live. Perhaps you're facing these possibilities while seeing this partner living in great prosperity. It may take a great deal of time to work through those feelings, and what you have learned about your partner means it would be unwise to reestablish that partnership, but that does not mean you are being unforgiving.

I realize a time may come when God gives a gift of grace, taking away the resentment and hurt. That happens, but generally, we can't count on that. And if it doesn't happen, we don't need to feel like we've done something wrong. It is disappointing, to be sure, but in the normal course of recovering from a deep wound, it takes time for forgiveness to come. Persistently pray for it; be patient as you wait for it.

Don't assume the burden of making forgiveness happen. Your part is to fill your mind with Christ. Pray for the grace of forgiveness to come through you to others, because it must, after all, come from God. It came to *us* through another—namely, Jesus Christ.

And then concentrate on the good to be done, first of all, in your own life. Sometimes this may mean simply paying attention to the beauty of the flowers in your backyard. God made them and gave them to you to fill your heart with joy, so pay attention to them.

DWELLING IN GOODNESS

Many of our troubles stay with us because we don't accept the little, wonderful things that God places in our lives every day, such as the simple pleasures of eating and resting. Even shallow talk between neighbors who love one another is a gift. Yes, *shallow* talk. I once had to learn the depth of shallow talk during a time of study in a Franciscan monastery in Belgium. I stayed there while doing research in a nearby university's library archives.

Surrounded by people who gave themselves fundamentally to service, meditation, and prayer, I observed how important it was for the brothers of the Franciscan order to greet one another and share small talk. I then understood that casual conversation is a way in which people reach out to one another and share life. There may well be nothing that goes more deeply than the ability of people to be with one another in shallow talk.

It was my pride that had once said, *Oh, I shouldn't waste my time with trivialities. Don't just say, "How's the weather?" I want to get right to the big ideas and deep thoughts.* I learned that loving people is a matter of being able to live with them at all levels.

People primarily live at the level of small things. Turn to those. God gave them to you. Pay attention to your garden, your dog, or whatever delights you, and enjoy the good that is there. You will find that doing this can help you forgive. It's hard to be angry with someone when you're looking at flowers or watching ducks. Perhaps that's why God made them.

BABY STEPS

Beyond the three basic suggestions listed above, you will want to occasionally concentrate your thoughts and prayers—in small, manageable amounts—toward the good of the individual who hurt you, especially in connection with the harm they have done. In doing so, be careful not to assume the role of being the one to straighten out their life. You are not their savior; Jesus Christ is their Savior. Try to reach the point where you can pray sincerely for their good.[§]

As Jesus hung on the cross, he was able to look at the soldiers who had nailed him there and say, "Father, forgive them, for they do not know what they do" (Luke 23:34). He truly meant the words he prayed, because he had a *heart proficient in forgiveness.* And when he said those words, his heart was full of generosity toward them. He wasn't praying through gritted teeth in an effort to impress God, but rather because he genuinely wanted what was best for them.

On the other hand, when *we* try to do this, we are apt to be distracted with thoughts of our own nobility or to indulge in a bit of self-congratulation. We may think, perhaps subtly, *Aren't I wonderful because I'm praying for the good of this person who has injured me!* That's why it's important to consider offering this kind of prayer in small, manageable amounts. Don't burden yourself with this until you feel that you're doing it genuinely and easily.

It will begin to come naturally to you when you engage in the previously mentioned efforts: occupy yourself in some other way;

---

§   Jesus gives practical advice on this in Luke 6:27–36.

don't try to will yourself to forgive; and acknowledge to God that you cannot forgive without his help. In time, you can come to the place where you will be able to pray for the person who hurt you without thinking about yourself at all. Then it will not be an exhibition of what a fine person you are—someone who didn't deserve to be hurt like you were.

Forgiveness can become a simple, straightforward act done because it is the best thing to do—not because you have to and not to try to prove anything about yourself. It's simply the wise thing to do. That's why God forgives.

THE GREAT HEART OF GOD

Forgiveness is available because of the great heart of God that played itself out in history and culminated on the cross where Jesus died. That event, foreseen from the foundation of the world (1 Peter 1:20–21), was never absent and will never be absent from God's mind. God arranged and made provision for our salvation in a way that invites us into his kind of life.

The incarnation of Jesus Christ was necessary in God's dealings with humanity in order for God to be able to forgive; for human beings to understand the significance of sin, redemption, and salvation; and for God to make his favor efficaciously possible for all human beings. Whatever God needed to be done to open the floodgates of his compassion on the world was done.

EARNING AND RECEIVING

Once we know we live by forgiveness, we're ready to extend forgiveness to other people. Jesus addressed this at the end of the Parable of the Unforgiving Servant: "So My heavenly Father also will do to you if each of you, from his heart, does not forgive his brother his trespasses" (Matthew 18:35).

Jesus taught about this elsewhere in Scripture, including in the Lord's Prayer: "And forgive us our debts, as we forgive our debtors. . . . For if you forgive men their trespasses, your heavenly Father will also forgive you. But if you do not forgive men their trespasses, neither will your Father forgive your trespasses" (Matthew 6:12, 14–15). Why is forgiveness from God tied to our forgiving others?

This teaching has been misunderstood to say that forgiveness from God is something to be earned, as if you can earn your forgiveness by the righteous work of forgiving those who have offended you. It isn't a matter of our *earning* our forgiveness; it is a matter of our *receiving* it.

It's always important to distinguish between *earning* and *receiving*. While you can do nothing to earn your salvation, there is something you can do to receive it, and you're so much better off for doing it. A gift is not imposed on you, forced on you, or fastened on you somehow. A gift requires *reception*.

I believe Jesus was saying that in order for us to receive the forgiveness that comes from God, we must have a certain kind of heart and life shaped by the grace of God in us. When we concentrate on the work of Christ (his coming for us, his life, and his way of living) as we apprentice ourselves to him, we step into the flow of that grace to receive a forgiving heart—a heart that can reach out in faith and accept forgiveness from God.

The Pharisees and the prodigal son's brother are examples of people who have no knowledge of a forgiving heart. They had not had an *experience* of forgiveness.

THE FLOW OF FORGIVENESS

It is impossible for us to forgive until we have experienced forgiveness ourselves. It's like love: "We love Him because He first loved us" (1 John 4:19). We find many hard, unhappy, unloving, unkind people in our world, some of whom even profess belief in Christ. Oftentimes, these are people who do not feel loved and have never experienced the reality that God is the One who "freely give[s] us all things" (Romans 8:32) and who haven't embraced the truth that nothing "shall be able to separate us from the love of God which is in Christ Jesus our Lord" (8:39). Like love, forgiveness becomes an active part of our lives because we are forgiven. The generosity of God that comes to us enables us to be generous and forgive those who have offended us.

When we experience forgiveness, it becomes a way of life we learn to identify with. When we think of our sins and our inability to meet the standards of God's righteousness, our faith will not be capable of moving out and receiving forgiveness from God unless we are standing in this *mode* of forgiveness. That's why many followers of Jesus continue to act as if they have not been forgiven. They are hindered and bound by things that have happened to them in the past, whether it was done to them, done by them, or some combination thereof. In their hearts and minds, they still see themselves as the person who did "that thing" rather than as someone who has been forgiven and cleansed.

Cleansed is a lovely word. To cleanse something is to take the spot away so that the dirt is gone. The place is still there where the dirt was, but it's no longer dirty. A lot of Christians still experience the dirt as being there. They still *feel* dirty. This may come from an inappropriate teaching of the gospel or a lack of the Spirit in fellowship. It may come because, in their hearts, they are unforgiving. There's someone in their life they have not forgiven. We all need to look deep into our hearts about these things and ask God if there is someone we have not forgiven.

The connection between God's forgiveness of you and your forgiveness of others is entwined with the reality of him living in you. And if you do not forgive, if you *cannot* forgive, it means, at least in some significant measure, that he does not occupy that part of your heart. If he is there, he is enabling you to forgive. And if he is there, you are forgiven. The experience of forgiveness comes to those who forgive, just as there is a connection between the experience of being loved and being able to love.

As we learn to forgive, we *receive* forgiveness and enter into it as a way of life. We pray, "Forgive us our debts, *as* we forgive our debtors" (Matthew 6:12, emphasis added), because it's a kind of totality. "Forgive us our sins as we forgive others." It's a whole. We choose to forgive because we are involved with God's action, and he's in the business of forgiveness. And so are we.

MAIN POINTS ABOUT THE KINGDOM OF GOD

- The Parable of the Unforgiving Servant is about the generosity of God's forgiveness toward us.
- It is safe to forgive in the kingdom of God because God forgives us and empowers us to forgive. In God's kingdom, there is no need for getting even.
- To receive forgiveness, we immerse ourselves in God's grace by concentrating on the person of Christ, his coming to earth, and his way of living that shows us how to step into the flow of his grace.
- Forgiveness is the simplest and best thing to do, and it is the most joyful way to live.

CHAPTER 12

THE OUTRAGEOUS COMPASSION OF GOD[*]

"For the LORD your God is the God of gods and Lord of lords. He is the great God, the mighty and awesome God, who shows no partiality and cannot be bribed. He ensures that orphans and widows receive justice. He shows love to the foreigners living among you and gives them food and clothing."

DEUTERONOMY 10:17-18 NLT

The unexpected, upside-down nature of the kingdom of God was a constant surprise to Jesus' disciples. God's kingdom was so different from what people thought it would be that Jesus' listeners would have considered his ideas scandalous. So he wisely used parables to lessen the shock and help them grasp the concepts of life in the kingdom.

---

[*] Since there was no audio recording of session 10 in the original series, the topics in Dallas's outline guided the creation of this chapter, using portions of Dallas's teaching about the Parable of the Hours in his 2012 Doctorate of Ministry class at Fuller Seminary and at the Renovaré Institute in 2010 and 2011.

The Parable of the Workers in the Vineyard, also called "the Parable of the Hours," is so contrary to worldly wisdom that it appears outrageous to us even today. It sometimes makes people angry because it seems unjust. But Jesus was redefining justice and helping people see that kingdom justice was not like anything we would normally think of as justice.

WHAT ARE *WE* GONNA GET?

Our uneasiness with this parable begins with the conversation that precipitated it. The disciples had witnessed Jesus' interaction with the man we call the "rich young ruler." This earnest young man had come to Jesus asking, "What good thing shall I do that I may have eternal life?" (Matthew 19:16).

Imagine the look on Peter's face as Jesus tells the man to give his money to the poor and then come and be his disciple. Peter and the other disciples were probably standing there aghast because they (like the rest of the people in their day) assumed that if you had money, you had God's favor. Why did the man need to do anything at all—especially give away his money? Then Jesus made it clear:

> "Assuredly, I say to you that it is hard for a rich man to enter the kingdom of heaven. And again I say to you, it is easier for a camel to go through the eye of a needle than for a rich man to enter the kingdom of God." (Matthew 19:23–24)

This contradicted what the disciples believed and caused a well-moneyed person to turn away from following Jesus. The shockwaves moved through the disciples:

> When His disciples heard it, they were greatly astonished, saying, "Who then can be saved?"

But Jesus looked at them and said to them, "With men this is impossible, but with God all things are possible."

Then Peter answered and said to Him, "See, we have left all and followed You. Therefore what shall we have?" (Matthew 19:25–27)

It's as if Peter blurted out, "What are *we* gonna get?" Jesus continued with words that must have helped reassure Peter:

"Assuredly I say to you, that in the regeneration, when the Son of Man sits on the throne of His glory, you who have followed Me will also sit on twelve thrones, judging the twelve tribes of Israel. And everyone who has left houses or brothers or sisters or father or mother or wife or children or lands, for My name's sake, shall receive a hundredfold, and inherit eternal life." (Matthew 19:28–29)

Then Jesus concluded with this:

"But many who are first will be last, and the last first." (Matthew 19:30)

The apostles clearly fell into the "last" category, and his choosing of them illustrates how the "nothings" of this world can become the "somethings" in the kingdom of God. The people Jesus selected were about as far removed from being "somethings" as you could imagine and certainly not the kind of people any rabbi would have chosen as their disciples. Instead, they were emblematic of the first beatitude in Matthew, "Blessed are those who have nothing going for them spiritually" (Matthew 5:3, paraphrased). The disciples were among the "last" who became "first" in the kingdom of God.

Jesus told this parable in response to Peter's question: "See, we have left all and followed You. Therefore what shall we have?" (Matthew 19:27). After telling them they would sit on thrones and receive one hundred times more than all they left behind, Jesus offered an illustration of the heart of God that is behind it all—the Parable of the Workers in the Vineyard.

> "For the kingdom of heaven is like a landowner who went out early in the morning to hire laborers for his vineyard. Now when he had agreed with the laborers for a denarius a day, he sent them into his vineyard. And he went out about the third hour and saw others standing idle in the marketplace, and said to them, 'You also go into the vineyard, and whatever is right I will give you.' So they went. Again he went out about the sixth and the ninth hour, and did likewise. And about the eleventh hour he went out and found others standing idle, and said to them, 'Why have you been standing here idle all day?' They said to him, 'Because no one hired us.' He said to them, 'You also go into the vineyard, and whatever is right you will receive.'
>
> "So when evening had come, the owner of the vineyard said to his steward, 'Call the laborers and give them their wages, beginning with the last to the first.' And when those came who were hired about the eleventh hour, they each received a denarius. But when the first came, they supposed that they would receive more; and they likewise received each a denarius. And when they had received it, they complained against the landowner, saying, 'These last men have worked only one hour, and you made them equal to us who have borne the burden and the heat of the day.' But he answered one of them and said, 'Friend, I am doing you no wrong. Did you not agree with me for a denarius? Take what is yours and

> go your way. I wish to give to this last man the same as to you. Is it not lawful for me to do what I wish with my own things? Or is your eye evil because I am good?' So the last will be first, and the first last. For many are called, but few chosen." (Matthew 20:1–16)

According to this parable, the kingdom of the heavens is like a vineyard owner who needed to hire some day laborers. He went out into the marketplace and found people waiting for jobs. He said, "Come work in my vineyard and I'll pay you a day's wages." When he came back after having coffee, more people were waiting. So he said, "Hey, come on and help me out. I'll pay you a day's wages." This pattern continued all day. After his afternoon nap and a cookie, the vineyard owner came out one last time and found some people still waiting, hoping to be hired. With only one hour of daylight left, he said, "Come on, come on! I've still got some work to do." This is such a wonderful teaching because the owner paid all the workers the same wage.

UPSIDE-DOWN JUSTICE

Suppose you were one of the workers who started sweating at 7:00 a.m. At the end of the day, you would have been exhausted and filthy. As you walked up to get paid, you might have thought, *Wow, I'm going to get paid more than those guys who got here so late.* But when the vineyard owner paid you both the same, you would have thought, *How can this be?*

This is an example of the great inversion where the teachings of Jesus seem "upside down." Those who viewed work from a worldly mindset would have gotten angry, saying, "Listen, we put up with the scorching heat of the day! We've been working hard, and now you want to pay us the same amount you paid to those guys who worked fewer hours? What do you think you're doing?"

Even though the owner was behaving justly because he paid

them exactly what he promised to give them, they wanted more. The owner had disrupted their sense of justice, but in God's kingdom, justice without love will never do justice to justice. Love and mercy permeate the kingdom, which then naturally means justice is taken care of. The workers who didn't get hired until the last hour had hungry babies at home. They received the sort of justice found only in God's kingdom.

If you look at this parable from the perspective of justice based on love, it is very touching. I have been a migrant field worker. I know what it's like to stand on a street corner, hoping someone will choose me for a job. We must have sympathy for these workers in the parable, especially those who had been waiting all day. By 4:30, they still hadn't been hired. They thought about their children at home who needed food to survive. They may have wondered if they had enough fuel at home. Maybe they didn't even have a house. Work gives you a place in life, a supply of resources, even if it's only for a day. The vineyard owner understood this.

The Parable of the Workers in the Vineyard is bookended by Jesus' teaching that "many who are first will be last, and the last will be first" (Matthew 19:30 NRSVue). This phrase is found in four major passages in the Gospels[†] and may seem insignificant, a throwaway line like, "Have a good day!" It shows up in various settings and stands as a foundational teaching that the kingdom of God reverses the order that is present in human affairs. What appears to be first in the human order could be last in the divine order, and what appears to be last may actually be at the front.

THE MERCHANT'S DUTY

Almost every culture desires recompense. People want to get compensated for everything they do. Expecting something in

---

[†] Matthew 19:30; 20:16; Mark 10:31; Luke 13:30.

return also means you might become resentful if you don't get repaid. The nature of the kingdom is not based on recompense, but rather on giving to those in need, such as dinner guests who are unable to invite you to dinner at their place:

> "But when you give a feast, invite the poor, the maimed, the lame, the blind. And you will be blessed, because they cannot repay you; for you shall be repaid at the resurrection of the just." (Luke 14:13–14)

In December 1995, Malden Mills, a textile manufacturing plant in Massachusetts, burned to the ground. The company's redbrick factory complex caught on fire, causing one of the largest blazes in Massachusetts history. The factory's employees couldn't keep working at the factory, but the owner, Aaron Feuerstein, kept paying them. Feuerstein is quoted as saying, "I'm not throwing 3,000 people out of work two weeks before Christmas."[17]

Some people must have been thinking, *Wow, this is a great opportunity for him. He can collect his insurance. He can build a factory where it's cheaper and make a lot more money.* Feuerstein didn't do it. He decided to let everyone in the factory keep their jobs and benefits, and he continued to pay their full wages during the rebuilding of the factory.

While many thought of him as a fool, Feuerstein was simply a good man. He wasn't thinking just about his gain; he was thinking about the people who worked for him. Such goodness in business owners isn't as uncommon as people think it is. Many see their responsibility toward their workers and respond to it. They set aside the worldly wisdom of what others think and do the right thing. It's a beautiful story.

John Ruskin wrote about this inversion regarding "the duty of the merchant" in a way that perfectly describes Aaron Feuerstein:

As the captain of a ship is bound to be the last man to leave his ship in case of wreck . . . so the manufacturer, in any commercial crisis or distress, is bound to take the suffering of it with his men, and even to take more of it for himself than he allows his men to feel; as a father would in a famine, shipwreck, or battle, sacrifice himself for his son.[18]

COMPARATIVE JUSTICE

Notice how Jesus emphasized the way the vineyard owner orchestrated his payment of the workers in this parable. When evening came, he didn't start by paying the ones who arrived at 7:00 a.m. Instead, he paid the one-hour workers first, then those who worked a few hours, and then those who worked a full day. This allowed the people who started early in the morning to stand and watch in anticipation of being paid more. But they were not, and so they complained. The vineyard owner said, "I didn't do you any wrong. I paid you what we agreed to." They had agreed to what they thought was a fair and adequate wage. The owner continued, "Take what belongs to you and go; I choose to give to this last the same as I give to you. Am I not allowed to do what I choose with what belongs to me? Or are you envious because I am generous?" (Matthew 20:14–15 NRSVue).

After the vineyard owner paid the last group who had worked the longest, they protested, "Wait a minute! This is not right!" Think about that: What was it that made it seem wrong? Was it that they were not adequately paid? No, it wasn't that; it was how they were paid in *comparison* to others. What if a person doesn't get as much money as they think they should, but thinks, *I'm really glad I have a job. I'm really thankful for what has been provided for me.* That changes their perspective.

One of the profound lessons from this parable is the effects of comparison. In the human order, this effect can be devastating.

When those who have enough or are well-off see others who are *better* off, they can suddenly feel they aren't so well-off after all.

Jesus understood that comparison can lead to all kinds of problems including envy, which was at the heart of the problem for these workers. Envy lays a foundation for resentment against others who have more—even for people who have enough.

Comparison is the heart of the problem and it is the root of what the human order calls justice. If we could pull comparison out of our idea of justice, we would more easily understand kingdom justice. Pilate recognized that the religious authorities crucified Jesus because of envy. The religious authorities were well-off and well-positioned, but they couldn't perform miracles or healings and couldn't earn the respect of the people, all of which Jesus could do. This comparison propelled them along the path to killing Jesus.

The kingdom of God is a place where you can live with a lack of concern about comparisons. The Beatitudes of Matthew 5 teach this. For example, a person who is poor can be just as well-off as a person who is rich—even better (Luke 6:20–21). We can see this is true when we understand that we live in two landscapes.

A DIVINE INVERSION

This parable draws a sharp contrast between those landscapes as we see the human order of justice and the divine order of love in action. This contrast goes right to the heart of life and how people make a living. Trying to earn a living brings out thoughts and feelings about justice, what is right and good, and what we believe we deserve.

Once we understand this, we can appreciate why Jesus repeatedly taught about the transformation of status for the lowly. The hand of God reaching into the life situation of the humanly hopeless may be the Bible's most pervasive theme.[‡] Some of the more significant passages stressing the transformation of status under God are the story of David and Goliath (1 Samuel 17) and Jehoshaphat's prayer and battle (2 Chronicles 20). Psalms 37, 107, and others celebrate the theme of God lifting up those who are cast down and casting down those who are considered lifted up in the human order.

One of the most outstanding Scripture sections in which the great inversion principle is exemplified are the songs of Moses and Miriam (Exodus 15:1–21). What was the inversion? The Israelites were facing the Egyptian army that was equipped with the latest instruments of death and destruction, such as horses and riders. The horse at that time was like the hypersonic missiles of our time. If you had horses and chariots and your enemy didn't, your victory was certain. In these songs, we see that the guys who were on top didn't win: "The horse and its rider He has thrown into the sea" (Exodus 15:1, 21).

Another example is Hannah's prayer of celebration at having given birth to Samuel—an infertile woman bearing a child—which is full of inversion language:

> "He raises up the poor from the dust;
> he lifts the needy from the ash heap
> to make them sit with princes
> and inherit a seat of honor.
>
> "For the pillars of the earth are the LORD's,
> and on them he has set the world."
> (1 Samuel 2:8 NRSVue)

---

‡ For further study on how this theme plays out in the Beatitudes, see chapter 4 in my *The Divine Conspiracy: Rediscovering Our Hidden Life in God* (San Francisco: HarperSanFrancisco, 1998).

You are probably more familiar with the song of Mary, the mother of Jesus:

> "He has shown strength with His arm;
> He has scattered the proud in the imagination of their
>   hearts.
> He has put down the mighty from their thrones,
> And exalted the lowly.
> He has filled the hungry with good things,
> And the rich He has sent away empty." (Luke 1:51–53)

Psalm 37 also offers assurance of the great inversion:

> Do not fret because of the wicked;
>   do not be envious of wrongdoers,
> for they will soon fade like the grass,
>   and wither like the green herb. . . .
> Yet a little while, and the wicked will be no more;
>   though you look diligently for their place, they will
>   not be there.
> But the meek shall inherit the land
>   and delight themselves in abundant prosperity.
>   (Psalm 37:1–2, 10–11 NRSVue)§

When you read these passages, you are reading about concrete instances of "the last shall be first, and the first shall be last." But this is difficult to believe unless you understand we live in the reality of both landscapes—the kingdom of God and the kingdom of humanity. We can't make judgments based solely on what is visible in the human kingdom. We have to discern in

---

§ Ezekiel 17:22-24 and Luke 1:70-75 are further examples of the inversion principle.

terms of both the visible and invisible and in the action that is being pursued there.

CHEAP GRACE

The Parable of the Workers in the Vineyard shows that God is not stingy with grace. If a family needs to be fed, the employer isn't cheating anyone if he hires the steadfast worker who hasn't given up and is still eager to work.

This divine justice and generosity sometimes cause people to ask me about those who wait until they are on the brink of death to accept Jesus into their life. Others may see Jesus' admittance to heaven of the thief next to him on the cross as a justice problem. They think the thief got a good deal or got off cheap. They see him as clearly not deserving eternity in heaven but getting in anyway. I don't see a problem with this. For my part, I think in terms of "trusting" (instead of deserving), with trusting being the positive side of surrendering.

While Dietrich Bonhoeffer's attack on "easy Christianity" or "cheap grace" is valid,[19] we have to understand that grace truly *is* cheap to us. This is not to minimize discipleship and obedience at all (which is Bonhoeffer's point). In fact, the years of the thief's life would have flourished so much more if he had lived a life of discipleship and obedience. Like all of us, the reward for good work is more work—more interesting, creative adventures as we rule and reign (Revelation 5:10; 22:5).

Often the question about the thief on the cross is followed by another justice question that has to do with the concept of purgatory and doing more work to gain entry into heaven. The problem with purgatory is that it is a merit system. People pay their dues by suffering there. At certain times during church history, they could have someone else pay *for* them. This is contrary to the entire concept of trust, grace, and the generosity of God.

HEAVEN'S TOUCHPOINT

Peter's question about what he and the other disciples deserved prompted Jesus to tell the Parable of the Workers in the Vineyard, illustrating that the last shall be first because of the lavish generosity of God—a generosity that knows that helping workers care for their families was more important than human justice.

As disciples, we are the touchpoint between the visible and invisible landscapes—that realm where the great needs of people around us are met by the generosity of God. Think about these guys who were waiting to get work so they could care for their families. Look at how the vineyard owner responded and what his response meant to them. Imagine being the instrument of God's compassion, grace, and generosity here and now, where "business as usual" can mean extending kingdom justice to those who are last in the human order of this world.

MAIN POINTS ABOUT
THE KINGDOM OF GOD

- The kingdom of God runs on the divine order of love and the lavish generosity of God, not the human order of justice. The workers in this parable received the sort of justice found only in God's kingdom.
- In the kingdom, the hand of God is always reaching into the life situations of the humanly hopeless. This may be the Bible's most pervasive theme.
- The nature of the kingdom is based not on recompense but on giving to those in need.
- The kingdom is a place to rejoice with those who rejoice, to choose to not be envious when God is generous, and to live without comparisons.

CHAPTER 13

WHAT IS YOUR LIFE?

And he said to them, "Take care! Be on your guard against all kinds of greed, for one's life does not consist in the abundance of possessions."

LUKE 12:15 NRSVUE

The ownership of possessions is an issue for everyone, rich and poor alike. The most seemingly insignificant possessions of the most destitute person are precious to them; those possessions are their treasures. Having them taken away would be as momentous a loss for them as losing huge fortunes in a stock market collapse would be for the rich. It's hard to get over such losses.

As we study some of the passages in this chapter, not everything of concern will be possessions and money. The primary concern is *gain*. No matter how much or how little we have, it sometimes feels like "the grass is always greener on the other side of the fence." It's impossible to know if this is true, of course, but we still compare and speculate about how much better things would be if we had more or had something better or different.

The Parable of the Rich Fool is about our relationship to riches, which includes money, possessions, treasures, and gain. The issue is not the *possession* of those things, but the *effect* of those treasures on our heart. The farmer in this story wasn't foolish because he was rich, but because his riches were his treasure. The issue is the *deceitfulness* of riches and how they can "choke the word, making it unfruitful" (Matthew 13:22 NIV).

Riches can deceive us about what our lives are, tempting us into thinking our lives consist of our riches. In this parable, we look at the deceitfulness of riches and how it relates to the question, "What is my life?"

Just like the Parable of the Workers in the Vineyard, this story challenges our trust in riches—whether ours or someone else's—and how we may treasure them or look to them to bring us happiness and well-being. We may suppose we are financially secure, like the rich fool, or even suppose we are better than those who are poor.

If we can think rightly about money, gain, and possessions, then we'll probably avoid many of the problems posed for human life by wealth and poverty. These are problems that reach to the foundations of our life before God.

I WANT MY MONEY!

Before telling this story, Jesus was approached by someone who was agitated about what he believed he deserved. This is one of those passages where what Jesus was saying makes us stop and wonder if we have understood him fully:

> "Then one from the crowd said to Him, 'Teacher, tell my brother to divide the inheritance with me.'" (Luke 12:13)

We've already learned that in this culture a man's possessions passed on to his children, primarily to his eldest son, and it was customary that the eldest brother would act as a trustee or executor of the estate. This story involves a situation where this younger brother believed his older brother was supposed to give him the share of the inheritance he was rightfully owed.

But people have a way of finding a reason for not doing something right away: "Well, why don't we wait six months and then we'll sell the bonds? They'll be worth more." This fellow who approached Jesus had been consumed by his situation and had one issue on his mind: *I want that money!*

The man complimented Jesus by calling him "Teacher," and Jesus responded in a way that is essential for each of us to learn—namely, not to be influenced by flattery. I'm sure Jesus' response shocked this fellow:

> "Man, who made Me a judge or an arbitrator over you?"
> (Luke 12:14)

Then Jesus disappointed the man even further. Instead of helping him out, Jesus admonished him with feedback on the state of his soul:

> "Take heed and beware of covetousness, for one's life does not consist in the abundance of the things he possesses."
> (Luke 12:15)

This younger brother didn't want a sermon; he wanted Jesus to do what he wanted him to do!

GREED AND IDOLATRY

Covetousness is wanting what another person has, and this fellow was being eaten up by wanting something that was in the possession of another. So as soon as he heard the degree of authority with which Jesus spoke, he thought, *This guy can solve my problem*. I'm not saying the younger brother was wrong; I'm simply pointing out where his mind was when he was listening to the teaching of the Lord and watching his ministry.

So the younger brother said, in effect, "Go talk to my brother." Perhaps he had heard the Lord speak to evil spirits and seen them cast out, or had heard Jesus speak to the sick and seen them healed. And so he said, "Speak to my brother. Lay the word on him, so I can have what I want."

I assume the younger brother had a legitimate problem, but Jesus' response focused on an even deeper problem: "Take heed and beware of covetousness" (Luke 12:15). The apostle Paul called a greedy person an idolater because when they covet something their heart is set on it (Colossians 3:5). They would do anything they could to get it. Jesus' response is important because it gives the right emphasis to the younger brother's deeper problem and how significant these matters are.

One of our problems in thinking about covetousness is the mistaken belief that the issue is one of giving. *Giving* our wealth is not the issue. *Keeping* our wealth is the issue; *having* it is the issue. God doesn't need our money. So this isn't about giving, but about how having riches might be done wrongly or rightly. Perhaps the question is, "Do you have them or do they have you?"

IN THE HANDS OF GOD

> Then He spoke a parable to them, saying: "The ground of a certain rich man yielded plentifully. And he thought within himself, saying, 'What shall I do, since I have no room to store my crops?' So he said, 'I will do this: I will pull down my barns and build greater, and there I will store all my crops and my goods.'" (Luke 12:16–18)

At this point, the rich man had done nothing wrong. In fact, he was being very sensible. But he made a mistake in his next breath, believing his life consisted in the abundance of the things he possessed.

> "'And I will say to my soul, "Soul, you have many goods laid up for many years; take your ease; eat, drink, and be merry."'" (Luke 12:19)

"Take your ease." You've got it made. You don't have to worry anymore. Just take a vacation. Watch your investments grow. Take it easy.

It's interesting that the farmer talked to his soul. That's a good thing to do, but what he said was troublesome. His plans to eat, drink, and be merry were fine; Jesus himself did that. Nor was there anything wrong with his soul being at rest, except for what it was resting *in*. The problem was making idols of riches and leisure, viewing them as the essence of his life.

In the way Jesus told the story, God was focused directly on the disposition of the farmer's soul:

> "But God said to him, 'Fool! This night your soul will be required of you; then whose will those things be which you have provided?'
>
> "So is he who lays up treasure for himself, and is not rich toward God." (Luke 12:20–21)

The rich man made the mistake of thinking it was up to him to dispose of his soul. It wasn't. None of us can predict or control the length of our life. *That's in the hands of God.* It's as if God said, "You've got all these barns stuffed with corn and all your cows are out in the field growing fatter. But your soul is going to be taken away. Your very self is not under your control." Now, that is the crux of the matter. Our very self is not ours to control. *It is under God's control.*

WHAT THE HEART WANTS

What is your life? Understand that this fellow thought his life consisted of enjoying his success, taking his rest, and trusting in his goods. Now, let's begin to try to sort these things out. This delusion meant the farmer was behaving foolishly, and Jesus offered the following diagnosis: "So is he who lays up treasure for himself, and is not rich toward God" (Luke 12:21).

We see in Jesus' diagnosis two issues—laying up treasure for yourself and being rich toward God. This parable isn't about being rich. It has to do with the way we *hold* our poverty or our riches. This man was holding them as if they were his own. He thought he was entirely in control of them, and so *he laid up treasures for himself.*

How does one know whether they are laying up treasures for themselves or are rich toward God? One of the best ways to figure this out is to work on this question: "What is your life?" Our life is what occupies our time, energy, and thoughts. It is, as Jesus says, what we have *set our hearts on.* "For where your treasure is, there your heart will be also" (Matthew 6:21).

People hold many things as treasure. One of those things is security—national security, social security, insurance, bank accounts. This is a reflection of the fact that human life is *in*secure apart from God. When people think of all the terrible things that could happen, they strive for security.

The musical *Fiddler on the Roof* contains an insightful line sung by Tevye, who knows that if he were rich, all the townspeople would come to him for advice: "When you're rich, they think you really know."[20] Riches make people assume they are smart and clever, that they've been able to get ahead because they know things others don't know.

GREAT GAIN

The apostle Paul wrote about riches in a prudent and insightful way in 1 Timothy 6, introducing the topic with a description of people who are always involved in quarreling, are deprived of truth, and believe godliness to be a means of gain. About them, Paul wrote, "From such withdraw yourself" (1 Timothy 6:5).

Some people confuse getting rich and being more secure (gain) with achieving a level of godliness. Or they think that being godly will bring them more riches and security. Whatever you do, don't confuse gain and godliness, and make sure you stay away from people who do. Gain is not godliness; godliness is not gain. But contentment with what we have, Paul says, is *great* gain:

> Now godliness with contentment is great gain. For we brought nothing into this world, and it is certain we can carry nothing out. And having food and clothing, with these we shall be content. But those who desire to be rich fall into temptation and a snare, and into many foolish and harmful lusts which drown men in destruction and perdition. (1 Timothy 6:6–9)

It's wise to stay out of the path of people who focus on getting ahead.* Those who desire to be rich hurt themselves and everyone around them because of their love of gain:

> For the love of money is a root of all kinds of evil, for which some have strayed from the faith in their greediness, and pierced themselves through with many sorrows.
>
> But you, O man of God, flee these things and pursue righteousness, godliness, faith, love, patience, gentleness.

---

* The book of Proverbs contains helpful instruction about this topic.

> Fight the good fight of faith, lay hold on eternal life, to which you were also called and have confessed the good confession in the presence of many witnesses. (1 Timothy 6:10–12)

And Paul instructs us, regardless of our poverty, wealth, or desire to be rich, with these words:

> Command those who are rich in this present age not to be haughty, nor to trust in uncertain riches but in the living God, who gives us richly all things to enjoy. (1 Timothy 6:17)

It is the pride and misplaced confidence that pose the problem. There was nothing wrong with the farmer having such full barns; he just shouldn't have let his trust rest in the contents of those barns. His faith was in the wrong place. He needed to place his trust in God:

> [He] gives us richly all things to enjoy. Let them do good, that they be rich in good works, ready to give, willing to share, storing up for themselves a good foundation for the time to come, that they may lay hold on eternal life. (1 Timothy 6:17–19)

What is your life? What does it consist of? Is your life filled with the knowledge of Jesus Christ, or does it consist of simply barns and business? Somebody has to take care of the barn, but God is more interested in your life. The barns are only a part of your life because your life is an eternal kind of life, lived in reliance on the resources of the kingdom of God, and that's the way it's supposed to be. If you are careful to distinguish between who you are and what you do, you'll have a place to stand in the face of the things that can mislead you. You will bring God into your work because you've allowed God to live in you completely.

And as you trust in God, "who gives us richly all things to enjoy," you will be rich toward him.

IN MAMMON WE TRUST

A thought exercise that will help you honestly answer the question of "what is my life" is to think of how you would react if everything were to be taken away. Picture in your mind an altar of fire where your house, bank account, retirement fund and all those things you treasure are consumed by fire. They're just gone. And then ask yourself, *How do I feel about this? Would I experience godliness and contentment in that situation?* We get so connected to what we have that we sometimes don't know what we're trusting. We think we've got peace and conclude that it has come from the Lord, but we might discover a different response if we were to imagine our possessions being taken away from us. That reveals what our life is.

To complete this exercise, it's important to carefully put our loved ones on the same altar. Imagine how it would feel if they were gone, because we need to turn them over to God too. And then when the moment of death comes, for them or for us, it will be altogether different because we've surrendered them to God. They're his. We can get an idea of where our treasures are through this exercise of letting them go.

It is easy to become dependent on people and things, which gives them power over us. Everyday worries and concerns also complicate our minds and do not allow us to simplify our lives. These anxieties lead to the desire to control and manipulate instead of allowing ourselves to be vulnerable in the hands of God. And so we compensate; we dress to impress and we accumulate to impress—all in an effort to make sure we feel secure and in control.

John Wesley pointed out how riches are a snare to good religious people. Wesley's ministry was so powerful that many people who lived on the brink of ruin in the lowest strata of society were redeemed. And then Wesley noticed a pattern. When men and women lived in relationship with God, they became hardworking, intelligent, grace-guided people. And the next thing you knew, they had more money than they'd ever seen before. But after that, they devoted themselves to that money.

Wesley commented that when you get right with God, you get right with the world; and when you get right with the world, you become prosperous. Often this is true. When we stop doing the unwise things that diminish our lives and dissipate our money and energy, we have the resources we need.

Thomas Aquinas is said to have noticed the same pattern. Once, when Aquinas was in Rome and in the presence of the pope, before whom a large sum of money was spread out, the pope observed, "You see, the Church can no longer say, 'Silver and gold have I none.'"

"True, holy father," replied Aquinas, "but neither can she now say, 'Rise and walk.'"[21]

When you trust in the power that belongs to riches, it's all the power you have. When you trust in the power of God, you're in touch with a different order and magnitude of power.

The church has repeatedly embraced the power of possessions and riches. Many church leaders have told me, "We had such a wonderful fellowship. The Lord was here and doing things left and right until we completed our new building." The building became the primary focus of their concern and affection.

It's interesting to consider that a church building can't heal anyone. Church property can't redeem anyone's soul. The church has been most prosperous spiritually in times when it was shut out from possessions, power, and influence. I'm not saying, "Tear the building down." But we need to remember what it is and isn't good for.

HOW MUCH MORE

After giving this parable, Jesus turned to nonparabolic teaching, using instruction and images to show what we need to do in order to be rich toward God.

> "Then He said to His disciples, 'Therefore I say to you, do not worry about your life, what you will eat; nor about the body, what you will put on.'" (Luke 12:22)

This takes us back to our central question: "What is your life?" Jesus was simply teaching us not to worry about our life, because God is taking care of it. You exist on this planet at the charge of God. You don't want to be here one moment longer than he appoints, and you do not need to be concerned about your death.

> "Life is more than food, and the body is more than clothing. Consider the ravens, for they neither sow nor reap, which have neither storehouse nor barn; and God feeds them. Of how much more value are you than the birds?" (Luke 12:23–24)

Jesus was saying to them, in essence, "Your life consists of much more than the food you eat, and your body consists of more than what you wear. Your body is the temple of the living God, so please don't think he's not going to take care of it. You're better than a raven. Look at how they get up early and work and yet don't worry." Jesus was not saying, "Don't work." He simply said, "Don't worry. Don't take things into your hands that don't belong to you."

USE ALL YOU CAN

John Wesley offered wise advice on how to deal with our riches so they don't entangle us: "Gain all you can; save all you can; give all you can."† The first statement, "gain all you can," is shocking until you understand what he had in mind. Wesley had the good sense to realize that we are put here on earth as stewards, and in that role we should strive to get all that we can.

I like to insert "use all you can" into this list before "give all you can." Use all you can for your health and well-being and for the glory of God. Take possession of property and use it for the glory of God, as well as for your own enjoyment of life. God guides us to take responsibility over the goods of this world. It's better that it be in the hands of those who will do good with it than in the hands of godless rulers or greedy people who don't know what to do with it except to strive to accumulate more. God wants it in the hands of the redeemed. What if all the land-lords in the city of Los Angeles were followers of Christ? What if all the bankers and business owners were disciples of Christ? How different would life be in that city?

When we use all we can, all of our monetary decisions (houses, cars, helping those in need, stocks, tithing, clothing, entertainment, and so forth) flow out of our discipleship to God in a way that exercises our stewardship under him. This comes from understanding our place in God's presence and in his kingdom and remembering that the outcomes are safely in his hands.

SHARE THE BURDEN

God never intended for people to bear all the burdens other people ask them to bear, even in religious activities. Early in my religious life, I was taken in by talk of "burning out for God." It had a good ring to it, but I learned that if we burn out for God,

---

† Wesley counsels to pursue *gain* without hurting either ourselves or our neighbors in soul or body as we apply ourselves to this with uninterrupted diligence and with all the understanding God has given us. He advises to *save* by cutting every expense that serves only to indulge foolish desire. See "Wesley's Sermon Reprints: The Use of Money," Christian History Institute, https://christianhistoryinstitute .org/magazine/article/wesleys-sermon-use-of-money, accessed May 2, 2024.

it's probably because we haven't been relying on the abundance of God to replenish our souls. We've been putting too much pressure on ourselves and others, rooted in misunderstandings about our place before God.

Being faithful does not mean overworking ourselves or taking on the work of other people. God never intended that only a few people should do his work, but that all the work to be done should be shared. We are all called to be priests and kings under God. We play different roles, but the ideal situation is not to have two or three powerful people doing the work but to have a powerful community through which the work is done *without any attention on who is doing it other than God himself*. That is the ministry of the unified church. Too often, the great expressions of effort we see are really exercises in self-righteousness and desperation that often end badly. Even when they don't, they still have the negative effect of depriving the majority of Christians of the challenge to exercise their responsibility to minister the kingdom of God where they are to those around them.

Jesus continued his teaching:

> "And which of you by worrying can add one cubit to his stature? If you then are not able to do the least, why are you anxious for the rest? Consider the lilies, how they grow: they neither toil nor spin; and yet I say to you, even Solomon in all his glory was not arrayed like one of these." (Luke 12:25–27)

Unlike the birds, plants don't even *work*. They just grow!

> "If then God so clothes the grass, which today is in the field and tomorrow is thrown into the oven, how much more will He clothe you, O you of little faith?
>
> "And do not seek what you should eat or what you should drink, nor have an anxious mind. For all these things the

nations of the world seek after, and your Father knows that you need these things. But seek the kingdom of God, and all these things shall be added to you.

"Do not fear, little flock, for it is your Father's good pleasure to give you the kingdom." (Luke 12:28–32)

God wants to *give* us the kingdom! This is God's grace coming to us here, right where we are.

PEOPLE MATTER

"Sell what you have and give alms; provide yourselves money bags which do not grow old, a treasure in the heavens that does not fail, where no thief approaches nor moth destroys." (Luke 12:33)

Jesus said not to store up more than we need or can use. He wasn't advising us to get rid of everything we have. We are to provide for ourselves. But the focus Jesus wanted us to have is the investment we make in people and their character: "As each one has received a gift, minister it to one another, as good stewards of the manifold grace of God" (1 Peter 4:10).

What are the "money bags which do not grow old"? We are the treasures in heaven—ourselves and other people. If you want to store up treasures in heaven, then embed "righteousness, godliness, faith, love, patience, gentleness" into your character and help others to do the same (1 Timothy 6:11). The difference you make in the lives of other people will go to heaven when *they* go to heaven. So you invest in people and their character. Anything you can do for someone else remains for eternity: "Therefore, encourage one another and build one another up, just as you also are doing" (1 Thessalonians 5:11 NASB).

People are what matter. They are the temple of God. They

are those whom God has chosen out of the world. They are his bride. What we can do for others, especially for "the least of these My brethren," is the treasure that goes on to heaven (Matthew 25:40). The answer to the question, "What is your life?" is not found in riches or possessions or gain, but can only be found in a heart that fully trusts God, is rich toward him, and loves others.

MAIN POINTS ABOUT THE KINGDOM OF GOD

- When we rely on God and his kingdom it changes our relationship with our wealth (money, possessions, treasures, and gain) and its effect on our heart.
- When we are "rich toward God," we no longer make idols of riches and leisure, and they no longer have a hold on us.
- Those who live in the kingdom of God have entered into the eternal life of God and find contentment in what God has graciously provided.
- We must pay attention to where we place our trust and allow ourselves to be vulnerable in the hands of God.
- Life in the kingdom is about investing in our own character and in the lives and character of others.

CHAPTER 14

PERSISTENCE AS THE PREREQUISITE TO GROWTH

Brothers and sisters, I do not consider that I have laid hold of it, but one thing I have laid hold of: forgetting what lies behind and straining forward to what lies ahead, I press on toward the goal, toward the prize of the heavenly call of God in Christ Jesus.

PHILIPPIANS 3:13–14 NRSVUE

The abundant life Jesus came to give us is a gift, but it does not come to those who are passive (John 10:10). It comes only through persistent, strenuous, and well-directed action. This is why Peter directed us to "grow in the grace and knowledge of our Lord and Savior Jesus Christ" (2 Peter 3:18). We need persistence—the will to stick with it, to consistently apply the means to our goal. We need patience—a willingness to let our life grow and to follow the wise courses of action. And we need confidence in the amazing promises of Jesus Christ.

These character traits are essential for a fruitful life because few things in life that are worth doing are pleasant in their early stages. As a teacher with some experience in the development of personality, I have found this to be true almost without exception. This may not be what we want to hear, because it means we must do some things that may not be enjoyable and may even be downright *un*pleasant.

For example, many of us took music lessons as children, but because we didn't have an attitude of patience and persistence to keep us practicing our instrument when we found it unpleasant, we didn't develop the skill our parents hoped would result from those lessons. Physical exercise is easy when you're in good shape, but when you're out of shape, it is torturous. Difficulty in the early stages of anything that is truly worth doing is a natural part of human life. This is true not only as we master new skills and talents, but also as we grow in areas of personality and human interaction where many things can be learned only through experience. This is the case as we learn to walk in the Spirit. Persistence is the prerequisite for a fruitful life in the kingdom of God.

We are taught, and rightly so, that the grace of God brings salvation. We do not earn it and could never deserve it, and it is not something we can attain on our own. But that isn't an indication that there's nothing left for us to do. Jesus said, "Strive to enter through the narrow gate, for many, I say to you, will seek to enter and will not be able" (Luke 13:24). *Strive!* Paul compared life to running a race or boxing against an opponent and concluded with, "I discipline my body and bring it into subjection, lest, when I have preached to others, I myself should become disqualified" (1 Corinthians 9:27). Even the apostle Paul, a mature disciple, was concerned about being disqualified.

On the one hand, we are saved by the grace of God, but on

the other hand, responding to the grace of God necessitates rigorous effort. This is a battle; it is a race. It's like a championship basketball game that comes down to the final few seconds. The following parables of Jesus will highlight four key areas in which persistence in our spiritual lives is a prerequisite—forgiveness, service, prayer, and humility.

PERSISTENCE IN FORGIVENESS

In Luke 17, Jesus taught about how his followers can advance in their faith, beginning with the subject of offenses and forgiveness. Whenever people come together, offenses are inevitable, so we shouldn't be surprised when we're offended (Luke 17:1). It is the nature of life that we will offend others and they will offend us.

Jesus began this way:

> "Take heed to yourselves. If your brother sins against you, rebuke him; and if he repents, forgive him." (Luke 17:3)

This idea of confronting someone or giving corrective feedback is not commonly practiced or even taught as a part of our life in community. Instead, if a brother or sister sins against us, we tend to go off into a corner and feel sorry for ourselves. But truthful and faithful correction is a part of the strenuous life of abiding in the way of Christ.

Be careful, though. Jesus didn't say, "Tell them off," or "Censure that person." We approach them in the loving and gentle manner of Jesus. The apostle Paul understood this: "Dear brothers and sisters, if another believer is overcome by some sin, you who are godly should *gently and humbly* help that person back onto the right path" (Galatians 6:1 NLT, emphasis added).

In that spirit, let the other person know they have hurt you. If they say, "I'm sorry. I didn't mean to do that. I will make restitution," forgive them. Remember that forgiveness is choosing not to hold an offense against someone, not bringing it up, and not making the other person pay for it in any way.

Jesus continued:

> "And if he sins against you seven times in a day, and seven times in a day returns to you, saying, 'I repent,' you shall forgive him." (Luke 17:4)

Why do you suppose Jesus said "seven times *in a day*"? I think he wanted to address our expectation that if you forgive someone, they're not supposed to do the same thing again.

You can almost hear the apostles saying in unison, "Increase our faith, Lord! Seven times is just too much. Twice would be more than enough, but not *seven* times!"

It's a wonderful thing to forgive. We don't forgive in order to manipulate other people; we forgive because it is good to forgive. The good that is in forgiveness is in the forgiveness itself, not only in the results that come from it. Even if the person is insincere, still, forgive them. Set yourself to forgive endlessly. The reason is very simple: we are far better off living that way than any other way. *Life in the kingdom goes beyond the minimum*, as each of the following parables will teach us.

UNDERSTANDING FAITH

When Jesus' stunned disciples asked him to increase their faith (Luke 17:5), he replied:

> "If you have faith as a mustard seed, you can say to this mulberry tree, 'Be pulled up by the roots and be planted in the sea,' and it would obey you." (Luke 17:6)

We can be misled by verses like these if we think, *Well, how much faith do I have? Let's see if I can move that tree.* Many people have attempted it and are ashamed it didn't work. The mulberry tree just stood there.

Notice that Jesus didn't say, "You will *pray*," but "You will *say*," just as God *said*, "Let there be light," and there was light.* Faith is a matter of knowing how to speak the creative word of God *with* God. In faith we see things as they truly are in the will and vision and purpose of God. In this way, we are joined *with God* in speaking the creative word.

Jesus was letting his disciples know, "If you think forgiving your brother seven times in a day is impossible, you don't understand faith." He was opening up to his disciples and to us a vision of what's possible in his kingdom.

After being told to forgive repeatedly, someone might think, *Oh no! I've gotta forgive seven times in a day? Another job I have to do?* But when you realize what faith is about, you won't be thinking about what you *have* to do; instead, doing whatever you can do to please the Lord will be foremost in your mind.

PERSISTENCE IN SERVICE

Jesus expanded on this idea with an interesting illustration that leads into an altogether different approach to what it means to serve the Lord. This story is intended to help us understand what *real* faith is like—that it's something that always goes beyond specifically assigned duties and minimum requirements (being ready to forgive someone *even more* than seven times). Real faith has a confidence that provides the initiative to enter into the *active life* of the kingdom of God without waiting to be told what to do. But often that's the picture we have of our relationship with God—just standing around waiting to be told what to do.

---

* See my in-depth discussion of the difference between praying and saying in *The Allure of Gentleness: Defending the Faith in the Manner of Jesus* (San Francisco: HarperOne, 2015), 160–62.

> "And which of you, having a servant plowing or tending sheep, will say to him when he has come in from the field, 'Come at once and sit down to eat'? But will he not rather say to him, 'Prepare something for my supper, and gird yourself and serve me till I have eaten and drunk, and afterward you will eat and drink'? Does he thank that servant because he did the things that were commanded him? I think not." (Luke 17:7–9)

The latter portion of this story described the way servants were typically treated in Jesus' day—treatment that may seem harsh to us today. It was customary for the servant, after working all day in the field, to take off his dirty clothes, clean up, put on his butler's uniform, bring out the food, and stand behind the master while he ate to make sure every little thing was just right. In that culture, the master would *never* have turned around and said, "Thank you! You're a wonderful person!" Jesus would certainly have caught his listeners' attention with this ludicrous idea.

The kind of servant who will be thanked by the master seeks and does those things he knows are pleasing and useful to the master without needing to be told. And then the master says, "Wow! Where did this guy come from? This person is *really identified* with my business. Thank you!" This is a *profitable* servant, and there's a good chance that servant will find himself profiting from the master's good pleasure.

PUT YOUR HEART INTO IT

> "So likewise you, when you have done all those things which you are commanded, say, 'We are unprofitable servants. We have done what was our duty to do.'" (Luke 17:10)

We often think, *I did what I was told to do. There's nothing more to be done.* Maybe you know people who always manage to do as little as possible. They do only what is asked of them. Does that please everyone? That isn't the idea of service one would hope for.

It is better to live and work with those whose heart is in what they do instead of folks who just wait for instructions, and then do only what they're told. You want people who can identify the key interests of the group and perhaps even take care of things better than you would.

Through this parable Jesus was teaching that *if our idea of service is doing only what we are told to do, we haven't yet begun to understand what life in the kingdom of God is like.* That sort of faith is not even the size of the mustard seed. It is *because* we don't understand these things that we still have to invest so much effort into day-to-day things like forgiveness, service, or honesty. When we have grown to the level of living our lives out of the abundant reality of the kingdom of God, these things, along with other things, will take care of themselves.

To identify with the mind of Christ, to the point where we are prepared to step forward and do his work without being told what to do, is fundamental to our ability to be persistent in serving the Lord.

Many people think all they need to do is make sure they never break any of the Ten Commandments. I would never downplay the importance of obedience, but there are many levels to that in our life with God. Jesus said that at the minimum level, when we've only done what we were told to do, we are to call ourselves "unprofitable." That kind of faith is below the level of the mustard seed, without an actively unfolding life of its own. Faith grows when we realize that we are unprofitable servants and strive to do more.

When people become concerned about doing God's will, they wonder, *What does God want me to do?* But God is there next to them, asking, "What do *you* want to do?" God wants to have conversations with us about what *we* want to do and about his purposes for our lives. God wants to help us grow and mature, and sometimes he does this by being quiet and allowing us to make our own choices based on our deepening relationship with him. *That's when we discover what we truly are before God.*

The Lord didn't make us to be sycophants or robots who simply stand around taking orders. God called us to be men and women who live in his world to *do* something. That's the vision of a co-laborer with God and a friend of God (2 Corinthians 6:1; James 2:23). Jesus called his disciples friends and made them partners in the family business (John 15:15).

Following Jesus is much more than asking, "What would Jesus do?" As you come to know Jesus and his ways, that knowledge allows you to recognize what you should do in most cases. I have been happily married to Jane Willard for most of my life, and because we've had this life together, I don't often need to ask what she wants and what she regards as good (at least most of the time). In the same way, it's our life together with Jesus in his kingdom that sharpens us and enables us to better understand what we're to do as we come to know him better. Paul prayed for this: "that I may know Him" (Philippians 3:10). And as we know Jesus, he speaks in our hearts.

Serving God in this wholehearted way helps us become more like a co-worker who sees what needs to be done and simply does it. That's a deeper level of relationship, of interacting with God and living in the kingdom of God here and now. We become so close to God that we do not have to wait to hear his words, but are engaged in freehearted collaboration with Jesus and his friends in the kingdom.

PERSISTENCE IN PRAYER

Another characteristic of someone with a diligent, persevering heart is illustrated by one of my favorite parables of Jesus—the next parable he tells in Luke's narrative, which is about a persistent widow who didn't give up or "lose heart."

> Then He spoke a parable to them, that men always ought to pray and not lose heart, saying: "There was in a certain city a judge who did not fear God nor regard man." (Luke 18:1–2)

To not lose heart means to not give up. The judge in this parable was not a good judge; he was a mean and ornery one. This crooked judge was more like a crime boss than a servant of justice (Luke 18:6). He had no respect for other people or for God. He said, "What is God to me?"

> "Now there was a widow in that city . . ." (Luke 18:3)

In those days, widows were regarded as the most helpless of persons. They were easy to push around because they didn't have a husband to defend them. This widow had no rights, placing her and the judge at opposite poles of social power. All she could do was come and ask.

> ". . . and she came to him, saying, 'Get justice for me from my adversary.'" (Luke 18:3)

She wanted justice because someone had wronged her. Perhaps some of her goods or land had been stolen. Jesus didn't say exactly how she had been injured, but simply told of her claim. She needed justice from the law and came to the judge, saying, in essence, "Correct this matter. Avenge me of my adversary. Set it right."

"And he would not for a while . . ." (Luke 18:4)

Since the judge did not fear anyone, why would he help? He probably wondered, *Who is this widow who is bothering me? I don't have time to waste on her!* But the widow did not let the matter drop and continued to plead her case while he tried to ignore her.

" . . . but afterward he said within himself, 'Though I do not fear God nor regard man, yet because this widow troubles me I will avenge her, lest by her continual coming she weary me.'" (Luke 18:4–5)

Now, *that* is persistence.

Jesus took the well-known tendency of many people to give in when they are continually asked something and used it to urge the disciples to keep praying. He knew that *asking* is not an incidental, trivial sort of thing but is among the most fundamental aspects of human relations. Asking and giving come from the deepest parts of human nature and personality.

After sharing the uncaring judge's response to the widow's persistent request, Jesus continued:

"Nevertheless, when the Son of Man comes, will He really find faith on the earth?" (Luke 18:8)

Jesus is urging us not to quit, not to give up on God. Remember, Jesus told this parable so that we would always pray and not lose heart. The Lord was calling out the tendency of so many to give up.

So we follow Paul's instruction to pray *always*, in whatever way we can, even when things are going well or when we don't feel like praying (1 Thessalonians 5:17). We are to pray not out of *duty* but out of *relationship*, not out of *obedience* but out of *love.* As our faith grows so does our desire to pray and speak with God.

What is prayer? It's talking with God. And yet we are often very slow to do it. And when we do get around to it, we say the prayer, move on, and don't come back to it for a while. This reveals the smallness of our faith. "Increase our faith, Lord!"

THE FRIEND IN NEED

Jesus also applied this need for persistence in prayer in the story of a man whose friend came to him at midnight and asked for some bread to feed an unexpected guest. You may recall how Jesus described the man's dilemma:

> "I have a friend who showed up on my doorstep. He was out late on the road, and the freeway was blocked off. He's hungry. I don't have anything to feed him. Give me three loaves of bread." (Luke 11:5–6, paraphrased)

The householder's whole family was in bed and the door was shut. He muttered words of protest to his friend but eventually ended up helping him.

> "I say to you, though he will not rise and give to him because he is his friend, yet because of his persistence he will rise and give him as many as he needs." (Luke 11:8)

The man gave in to his friend's "persistence"—an interesting term to translate that essentially means "shamelessness."† It's kind of like when you eat in front of the family dog that watches utterly without shame until you give it some of whatever

---

† The Greek word is *anaideia*. It is translated as "importunity" in the KJV and "persistence" in the NKJV. *Thayer's Greek Lexicon* defines it as "shamelessness, impudence."

you're eating. This fellow just stood at the door bearing no shame whatsoever. Eventually, the householder gave his friend what he asked for.

In the process of asking God for something, we recognize and welcome his presence with us. We make ourselves present to him. That's the nature of the request—simply the presence of one person to another. Why does God give us what we ask for? Because we ask. In these two cases, the effective component is simply the power of asking—and continuing time and time again.

DOING BUSINESS WITH GOD

God answers prayer and *wants* to do so. He is not like the unjust judge who only yields "lest" the widow wear him out. This is part of what it means to live in a universe where the ultimate reality is a community of persons—Father, Son, and Holy Spirit. Matthew 7:7–8 gives us a glimpse into this reality: "Ask, and it will be given to you; seek, and you will find; knock, and it will be opened to you. For everyone who asks receives, and he who seeks finds, and to him who knocks it will be opened." That's why the law of request that Jesus gave us in these teachings is more foundational than the law of gravity.

Why does prayer work? Because asking and giving is a fundamental law of the universe. People will cross the street to avoid making eye contact with someone who is begging. They don't want to get close enough to be overwhelmed by the power of the request. They don't want to feel that tug to give.

Let me ask you to thoughtfully consider the idea that prayer is not primarily trying to get someone to do something, nor is it an exercise in self-talk—a form of self-adminstered therapy—though it often has a healing effect. Prayer is doing business with God.

When we pray, we are entering into a working relationship

with God—namely, one that includes speaking with God: "If you had faith like a mustard seed, you would *say* . . ." When you understand that, you see how prayer is doing something together with God. Prayer and speaking with God are on a continuum together.

Now, when you start to pray for something, you are entering into a profoundly complex relationship, because most people are going to be praying about things that involve themselves intimately—members of their family, neighborhood, church, loved ones. When you start praying about those kinds of things, it is likely to change you as well.

For example, I've watched many women pray that their husbands would open themselves up to a relationship with God. Within the close relationship of marriage, that prayer will probably not be answered without the wife changing as well. Once when praying for my son and not seeing any change, I sensed the Lord saying to me, *Why don't you stop being angry with him?* And when I did move away from anger, my son immediately began to change. God is working with everyone involved, and we have to be open to *changing ourselves.*

JOY WITH THE LORD

It's ironic that many people think they have something more important to do than to pray. Yet when prayer is conversation, it can be delightful—a "sweet hour of prayer" as we used to sing.[22] Think of the most delightful interactions you've had with your loved ones, and ask yourself, *Would I hesitate to do that again?* We can understand what the psalmist had to say about the joyous time in the temple of the Lord—time in the presence of God—and how he would rather be a doorkeeper in the house of God than dwell in the tents of unrighteousness (Psalm 84:10).

When we grow beyond the level of faith that meets only minimal requirements—beginning to forgive freely because it is good for us and entering into the work of God as his partner and friend—we open ourselves to experience the sweetness of prayer, the *joy* of time spent in the presence of the Lord. We even start thinking that every moment spent away from God is a loss of valuable time.

Prayer requires us to be willing to change as we work with God to accomplish things together. Change is growth, and growth takes time. Anyone who is unwilling to consistently lift their requests before the Lord in prayer is like a person who learns that a plant needs a full day of sunshine but only sets it outside for five minutes every morning. Prayer is a kind of service we offer the Lord as coworkers whose hearts are in what we do.

PERSISTENCE IN HUMILITY

Jesus follows the parable of the unjust judge in Luke 18 with a parable about humility in prayer as he concludes this series of parables focused on increasing the disciples' faith. Humility and prayer are deeply connected because one of the things that keeps us from prayer is a lack of humility. When the widow went into court to plead her case, she came in humility, not pride. If she had been proud, she wouldn't have gone to the judge for help. She would have thought to herself, *I'm not going to take this from that mean guy! He treats me as if I'm nothing!*

Humility is one of the main ingredients in prayer because humility shows dependence on God. When we're not praying, it can be because we have more confidence in ourselves than in God, despite all our failures. We keep thinking, *I can handle it; I'll work it out,* rather than crying out, "Lord, help me!" We can get so consumed with trying to prove ourselves and get what we want through our own abilities that we leave no space for God to work with us. We trust only in ourselves.

Humility is the secret to maintaining our persistence in our efforts to increase our faith and move forward in the kingdom of God. Jesus' listeners probably didn't realize they lacked humility or trusted only in themselves, so Jesus told a story to help them understand:

> Also He spoke this parable to some who trusted in themselves that they were righteous, and despised others: "Two men went up to the temple to pray, one a Pharisee and the other a tax collector." (Luke 18:9–10)

You may recall that tax collectors were appointees of the Roman government, political figures who were, by and large, corrupt in their business dealings and greatly despised. The Pharisees "trusted in themselves that they were righteous." They thought they had to impress God, as if somehow, there must be a catch. The only catch is, just ask. But if you trust in yourself, you will probably not pray; you won't excel in service; and you will struggle with forgiveness. Trusting in ourselves hamstrings our persistent efforts to go forward in the kingdom of God. But the Pharisees trusted in themselves and viewed others with contempt:

> "The Pharisee stood and prayed thus with himself, 'God, I thank You that I am not like other men—extortioners, unjust, adulterers, or even as this tax collector. I fast twice a week; I give tithes of all that I possess.' And the tax collector, standing afar off, would not so much as raise his eyes to heaven, but beat his breast, saying, 'God, be merciful to me a sinner!'" (Luke 18:11–13)

The tax collector didn't stand on his own personal qualifications as the Pharisee did. He just said, "God, be merciful." Beating his breast was an honest expression of anguish and despair. The tax collector presented himself humbly before the God of the universe, a God whose nature is to give when he is asked. Jesus pointed out that the result of these two men's prayers was the opposite of what would have been culturally assumed:

> "I tell you, this man went down to his house justified rather than the other; for everyone who exalts himself will be humbled, and he who humbles himself will be exalted." (Luke 18:14)

Humility enables us to get ourselves out of the way and connect with God. If you "humble yourselves under the mighty hand of God," then in due time what will happen? He will "exalt you" (1 Peter 5:6). Notice, *you* will not exalt you, but *God* will exalt you when the time is right. "Let your light so shine before men, that they may see your good works and glorify . . ." *you*? No. When this light displays the life, love, and power that is in you, they will "glorify your Father in heaven" (Matthew 5:16).‡

True humility is based on a high view of God and others, not on a low view of the self. We become humble by elevating others. As the apostle Paul wrote, "Let each think of the other as better than themselves" (Philippians 2:3, paraphrased). But sometimes people say, "I know I'm doing better than she is, but I have to think about *her* as better than *me*?" So they decide to fake it: "I'll just *tell* her she's better than I am." How do we learn to *truly* think better of others than ourselves?

Paul's way of doing this is found in 1 Corinthians 2:2: "For I determined not to know any thing among you, save Jesus Christ, and him crucified" (KJV). When I see in you what Christ can be, then I am in a position to think better of you than of myself. And when I am caught up in love and adoration of God and love for my neighbor because of their relationship to God as his children, I will not be thinking about myself at all. This is especially true since I know I am always thought of by God and he is taking care of me.

---

‡ Light usually symbolizes love, power, and truth in the Bible.

Having a low view of others is a desperation ploy. Our praying Pharisee was attempting to secure himself by deflating other people. Sadly, tearing one another down is a normal way of life. I almost dread hearing someone say, "Well, Joe is a good man . . ." because what typically follows is, "But here's what's wrong with Joe . . ." There may be a time for making judgments, but there is absolutely no place for condemnation in the fellowship of love and humility.

CHILDLIKENESS

Jesus underscored this parable about humility with an example of how childlikeness reflects the kinds of attitudes we need to enter the kingdom of the heavens.

> Some people brought their little children for Jesus to bless. But when his disciples saw them doing this, they told the people to stop bothering him. So Jesus called the children over to him and said, "Let the children come to me! Don't try to stop them. People who are like these children belong to God's kingdom. You will never get into God's kingdom unless you enter it like a child!" (Luke 18:15–17 CEV)

Children excel at persistence and humility. When children fall down, they get up and try again. They learn to talk by steadily babbling. As little children grow, they possess an unlimited ability to humbly persist in learning things and never quitting.

The humble person is also like a little child in their ability to forgive. Small children cannot hold a grudge (at least not until they have had considerable practice). A child says, "I'm never going to play with Jimmy again. Never! I *hate* Jimmy!" Five minutes later, she looks out the window at Jimmy, and then, after a few more minutes, she thinks about what she could give Jimmy. A cookie maybe? Soon they're back playing again, and all is forgotten.

The humility of little children shows in how they don't have to think about "saving face." "Saving face" is a *façade*-saving device. Grown-ups are not saving face, but saving the façade they have created to manage how they appear to those around them. A little child doesn't yet have a façade to save. This kind of honesty—tearing away all the pretenses and just being who we are—is what enables us to have a tender heart that is honest and vulnerable.

This idea is also seen in the Gospel of Matthew, where Jesus called a little child to stand alongside his disciples and said these words:

> "Verily I say unto you, except you are turned around, and become as little children, you shall not enter into the kingdom of the heavens. Whosoever therefore shall humble himself as this little child, the same is greatest in the kingdom of the heavens." (Matthew 18:3–4, paraphrased)

If we are to be humble like a little child and be great in the kingdom of the heavens, we must turn from the normal human attitude that says we are competent and quite capable of managing our lives on our own. Children are defenseless in themselves, and hence physically and spiritually vulnerable, leaving them no choice but to request guidance, protection, and help from those around them. When we understand our place in the rule of God, we naturally humble ourselves under his mighty hand and depend on him to care for us.

Presumption is another aspect of a child's humility. They expect to receive others' attention and even affection. We normally think of presumption negatively because of the way people presume upon each other. But very young children—so young they haven't yet been made to feel like they have to justify their existence—live with an assurance that they will be loved and accepted. You may be sitting in a waiting room and a toddler comes over to you. This tiny person starts talking to you, and may even reach out and smear chocolate on your shirt. He doesn't ask permission and fully expects you to receive his attention with joy.

Presumption can be a wonderful thing. It says, "Here I am. I'm worth paying attention to!" Children who have not been deprived of their sense of worth can be relaxed, trusting, and spontaneous. But as they grow up, they learn they must defend and validate their worth and no longer live with the presumption that they will be loved and accepted. Many of us have much to learn (and unlearn!) about ourselves and God in this area.

PERSISTENCE TAKES PRACTICE

Persistence in forgiveness, service, prayer, and humility has to be undertaken consciously and cultivated intentionally if we are to run the race like the apostle Paul (1 Corinthians 9:24–27). Our persistent efforts to forgive freely, serve wholeheartedly, pray unceasingly, and humbly regard others as better than ourselves with childlike abandon will most certainly increase our faith in, confidence in, and dependence on God. We need to seriously consider how we experience this way of life and receive the grace of God for a fruitful life in his kingdom.

You can train yourself in this. To get started, you may want to have some special devices associated with your daily routine that remind you to forgive, serve, pray, and live in humility and child-like dependence on God. For example, you can put a sign on the coffee pot or on your bathroom mirror that reminds you to pray in the morning. God can lead you toward developing customized habits suited to the circumstances in your home and workplace.

The key is simply to change your habits by associating the desired practices with the simple things that make up your life. And if you are persistent, everything about you will begin to change, and you will find that God will give you the gift of increased faith.

MAIN POINTS ABOUT THE KINGDOM OF GOD

- Persistence in forgiveness, service, prayer, and humility is the prerequisite for a fruitful life in the kingdom of God.
- Service in the kingdom is done with a heart of love for and connection with God, being prepared to step forward and do the next right thing.
- We are to pray out of the loving relationship we have with God. As our faith grows, so does our desire to pray and speak with him. When we pray, we enter a cooperative working relationship with God, where we are open to being changed ourselves.
- Humility enables us to stop trusting only in ourselves and depend on God.

CHAPTER 15

MOVED BY COMPASSION

"Then a despised Samaritan came along, and when he saw the man, he felt compassion for him."

LUKE 10:33 NLT

The Parable of the Good Samaritan displays the outworking of the Word of the kingdom. I am tempted to say this is Jesus' greatest parable, but I wouldn't want to defend that claim. This parable is a fitting way to close our study together because it best embodies what it means to live in the welcoming and accessible kingdom of God. In many ways, it includes in its entirety the message Jesus proclaimed about the kingdom of God and what it means to live it out in practical ways.

This parable teaches about our responsibility for others, which is one of the oldest messages in the Bible. When God came to Cain and said, "Where is Abel your brother?" Cain responded, "Am I my brother's keeper?" (Genesis 4:9). Cain answered this way because he knew he was, in reality, his brother's keeper. He knew he was responsible for his brother.

And we all know this in our own lives too. We know we have a responsibility for others.

We have studied several aspects of the Word of the kingdom, including the Word as a seed, as a life, and as a principle, but now we look at its *practical* side, which is focused around a single word—*neighbor*. This interesting word comes from the Middle English *neigh-boor*, and is from a time when the word *boor/bor* described a citizen who was a peasant or a rustic individual. This term represented a person (the *bor*) who was *neigh* (nigh/near) to you (*neighbor*).

In Jesus' culture, having a neighbor carried with it a sense of responsibility. And in our time, at least prior to the days when we could count on government assistance like Social Security or Medicare, and before we could call 911 in an emergency, people have relied on one another to look after those who were located near them. They needed each other and took care of each other.

Every language has a word like *neighbor* that carries the sense of a person who is near to you and for whom you have some degree of responsibility. In our world today, who my neighbor is largely depends on me. A large portion of my neighbors are the people I pay attention to in a special way, who are closely involved in my life. The most intimate of my neighbors are the members of my family. We don't often think of family as neighbors, and all too often we wind up ignoring them and not being compassionate toward them. But we want to start there and move outward.

Our neighbors are people for whom we can do things that will be helpful. In this day and age, we can help people on the other side of the world. We feed hungry children and support missionary efforts. But because of the fallen condition of the world, there is a great temptation to despair and to disown our responsibility toward others because so much need exists and we can't effectively help everyone. Misunderstanding our responsibility toward others can cause us to feel powerless and hopeless. We can't help everyone. Only God can do that, but each of us has a responsibility to help in some way.

We can also be tempted to be satisfied with doing our own religious activities—like the priest and Levite in the parable— instead of helping others. These influential leaders didn't help the man in trouble because they thought it was okay for them not to do so. Something in their minds believed, *It's alright for me to turn away and not help.* They were using their religious standing as an excuse, which may be why Jesus chose to insert characters with these particular religious roles into the story. They kept their righteousness someplace else, tucked away in another pocket, so to speak. When they saw someone in need, they checked that pocket and thought, *Yes, it's all right there.* And right on down the road they went.

ORDINARY PEOPLE CHANGING THE WORLD

Jesus told this parable as he talked with his followers after they had healed people in the power of the kingdom of God (Luke 10:1–23). He thought those acts of healing were so marvelous that he exclaimed, "I saw Satan fall like lightning from heaven" (10:18). This settled in his mind the plan by which he would work to evangelize the world. He knew he had triumphed by committing himself to ordinary people—fisherfolk and tax collectors—exercising the *power* of the kingdom of God. This is not irrelevant to our parable—keep in mind what I said about how the lack of power can cause us to feel hopeless.

> Then He turned to His disciples and said privately, "Blessed are the eyes which see the things you see; for I tell you that many prophets and kings have desired to see what you see, and have not seen it, and to hear what you hear, and have not heard it." (Luke 10:23–24)

In the midst of Jesus' celebration, a certain lawyer questioned him. A lawyer was a person of great power in that society, both as a religious and public figure, and might also have been identified in the Gospels as a scribe who wrote primarily about the law. Because the law was central in Jewish culture, the people who studied it held positions of great authority and power.

I imagine this lawyer considered what Jesus said and had a lot of questions in his mind because he believed it was mainly people like himself who were especially blessed. But he had seen this ragtag group of fisherfolk, merchants, and farmers coming back from their outings and saying, "Lord, we have exercised the power of your kingdom!"

PEOPLE ALREADY KNOW

The lawyer seemed offended by these common folk exercising kingdom power and felt like his own standing was being called into question. He was put on edge and may have thought to himself, *Well, now wait a moment . . .* He decided to take the offensive and test Jesus to see if he knew what he was talking about—or, even better, to prove him wrong.

> "Teacher, what shall I do to inherit eternal life?"
>
> He said to him, "What is written in the law? What is your reading of it?" (Luke 10:25–26)

Jesus replied to him using the same requirements the lawyer would understand: "You're a lawyer, you tell me. What do you do to inherit eternal life?"

Jesus did not need to create any arguments; he simply asked the man what he already knew. The interesting thing about witnessing and teaching is that most folks already know what they need to know. They already have an idea about the answers.

Sometimes they need something clarified or confirmed, or maybe they need an example laid out for them, but basically they know.

This same concept applies to condemnation. We hardly ever need to condemn anyone because they've already condemned themselves. People already know the things they've done wrong. Jesus said, "I did not come into the world to condemn the world" (John 3:17, paraphrased). If you choose to condemn someone and they respond somewhat vigorously, it's usually because you have touched the spot in them that is already sore from their own harsh criticism.

So the world doesn't need another ounce of blame. And so much of blaming is just an exercise in self-righteousness so everyone will know we really know what is right and are on the right track. Sometimes a tender word needs to be said about what they should do. If that's our role, we need to speak in a spirit of helpfulness and firmness.

Here the lawyer answered his own question:

> So he answered and said, "'You shall love the Lord your God with all your heart, with all your soul, with all your strength, and with all your mind,' and 'your neighbor as yourself.'"
>
> And He said to him, "You have answered rightly; do this and you will live." (Luke 10:27–28)

No sooner had the lawyer given the right answer than he began to feel uneasy. He had condemned himself with his own mouth. The lawyer knew in his heart that he had not loved his neighbor. He may have heard his mouth say, "You shall love your neighbor as yourself," and simply *thought* of someone he did not love. So immediately he thought up a clever question. (That's one of the things education is good for—to teach us how to dodge and ask clever questions.) So the lawyer asked, "And who is my neighbor?" (Luke 10:29). Perhaps he thought Jesus would need some time to work on that question.

Jesus' response is a perfect example of the way parables work because when he heard this question, he didn't define the word *neighbor* or give the lawyer a list of who his neighbors might be. Instead, Jesus offered this intriguing story to help him explore the kingdom of God. The story changed the question from, "Who is my neighbor?" to "To whom will I *be* a neighbor?" The question, "Who is my neighbor?" is the wrong question because there's no end to the way it can be debated and discussed. The kingdom question is, "To whom will you be a neighbor?"

To "love your neighbor as yourself" is not a matter of identifying and making a list of neighbors and then making it a project to go around and love those people. It's an active love, where we are alert and aware because the next person we come across—though we may have never seen them before and though they are very unlike us—may turn out to be someone to whom we will choose to be a neighbor. This places the emphasis on neighbor-*ing*. Neighboring is an opportunity in the kingdom of God.

COM-PASSION

We need insight, understanding, power, and, above all, compassion (that wonderful quality possessed by the Samaritan) to be a neighbor to someone. *Compassion* is the Latin correlate of the Greek word *sympatheia*, from which we get our English word *sympathy*, meaning "suffer with or feel with"—"com-passion." The Samaritan had the ability to suffer with another person, to feel with another person, and to allow himself to demonstrate compassion. The other two chaps we meet in the story couldn't do that.

A person of compassion is one who feels the struggles of others and is moved by the distress of someone else. To do so requires resources of personal strength, as well as wisdom in action. Loving your neighbor as yourself is primarily a matter of who you are, not of what you decide to do.

If you're going to love your neighbor as yourself, you must first understand what love is and understand that *you yourself are loved*—abundantly loved and provided for by God. Out of that love and provision, you can commit to be a person of compassion and mercy who will have pity on your neighbor. This explains why the Great Commandment says to love God first and then to love our neighbor. They are not two separate commandments, but one with two aspects, similar to the teaching about being forgiven by God and forgiving others.

Having mercy or compassion on people is one of the main elements in learning to love our neighbors. People who don't love their neighbors are usually too hard on them. Instead of being hard on people, we need to decide to pay attention to the way they must be feeling as they face their challenging circumstances. That's what being compassionate is all about.

You can afford to be compassionate only when you know that abundant compassion is provided to you by someone who has appropriate means—and this is primarily God: "We love because he first loved us" (1 John 4:19 NIV).

When you commit to being a person of compassion, you have to use your intelligence instead of just being a people-pleaser. You must look at your resources and make wise decisions. Apparently, it didn't break the bank of the Samaritan to do what he did. "If you need more money, I will come back this way and will pay it," he told the innkeeper (Luke 10:35, paraphrased). You must have consideration for yourself: *Will helping this person still make it possible for me to carry on with my life, including my relationships with others?*

As we show compassion, we need to be talking to the Lord in the process, because God will undoubtedly have something to say. There will be times when he will say, in effect, "You make the judgment." When we are moved to open ourselves up to the possibility of a messy, vulnerable situation as we act on behalf of someone in need, we have to be responsible in making judgments about where this kind of intimacy lies and how it might impact our broader responsibilities.

Intimate involvement in someone else's life might not lead to a long-lasting relationship, but it will express itself in the ordinary events of life. The Samaritan was thrown into intimate engagement with a victim of violence by merely being on the same road, and he responded accordingly. When the Samaritan and the wounded man were thrown together in this circumstance, the Samaritan seemed to be thinking, *I am going to make that one my neighbor*—and he did.

SO JESUS TELLS A STORY

> Then Jesus answered and said: "A certain man went down from Jerusalem to Jericho." (Luke 10:30)

This description makes us believe that this man was a Jew and a resident of Jerusalem—a man Jesus' listeners would expect a priest and a Levite to care about and respond to favorably. In other words, this man was a neighbor, at least in a *spatial* sense. In effect, Jesus is saying that one of their neighbors went down from Jerusalem to Jericho:

> "A certain man . . fell among thieves, who stripped him of his clothing, wounded him, and departed, leaving him half dead." (Luke 10:30)

To get the picture, imagine driving down a dangerously curving road (like the Jerusalem to Jericho road is yet today), and seeing something alongside the road that looks suspiciously like a human being. Or maybe it looks like part of a cardboard box. (When you read the Bible, it's helpful to think about the details to get some sense of what was really going on.)

> "Now by chance a certain priest came down that road. And when he saw him, he passed by on the other side." (Luke 10:31)

We don't know what the priest might have been thinking, but he didn't bother to stop and look. One of the tricks we learn early in life is not to look, because if we look, we may feel a certain responsibility. So just as when we see someone on the street corner who may ask something from us, we turn away and focus on something else. Perhaps the priest didn't want to be the next victim of the robbers. Perhaps he was memorizing Scripture and thought to himself, *I've got to concentrate here. I can't be distracted.* By the time that thought flashed into his mind, he had passed by and the man alongside the road had faded from view.

Since Jesus chose to make two religious leaders his first and second passersby, he seemed to be making a point about the religious life. Perhaps in that day, people assumed a priest had more important things to do than to help people. Unconsciously we begin to assume that anyone in spiritual leadership is too busy to stop and help anybody, that devotions and church activities are more important than helping someone in need. When our religious practices blind us to the needs of people, those practices become a snare.

> "Likewise a Levite, when he arrived at the place, came and looked, and passed by on the other side." (Luke 10:32)

The Levite actually *looked*, which fits well with his position because the Levite in his priestly work was a helper more than anything else. He was not the person up front, but the one who set up the stage, got the chairs out, and positioned the sound equipment. So Jesus described the Levite as having looked, but the outcome was no different.

As far as we can tell, the priest didn't even slow down. The Levite, at least, paused or maybe stopped altogether. But neither person went near the badly beaten man. One of the main things in the religion of the Jews was to avoid at all costs the uncleanness that came from touching a sick or dead person. Perhaps the priest and Levite imagined the fellow was dead and thought that if they touched him, they would be out of commission for several days. Perhaps the priest was going to Jericho for an evangelistic rally and the Levite was going there to help him. If the Levite had done something that made him ceremonially unclean, he couldn't have aided the priest.

The priest and the Levite had what they regarded as good reasons for not helping this man. We won't understand Jesus' teaching if we can't see that. Jesus was not trying to make them look bad, just as he wasn't trying to make the Samaritan look like a spiritual hero. We have to be very careful about our interpretation here. Jesus never called the Samaritan "good," but just "a certain Samaritan," which had all kinds of difficult implications.

POLITICALLY INCORRECT

In order to understand this parable in the context of how Jesus taught it, we must recognize the offensiveness of the term *Samaritan*. John 8:31–59 records one of the most heated exchanges between Jesus and "those Jews who believed Him" (verse 31). During this exchange, questions of lineage, righteousness, and propriety were being hotly debated. This fight degenerated into name-calling. The Jews defended themselves as "Abraham's descendants," to which Jesus responded, "You are of your father the devil" (John 8:33, 44). Jesus told them the reason they did not hear the words of God that he was speaking was because "you are not of God," to which they replied, "Do we not say rightly that You are a Samaritan and have a demon?" (8:47–48).

To call a Jew a Samaritan was the most offensive thing that could be said at that time. You would be hard-pressed to find a modern equivalent that evokes the same shock and disgust. So a story about a Samaritan helping a Jew would have been appalling and offensive. To witness Jesus talking to a Samaritan woman or healing a Samaritan leper would have been equally alarming (John 4:5–42; Luke 17:11–16). Jesus periodically involved a Samaritan in what he was doing because he wanted to break down the idea that a person couldn't be good if they were a Samaritan.

To offer a story in which a despised Samaritan served as a role model was intended to cause an earthquake in the listeners' prevailing cultural beliefs. Perhaps this is Jesus' most scandalous parable of all. Some modern equivalents of this Samaritan and Jewish pairing that could potentially cause the same reaction today might be Nazi and Jew, Ottoman and Armenian, imperialist Japanese and Chinese civilian, or Hutu and Tutsi.

The term *Samaritan* was a holdover from the days when the ten northern tribes of Israel intermarried with the people of the land who were not Israelites. As a result, a proper Jew felt disgust for these people of mixed heritage. Jews who were sufficiently holy wouldn't even go through Samaria to get to Jerusalem for the feasts, but would cross the Jordan River and go down the other side to avoid coming into contact with Samaritans.

Jesus chose to include a Samaritan in his story because he was profoundly conscious of how the religion of the Jews had blinded them.

"But a certain Samaritan, as he journeyed, came where he was. And when he saw him, he had compassion." (Luke 10:33)

This "certain Samaritan" came along and looked. And when he looked, he *felt*. He had compassion on the man who was in the place of suffering. Sometimes it is hard for us to put ourselves in the shoes of other people, especially when they are not like us. It's easier to identify with people who are like us. We can train ourselves to be compassionate toward other people and eliminate our indifference toward those who are not like us.

It is sometimes hard to believe that people who are different from us truly do experience many of the same feelings we have. If a person is a member of another race or another culture, we may find it hard to imagine that they'd have the same feelings, virtues, or character. So if we see them hurt badly, we may not easily identify with them and have compassion on them.

WILLINGNESS TO ENTER IN

One of the great things about Jesus was that he exhibited compassion for everyone. When we read the Gospels, we see repeatedly his compassion for people of different social, racial, and cultural backgrounds. Jesus focused primarily on the Jews because they were a people who had been prepared to receive him, but he cared for everyone he came into contact with. He had an intuitive sense of their suffering, and he knew that the gospel of the kingdom of God is available to all.

A foundational test of our spiritual life is how deeply we can feel with people who are different from us. You see, Jesus' great command to "do unto others as you would have them do unto you" just isn't practical until we can feel how others feel (Matthew 7:12, paraphrased). That way we have some idea of what they would like us to do by working out what we would like *them* to do if we were in their place. The key attribute of the Samaritan man was that he could feel with other people. He wasn't so wrapped up in his religion or his righteousness that he couldn't take time to look and help. His heart and hands were open to compassion.

Bob Pierce, who founded World Vision, often prayed, "Let my heart be broken by the things that break the heart of God."[23] Praying this prayer helps us identify with others, feel with them, put ourselves in their place, and imagine what it would be like to walk in their shoes. To share the mind and heart of Christ is to be prepared to feel toward people and situations the way he did. And if we do that, we may cry a great deal more than we do now. We may also laugh a great deal more than we do now.

The admonition to "rejoice with those who rejoice, and weep with those who weep" (Romans 12:15) is a way to reinforce the necessity of being able to feel for other people. Paul was not saying, "When you find someone happy, say 'Praise the Lord!' or if they cry, shed a few tears, whether or not you feel like it." He wasn't saying, "Fake it"; he was saying, "Enter into their joy; enter into their sorrow." The Samaritan had the ability to enter into another person's situation, and this is a great gift that God can give us.

The thought of "entering into" may give us pause, causing us to hesitate and even be frightened. We may think we can't handle feeling deeply with every person who comes by. By the end of the day, we'd be utterly wiped out! But though there is a demand that comes through it, there is also a source of strength in it. And it is a life in which there is a getting as well as a giving.

We need to regularly remind ourselves to weep with weepers and rejoice with rejoicers to counter our well-trained gift for a stiff upper lip and an "I am not gonna give in to my feelings" mentality. We need to understand that Jesus' way is one of compassion, a way of tears and smiles.

Don't be afraid of tears. If you're a member of a church where no tears are shed and no true joy is experienced, if your life is devoid of those things, diligently and fervently seek them. God wants you to have them. You're not alive until you have them. Tears and joy are a part of the full dimension of the life

God intends us to live. And he invites us to experience them in relationship with others as well.

MOVED WITH COMPASSION

After the Samaritan had compassion, he acted. That is the connection between the head and the feet, hands, and heart. The man looked, he felt, and then he acted. Now, what he did was a simple thing. He did not stand aside, but rather entered into the situation:

> "So he went to him and bandaged his wounds, pouring on oil and wine; and he set him on his own animal, brought him to an inn, and took care of him." (Luke 10:34)

He took the injured man down the road to an inn and rented a room. He ministered to him, stayed with him, put his hand on his brow and cooled him, and took care of his needs through the night. When the next day came, he made plans for the wounded man's care:

> "On the next day, when he departed, he took out two denarii, gave them to the innkeeper, and said to him, 'Take care of him; and whatever more you spend, when I come again, I will repay you.'" (Luke 10:35)

It's very possible the Samaritan was a fellow who traveled that road regularly—maybe as a traveling salesman or something of that sort. And he made sure the innkeeper knew he would return: "When I come back . . ."

I want to stress the simplicity of this act. This wasn't a great act of self-sacrifice. He didn't say, *Well, I guess I'll have to sell my donkey and mortgage my business*. It isn't so much the big sacrifices that defeat our movement toward compassion as it is the little things. Song of Solomon contains this poetic section:

> Catch us the foxes,
> The little foxes that spoil the vines,
> For our vines have tender grapes. (Song of Solomon 2:15)

The speaker in this verse sees the need to get the "little foxes" of destruction out of the vineyard. And that's what ruins our lives—just as the "little fox" of religious busyness spoiled the priest, and the "little fox" of cleanliness spoiled the Levite.

LITTLE THINGS

Our lives consist primarily of little things that can either defeat us or move us to "redeem the time, to buy back the moments because the days are evil" as Paul admonishes us in Ephesians 5:16 (paraphrased). Perhaps the priest and the Levite thought to themselves, *I'll certainly have another chance. There will be other people I will need to help.* But if we think like that day after day, we will look back on a life full of missed opportunities. "Today is the day of salvation" is an all-encompassing statement about our lives (Isaiah 49:8; 2 Corinthians 6:2).

When we redeem something, we buy it back. Our time needs to be brought back into the life of God and redeemed, or it will be lost. Paul repeats this instruction in Colossians 4:5. It's unfortunate that only the older versions of the Bible use the idea of redemption, because redemption is a special kind of relationship. It's quite different from urging us to make the most of our time and opportunities, as we find in many Bible translations today. Our time is already poised to be wasted. It is in the pawnshop of souls. It must be "bought back" by proactive provision.

REDEEMING OUR TIME

The challenge to you and me today is to be active in bringing everything that fills our time back into God's time and make it count for him. God is in our moments. That's where we meet him, and that's where we live with him. We have to redeem our time by viewing everything we're involved in as being in the hand of God.

Here are a few practical steps for redeeming our time:

- *Be thankful.* You can't make much progress without being thankful, and this is a crucial attribute in your life with God. If you want to redeem your time, start with being thankful for the next thing that's in front of you. Redemption is a concrete experience that we live out in the events of our lives and in our relationships with other people. To be thankful for that is to acknowledge that God is there.

- *Fill your life with God.* The world around us is programmed to waste our time. And its main tactic is to convince us that what we're engaged in is not of great value. We often respond by allowing ourselves to be distracted, and distraction is one of the main enemies of the human soul because we are investing our time in things that don't matter.

  Make sure that your gentle but persistent focus is on doing the things that are righteous and true and good (Ephesians 5:9). We do this by constantly submitting our place and time to love, to joy, to peace, and to all the aspects of the fruit of the Spirit, and by taking God into those moments.

- *Plan in faith.* We have plenty of time available to us, but if we do not take mastery over our time, it will be wasted. We will not do the things we want to do, and we will believe we never have enough time. Of course, "not having time" is a choice. God does not manage your book of appointments; you do. The reality is this: if you do not work hard to make the time, you will never "find" it.

  Planning involves saying no more than saying yes. It's the only way to avoid the kind of frantic scurrying about that comes to us as we're constantly bombarded with demands. In *The Art of Pastoring*, William Martin writes, "Take a long, prayerful, meditative look at your calendar. Who are you trying to impress? God? Give me a break. The congregation? Possibly. Yourself? Bingo! Now cut some big chunks out of each week for family, rest, meditation, prayer, and flower sniffing. When you've done that we'll talk more about the path to God."[24] We must make our plans in reliance on God with an expectation that he will bring to pass the things we set before ourselves.

Ask yourself how much of your time really centers around the renewal and development of your life. How much of your time is spent doing *little things* you think you just have to do instead? That's failing to redeem the time. Another threat is when we believe we can only redeem our time by doing things that are religious. *Religion* can be a very good thing, but it's never life itself, and *redemption* has to do with life. It has to do with all our moments, our days, and our relationships with other people. That's the way we bring all of our time back into the life of God and expect his blessing on it.

ETERNAL TREASURES

Leo Tolstoy told a wonderful story about Martin, a devout Russian shoemaker who regularly read his Bible.[25] One day as he was reading, the message came to him that Jesus would come and visit him that day. So he arose expectantly and went through the morning working on shoes. He lived in a little basement where through the window he could see the feet of the people as they passed by, and he would look for the feet of the Master. And he thought he would surely recognize him.

By noon, Jesus still hadn't come. As the afternoon wore on, a penniless soldier friend came in. They talked, and as the man went away, the cobbler gave him a coat to keep him warm knowing that he would be freezing out on the streets.

Later that day, the cobbler went to buy some bread for the

evening. He found a little child who was lost and took him to his mother. And finally, he met an old woman on the street who needed food, and he took her in and gave her some soup and bread. As the evening drew to a close, he said, "Lord, was I wrong? The day is over, and you haven't come." Then he heard the words, "Inasmuch as you did it to one of the least of these My brethren, you did it to Me" (Matthew 25:40).

We will have many occasions to invest in people, to be a neighbor to someone in need, and store up eternal treasures in heaven. We don't control who comes into our lives; God does. He sends us the people to whom we can be a neighbor.

The message we're hearing from the Good Samaritan, as we've come to call him, is simply the message of redeeming our time as servants in the kingdom of God. There's nothing better to do than that. Buy back the moments. But how swiftly they fly.

Watch for the opportunities.

Be ready.

MAIN POINTS ABOUT
THE KINGDOM OF GOD

- The Parable of the Good Samaritan displays the outworking of the Word of the kingdom and best embodies what it means to live in the welcoming and accessible kingdom of God.
- Neighboring is a daily opportunity in the kingdom of God where he brings people into our lives who prompt us to ask, "To whom will I be a neighbor?"
- In the kingdom of God, we learn that we are loved— abundantly loved. Out of that love, we are free to be persons of compassion.
- Neighboring means we can freely laugh and cry with others in their joy and sorrow, and extend mercy to the next person God brings into our lives.
- To redeem our time means to draw all of our moments into the kingdom through the grace of God.

IN CLOSING

My hope is that this study of what Jesus taught in his kingdom parables will deepen your understanding about *the message of Christ* and provide a compelling vision of life in the kingdom of God. May the Lord make these things sweet and clear to your mind, enabling you to take *the faith of Christ* into yourself and enter more deeply into the present reality of the kingdom that is always at hand.

With that in mind, I offer this prayer for all who read this book:

Our gracious Father, Holy Spirit, Lord Jesus, we are so thankful for the opportunity to explore what you have said about your kingdom through these beautiful stories. We pray that you will take them and bless them by your Spirit in the power of a constant relationship of communication, guidance, love, and service.

Plant the seed of your living Word deep within us so that our hearing of it may be profitable to the upbuilding of our soul and to the advancement of your kingdom that is available to us all. Help us to receive the grace we need each day to see clearly and to hear the Word of the kingdom—to the very foundation of our lives.

Fill all of the space of our minds and hearts with the presence of your Spirit, that there might not be one part of us that is not possessed for your purposes, by your glory, by your person. May you rise above everything in our lives and hold us fast in the grip of adoration of who you are. We are amazed at ourselves— how we can so easily be enchanted and distracted by trivial things when your feast is waiting. Teach us, dear Lord, the sweetness of your kingdom and how everything we lay aside that might look like a sacrifice is of no cost at all when compared to the glory and the power of living fully and freely in your kingdom.

Touch our hearts with your heart. Touch our minds with your mind. Move through us with your power and transform us into your likeness. Give us eyes to see your majesty and glory in all that we do with you, and lead others into your eternal life. Help us walk in and conform to your image in this world, holding forth the Word of life to those around us with gentleness, confidence, and patience.

Fill us with compassion for those who are not yet of your kingdom, those who are lost or not yet fully surrendered to your will and purposes. May we so live and speak with clarity and force that others will come to be your disciples and walk with you always before them, walking in the light you provide, following you as you've called us to do.

Keep us mindful of the value of the small things that make up our lives, and show us how to bring them into your kingdom. May we come to know more and more each day that you will care for us and bless our faithfulness.

Help us to understand the liberty and the responsibilities of living in this world before you with the possessions and material goods you have given us to steward. Help us to lead our lives always surrendered to you, knowing the joy of godliness with contentment, which is great gain.

Keep us with our inward ear and inward eye always open to

you. Keep us ready. Make us alert, and teach us how to redeem each moment. May there not be a single thing we would be unprepared to drop if you were to come right now. And we would be happy if you would.

Help us to understand and to grow in your ways. May we continue in our studies of your Word, that it may flourish in the deepest recesses of our hearts and souls. Dear Lord, have your way in us and cultivate our minds, that they might grow, and our hearts, that they would be always soft toward you. May your seed find rich and fertile soil to bring forth the fruit of your kingdom in whatever measure is right for your purposes. Bless each heart and each mind to this end.

We ask these things in Jesus' name. Amen.

ON MAKING
THIS BOOK

Publishing a new work from a beloved and bestselling author after their death presents unique challenges to an estate and a publishing team. There are many ways such projects can go wrong, and only one way they can go right—by being faithful to the author's character, voice, and life, while also presenting something fresh and worthy of being added to their body of work. We care deeply about this stewardship and consider it a great honor to be entrusted with Dallas's words and work. Thus, here are some brief notes for anyone who may be interested in how this book was made.

Most of the content came from a thirteen-week series of talks given by Dallas Willard in 1983 titled "The Parabolic Teaching about Christ's Kingdom by Christ Himself." Supplementary content, where further context was called for, came from a variety of Dallas's unpublished sermons, talks, and writings, and a few published ones, especially on material relevant to his theology of the kingdom, which he covered in detail in previous works, most prominently *The Divine Conspiracy*. Concepts from previously published material have been cited, and editorial notes have been added in places where we feel they will help the reader.

We have minimized changes and have added or omitted words or phrases when necessary to allow for smoother reading. In blending it all together, our goal has been to maintain Dallas's pastoral tone, convey his interpretations and ideas without encumbrance, and give readers a sense of what it was like to be in the room with Dallas and the "fellow pilgrims" with whom he spoke. We pray that this book will help you venture more deeply into the wondrous landscape of the kingdom of God. May you find in your reading and contemplation of the parables the heart of God that desires to know you and to be known by you.

THE EDITORS AND THE ESTATE OF DALLAS WILLARD

IN GRATITUDE

This book has truly been a team effort. Many thanks to . . .

- Jane Willard, without whom neither I nor this book would be here. She has championed the publication of this teaching series for many years, and, as my father once said about *The Divine Conspiracy*, this is her book.
- Jan Johnson, for spending a year collaborating with me to bring transcripts into book form. And she then agreed to write a workbook to go with it! Her knowledge of Dallas and the corpus of his teaching was indispensable as the chapters were assembled, and her experience of him as a friend and teacher helped guide the spirit of our work.
- Our backup editors: Larry Burtoft, who provided an insightful and complete editorial review, and especially Bill Heatley, whose knowledge of Dallas's heart and work was invaluable in refining this material.
- The advisers and partners who have engaged with us in various aspects of the work, including Keith Matthews, James Catford, Greg Hinkle, Steve Hanselman, Dara Jones, Gloria Ketchum, Teri Reisser, John Willard, Keas Keasler, Aaron Preston, Brandon Rickabaugh, Mike Robb, Steve Porter, Ken Lumley, J. P. Moreland, and James Hutter.

- Paul Pastor, Dirk Buursma, and the rest of the team at Zondervan for the gifts and talents they have contributed to bringing *The Scandal of the Kingdom* to its final form.
- Roger Minor and the students of the Hour of Discovery class at Harbor Church (Harbor City, California), who invited Dallas to teach this series in 1983.
- The Martin Institute for Christianity and Culture, the Renovaré Institute, Denver Seminary, The Neighborhood Initiative, Fuller Theological Seminary, and Renovaré Korea, whose recordings of Dallas were used in supplementing the primary teaching material.
- The team at Dallas Willard Ministries and our family and friends, who have encouraged and prayed for us along the way.

Our deepest gratitude goes to our Lord and Savior, Jesus Christ, who came to teach us the ways of his upside-down kingdom. Like the father of the prodigal, he ran down the road to meet us and welcome us home—"pig stink and all."

May the seeds sown in these chapters be allowed to reorganize the reality of all of our lives as they take root in the fertile soil of our hearts. Dallas has planted, we have watered, and may God give the increase.

REBECCA WILLARD HEATLEY

NOTES

1. Elisabeth Kübler-Ross, *Death: The Final Stage* (New York: Scribner, 2009), 96.
2. Hebrews 11:38.
3. Dallas Willard, "Biblical and Theological Foundations for Spiritual Formation in Christ 2," Renovaré Institute, Atlanta, GA, October 11, 2011, https://conversatio.org/biblical-and-theological-foundations-for -spiritual-formation-in-christ-2.
4. Dietrich Bonhoeffer, *The Cost of Discipleship* (1959; repr., New York: Macmillan, 1963), 99.
5. John 1:23.
6. See "Heaven," in John McClintock and James Strong, *Cyclopedia of Biblical, Theological, and Ecclesiastical Literature*, vol. 4 (New York: Harper Bros., 1891), 122–27.
7. Philip P. Bliss, "Whosoever Will," 1870, published in 304 hymnals. Public domain.
8. C. S. Lewis, *The Screwtape Letters* (1942; repr., San Francisco: HarperSanFrancisco, 2001), 1–4.
9. Mother Teresa, *A Simple Path*, compiled by Lucinda Vardey (New York: Ballantine, 1995), 79, 94.
10. Quoted in William R. Parker and Elaine St. Johns, *Prayer Can Change Your Life* (Carmel, NY: Guideposts, 1957), 40.
11. J. B. Phillips, *Your God Is Too Small: A Guide for Believers and Skeptics Alike* (1952; repr. New York: Simon & Schuster, 2004).

12. "Lord, I Want to Be a Christian," African-American spiritual (ca. 1754). Public domain.

13. "He's Got the Whole World in His Hands," African-American spiritual (1927). Public domain.

14. Erdmann Neumeister, "Christ Receiveth Sinful Men" (1718). Public domain.

15. Steve Saint, *End of the Spear* (Wheaton, IL: Tyndale House, 2007), 184 (verified by email from Jaime Saint, October 19, 2023).

16. George Eldon Ladd, *The Gospel of the Kingdom: Scriptural Studies in the Kingdom of God* (Grand Rapids: Eerdmans, 1990), 71.

17. Quoted in "Back from the Ashes," *Hartford Courant*, November 13, 2005, www.courant.com/2005/11/13/back-from-the-ashes-2.

18. John Ruskin, *"Unto This Last": Four Essays on the First Principles of Political Economy* (London: Smith, Elder, 1862), 36.

19. See Bonhoeffer, *Cost of Discipleship*, especially chapter 1.

20. Sheldon Harnick and Jerry Bock, "If I Were a Rich Man," *Fiddler on the Roof* (1964).

21. Cited by F. F. Bruce, *The Book of Acts*, rev. ed. (Grand Rapids: Eerdmans, 1988), 77–78. While the internet often attributes this story to Thomas Aquinas, other sources point to the thirteenth-century Catholic preacher and friar Dominic.

22. W. W. Walford, "Sweet Hour of Prayer" (1845). Public domain.

23. Quoted in "Let My Heart Be Broken by the Things That Break the Heart of God," Samaritan's Purse, January 25, 2020, www.samaritanspurse.org/article/let-my-heart-be-broken-by-the-things-that-break-the-heart-of-god.

24. William Martin, *The Art of Pastoring: Contemplative Reflections* (Pittsburgh: Vital Faith, 1994), 9.

25. Leo Tolstoy, "Where Love Is, God Is" (also known as "Martin the Cobbler"), first published 1885, available in many collections.

Companion Workbook
Also Available

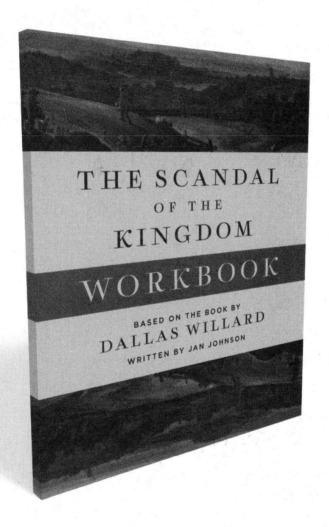

Use alongside the book for
greater understanding.

Dallas Willard
MINISTRIES
Living In The Kingdom Now

Resources for the
WITH GOD LIFE

ABOUT US

Dallas Willard Ministries exists to proclaim, teach and manifest the love, truth and transforming power of Christ and the Kingdom of God. Abundant life through union with God is available here and now to all who place their confidence in Jesus Christ and become his disciple in Kingdom living.

We are a 501(c)(3) organization dedicated to developing and disseminating the ideas, writings, and teachings that the Lord brought to life through Dallas. Our efforts are not centered on Dallas himself, but on the truth he continuously encouraged his "fellow pilgrims" to pursue.

Dallas taught that the most important thing you and God get from your life is the person you become. We are here to support and encourage you in your journey into Christlikeness. We warmly invite you to connect with us and explore our resources and learning opportunities as you seek to "grow in the grace and knowledge of our Lord and Savior Jesus Christ."

WHAT WE OFFER

Our website offers videos, audios, articles and accompanying resources for individuals and churches.

School of Kingdom Living

An immersive discipleship experience intended for anyone seeking a richer, fuller life with God.

DWM's YouTube channel houses an extensive library of Dallas Willard videos.

YouVersion

The YouVersion Bible App is home to Dallas Willard study plans for individuals and groups.

 DWMinistries@dwillard.org   @dallas_willard_ministries

 /dallas.willard.0717   www.dwillard.org